THEY CAME BEFORE COLUMBUS

IVAN VAN SERTIMA

THEY CAME BEFORE COLUMBUS

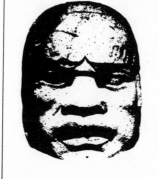

RANDOM HOUSE NEW YORK

Library of Congress Cataloging in Publication Data
Van Sertima, Ivan.
    They came before Columbus.
    Includes bibliographical references.
    1.   America—Discovery and exploration—African.
2.   Blacks—America—History.   3.   Indians—Culture—
African influences.   I.   Title.
E109.A35V36   970′.019   76-14186
ISBN 0-394-40245-6

Manufactured in the United States of America
23456789B

PHOTO CREDITS

PLATE 2   Leih-Foto/By permission of Holle Bildarchiv, Baden-Baden, Germany

PLATE 3   Leih-Foto/By permission of Holle Bildarchiv, Baden-Baden, Germany

PLATE 4   Leih-Foto/By permission of Holle Bildarchiv, Baden-Baden, Germany

PLATE 5   Leih-Foto/By permission of Holle Bildarchiv, Baden-Baden, Germany

PLATE 6   Leih-Foto/By permission of Holle Bildarchiv, Baden-Baden, Germany

PLATE 7   By permission of Museo de America, Madrid, Spain

PLATE 11   Redrawn from illustration on page 214 of *The African Genius: An Introduction to African Social and Cultural History* by Basil Davidson. Copyright © 1969 by Basil Davidson. Reprinted by permission of Little, Brown and Company, in Association with Atlantic Monthly Press.

PLATE 12   Reprinted by permission of Dr. Thor Heyerdahl from his book *The Quest for America* (Phaidon Press Ltd.)

PLATE 14   From *Unexpected Faces in Ancient America* by Alexander von Wuthenau. Copyright © 1975 by Alexander von Wuthenau. Reprinted by permission of Crown Publishers, Inc.

PLATE 18   Leih-Foto/By permission of Holle Bildarchiv, Baden-Baden, Germany

PLATE 20   Illustration from *Egyptian Antiquities in the Hermitage* by B. Piotrovsky (Aurora Art Publishers). Reprinted by permission of the Copyright Agency of the U.S.S.R. (VAAP) and the publisher.

PLATE 22   Reprinted by permission of Dr. Thor Heyerdahl, from his book *The Quest for America* (Phaidon Press Ltd.)

For
MARIA,
WILSON
and
JAN

ACKNOWLEDGMENTS

The author wishes to make special mention of his debt to the following:

Professor Jan Carew, for introducing me in 1970 to the Leo Weiner trilogy, thereby initiating my researches into pre-Columbian African presences in the Americas.

Ms. Elizabeth Farrah, for her assistance in the collection of hundreds of references, particularly those upon which the oceanographic and botanical sections of this work are based.

Ms. Mary Falk Horwitz, for translation of large sections of Jules Cauvet's *Les Berbères en Amérique* from the Yale copy of this now-unavailable work.

Ms. Harriet Lehmann, for translation of Spanish documents, particularly Gonzalo Aguirre Beltran's "La Ethnohistoria y el Estudio del Negro en Mexico."

Ms. Barbara Dazzo, for her research notes on the black African presence in the multiracial navies of the Ramessids.

Ms. Jeanne Mooney, for acquainting me with the African presence in Irish pre-Christian history.

Professor Edward Scobie, whose encouragement and companionship often sustained me during the preparation of this work.

CONTENTS

INTRODUCTION

Six years ago, during my first brief visit to America, I came across three volumes in the private library of a Princeton professor. They had been published half a century ago and their title fascinated me—*Africa and the Discovery of America*. They represented a lifetime of dedicated scholarship by a Harvard linguist, Leo Wiener. Professor Wiener had been working on a grammar of American languages in the early years of this century when he stumbled upon a body of linguistic phenomena that indicated clearly to him the presence of an African and Arabic influence on some medieval Mexican and South American languages before the European contact period. As I say, I was fascinated by the subject. The thesis was revolutionary, the evidence novel and startling. The implications of such a thesis, if proven, could have far-reaching consequences for both American and African history. But I returned to my home in London after reading these books, only partially convinced. I was intrigued and impressed but very skeptical. I felt like a man who had come upon a dozen clues to a sensational murder but did not feel too confident about the evidence. The smell of the blood, even the marks of the bullet, were there, but far more important things—the body and the gun —were missing.

Later that year I returned to live and teach in the United States. I returned also to that obscure trilogy of Wiener. I began to see far more than I had at first. I began to understand what was the source of my doubts. Professor Wiener was writing too early, when too many bits of the puzzle were missing. Furthermore, while he was a trained linguist and his reading was wide, his method of dealing with anthropological data was naïve. He depended too heavily on the fragile pillars of philology to support the great weight of his thesis. Yet in spite of these inadequacies, something of lasting value emerged. It sank to the bottom of my mind and began to radiate quiet, flashing signals that haunted me.

In the fall of 1970, at the request of a magazine editor, I sat down to simplify and summarize Wiener. I also began to examine some of his primary sources. I felt the case was an unproven case but by no means a closed case. I was in no position then to explore it to its limits but I felt the information should not remain buried under fifty years of silence. It should be circulated afresh. Then something happened that started me off on a hunt that has been like the leads in a detective story, from suspect to suspect, print to print, clue to clue, until finally I came upon what lawyers like to call "the smoking gun."

On the very day I submitted my summary of the Wiener case to a magazine the novelist John Williams submitted to the same an interview with a lecturer in art at the University of the Americas in Mexico City, Professor Alexander von Wuthenau. Professor von Wuthenau had done extensive searches of private collections and museums in the Americas and also his own excavations in Mexico. A generation of work in this area had unearthed a large number of Negroid heads in clay, gold, copper and copal sculpted by pre-Columbian American artists. The strata on which these heads were found ranged from the earliest American civilizations right through to the Columbian contact period. Accidental stylization could not account for the individuality and racial particulars of these heads. Their Negro-ness could not be explained away nor, in most cases, their African cultural origin. Their coloration, fullness of lip, prognathism, scarification, tattoo markings, beards, kinky hair, generously fleshed noses, and, even in some instances, identifiable coiffures, headkerchiefs, helmets, compound earrings —all these had been skillfully and realistically portrayed by pre-Columbian American potters, jewelers and sculptors.

Terra-cotta sculpture of faces was the photography of the pre-Columbian Americans and what von Wuthenau had done was to open new rooms in the photo gallery of our lost American ages. No longer was the African chapter in American pre-Columbian history an irrecoverable blank because of the vicious destruction of native American books. Here were visible witnesses of a vanished time and they were telling us a remarkable new story. Wiener and von Wuthenau, two ostracized German-American scholars, fifty years apart, their works unknown to each other, joined forces that day in my mind to establish a base for the hypothesis that Africans were here in the Americas before Columbus.

Thus began my research. Over the years it has led me into many fields where important and recent discoveries have been made but always, it seems, in isolation. Schwerin and Stephens in botany; Stirling and the Drucker-Heizer-Squier team in American archaeology; Lhote, Mori, Arkell, Delcroix and Vaufrey, Thomson and McIver, Davies, Summers and Wild in African and Egyptian archaeology; Wiener, Cauvet and Jeffreys in philology; von Wuthenau in art history; explorers like Heyerdahl and Lindemann in ancient seacraft and oceanography; de Quatrefages, Hooton and Dixon in ethno-anthropology; Wiercinski in craniology; Davidson and Diop in African and Egyptian cultural history; Hapgood in cartography; de Garay in serology; Fell, Gordon and the Verills in their decipherment of Old World scripts on ancient New World stones, all contributing to a confirmation of the hypothesis and yet, with a few exceptions, unaware of the work that has been done or is being done by the others.

What I have sought to do in this book, therefore, is to present the whole picture emerging from these disciplines, all the facts that are now known about the links between Africa and America in pre-Columbian times.

Ivan Van Sertima

AUTHOR'S NOTE

The word "Negro" has become a very sensitive term, loaded with negative connotations. Whatever its original meaning (a specific race of Africans, or just black-skinned people of general African descent), that meaning has deteriorated in the popular imagination. It is not surprising that many blacks, particularly in North America, now react to the word with varying degrees of pain and disgust. I therefore consider it necessary to explain my particular understanding of the word and my use of it in this book.

I have searched for alternatives, and I have used several in different parts of the text. For example, I have often used the term "Negroid," since the adjective, strangely enough, seems to de-fuse some of the negative connotations of the noun. I have tried to confine the use of the term "Negro" to quotations and direct reference to quotations. The word cannot be deleted, however, whatever the sensitivity of certain readers, from early and present anthropological and archaeological texts.

The term "black," although it is the fashionable and more acceptable term, presents problems in several contexts. To speak of a black skeleton would be ridiculous. Skin coloration, as such, means nothing in the study of bones and other ancient physiological remains. The classical distinctions between the three main racial categories—Negroid, Mongoloid and Caucasoid—have to be determined by reference to certain structural features, measurements and relationships that are not derived from superficialities of color. It is unfortunate that the early misuse of skeletal evidence to prove evolutionary differences between races, a blatant fiction, has placed the fairly precise science of craniology in popular disrepute.

Black also means nothing when we are talking about gods among the native Americans. Tezcatlipoca is a black god because black is his symbolic and ceremonial color. He is not African, as is Naualpilli, the Mexican god of jewelers, whose indisputably Negroid features were sculpted in green stone by the Mexicans while his kinky hair was cast in pure gold.

I have sometimes found hyphenated terms similar to those used by certain French African writers—terms like "Negro-African"— useful. I have also used hyphenated terms like "Negro-Nubian" and "Negro-Egyptian." Some may object to this. Why should one append Negro to Nubian? Either the Nubians are Negroid or they are not. This is a simplification of the complexity that one faces as an anthropologist and historian. The terms, which are used in this book to highlight the racial identity of Nubians in the Twenty-Fifth Dynasty, stand in contradiction to attempts by several anthropo-historians, particularly the British scholars Arkell and Shinnie, to deny the Negroid ancestry of the Nubian pharaohs. In spite of the excavations at Karanog, which demonstrate the overwhelming "Negro-ness" of the Nubians in this period, and the existing Negroid portraits of Nubian kings like Taharka, Arkell declares, "It is most improbable that Taharka was a negro, although he may have had some negroid blood in his veins."* Only recent and isolated studies have exposed the Negrophobic biases and distortions of these authorities, and thus the hyphenated coupling of Negro with Nubian emerges as a corrective.

The use of "Negro-Egyptian" is even more necessary in the light of the mixed and confused racial situation in the North during certain dynasties. These racial distinctions would not need to be so heavily emphasized were it not for the attempt, deliberate and sustained over the centuries, to deny the contribution of the black African to ancient Egyptian civilization.

* A. J. Arkell, *A History of the Sudan: From the Earliest Times to 1821*, London, The Athlone Press, 1955, p. 128.

Obviously these terms are in transition and certain confusions exist. All a writer can do in such a situation is to avoid further confusion by explaining his own particular understanding and use of these terms.

Ivan Van Sertima

THEY CAME BEFORE COLUMBUS

THE SECRET ROUTE
FROM GUINEA

. . . and he [Columbus] wanted to find out what the In-
dians of Hispaniola had told him, that there had come to
it from the south and southeast Negro people, who brought
those spear points made of a metal which they call guanin,
of which he had sent to the king and queen for assaying,
and which was found to have thirty-two parts, eighteen of
gold, six of silver, and eight of copper.

—*Raccolta,* PARTE I, VOL I.

African guanines *were alloys of gold containing copper*
for the sake of its odor, for it seems that the Negroes like
to smell their wealth. The guanines brought home by Co-
lumbus were assayed in Spain and were found to contain
the same ratio of alloy as those in African Guinea.

—FREDERICK POHL, *Amerigo Vespucci, Pilot Major*

On Saturday evening, March 9, 1493, a week after Columbus
had been driven by a storm into Lisbon, following his first voyage
to the Indies, he sat down to dinner with the Portuguese king at
his court in the valley of Paraiso.[1] Don Juan seemed to be in an
extremely good mood. He talked to Columbus as to a close friend,
with great candor and sweetness, insisting that his guest not stand,
bow or accord him any special deference, but sit beside him at
table as an equal. The admiral was surprised, deeply warmed by
this hospitality, but marveling, nonetheless, at the apparent absence of resentment or envy in the king. All through dinner he

looked at Don Juan closely, wondering whether the mask would suddenly slip to reveal the malice Columbus believed was beneath. Had not Don Juan sent three armed caravels to track him down last September as he was setting out on his Atlantic journey? Had not the king given orders that on the islands of Madeira, Puerto Sancto and the Azores, and in the regions and harbors where there were Portuguese, Columbus should be taken?[2] Only last Tuesday Bartholomew Diaz, patron to the king's ship, armed to the teeth, had confronted him, as he lay helpless in the port of Lisbon, his sails split in half by the storm. Diaz had ordered him to leave his ship and render an account to the factors of the king and had pulled back only because Columbus had responded with fighting words, saying he was the Most High Admiral to the Sovereigns of Castile and had to give an account to no one.[3]

Perhaps, thought Columbus, he had overreacted to the event because of the fatigue and terror he had suffered in the storm. After he had formally presented his letters to Diaz, had not Alvaro Dama, the Portuguese captain, come to his caravel in great state, with kettledrums and trumpets and pipes?[4] The king too had received him with the highest honors, as befitted a foreign prince. There was nothing, therefore, to be alarmed about. Diaz had issued a routine challenge to a foreign fleet lying at anchor in his country's port. And the *talk* of the three caravels last September (for he had never *seen* them) may have been just alarmist talk. Yet as he sat there, balancing these interpretations in his mind, Columbus felt uneasy and afraid.

He had brought with him some of the Indian hostages he had seized on the island of Guanahani (Watling Island).[5] These strange guests fascinated the Portuguese court. Not since 62 B.C., when the king of the Suevians presented Quintus Metellus Celer, the Roman proconsul in Gaul, with a gift of "Indians" cast up on the shores of Germany by a storm, had men with skin the tint of red sand been seen in Europe.[6]

If the faintest shadow of his true feelings passed across Don Juan's face during his talk at dinner, it was when he looked at these men. Captives though they were, they became inverted in the king's agitated mind into a triumphant troop, their vigorous young bodies branded already with the rival insignia of the Spanish crown. He saw them as King Ferdinand's little puppets, signaling with their hands and limbs for the lack and loss of words. Some of them had paint on their faces, as puppets do, and their hair was unreal, as is the hair of puppets, as coarse and black as a horse's tail drooping over the eyebrows. Some appeared to the king like dolls, oriental dolls with eyes of hard, black glass, void of all expression. Within the glass of those eyes he saw the lands he too had dreamed about, and about which mariners and traders in his African service had spoken.[7] Had he taken the rumors from Guinea more seriously he would have been sitting there that evening, emperor of two continents. The thought of it tormented him. The deep resentments he felt against Columbus, which for diplomatic reasons he had suppressed, crystallized into a beam of mischievous energy directed at the men of the Indies.

After dinner that evening, while he was talking with Columbus, "he ordered a dish of beans brought and placed on a table near them, and by signs ordered an Indian from among those who were there, to designate the many islands of his country that Columbus said he had discovered. The Indian at once showed Española and Cuba and the Lucayos and others. The king noted it with morose consideration and in a moment, as though inadvertently, he undid with his hand what the Indian had constructed. In a few moments he ordered another Indian to do the same with the beans, and this Indian quickly and diligently showed with the beans what the other Indian had shown, adding more islands and lands, giving the reason in his language for all he had shown, though no one understood it. And then the king, recognizing clearly the greatness of the lands discovered and their riches, was unable to conceal his grief at the loss of such things and cried out loudly and impetuously, giving himself a blow with his fist in the breast: 'O you wretched fool! Why did you let an undertaking of such importance slip through your fingers?' "[8]

The mask had fallen with spectacular suddenness. Columbus' fears were realized. Several members of the court surrounded the king. Some of them attributed his grief to the boldness of the admiral and begged leave to kill Columbus on the spot, destroy all the ships awaiting him in Lisbon, nine leagues from the court, so that news of the discovery would not go back to Castile. But Don Juan said that God would damn his soul to hell for it, and that they should not touch the man.[9]

After this frenzied, whispered session with his advisers, Don Juan resumed his conversations with Columbus as if nothing had happened. His face was flushed, but his manner showed none of the agitation which had driven him to that extraordinary outburst. He made it clear, and with a certain grave candor and graciousness, that regardless of his grief and disappointment at not having been Columbus' patron, "he felt great pleasure, nevertheless, that the voyage had been made and had terminated favorably."[10] The whole Christian world should rejoice at this, Don Juan said. His queen was staying in the monastery of San Antonio near the village of Villafranca on the right bank of the Tagus, less than a day's journey from the court. She too would like to see Columbus and accord him every honor before he left for Spain.[11]

The truth was, having failed to intercept Columbus both on his outward journey and his return, and having no heart now to order his assassination, as some of his advisers had urged, Don Juan quickly reconciled himself to the implications of this breakthrough to the islands and lands west of the ocean-sea. These implications, he knew, could be serious for Portugal. They would call for a repartitioning of the Christian world, a redefinition of the spheres of power and influence assumed by the two great maritime powers.

Before there could be any more Spanish claims to islands and lands within the ocean-sea, he must negotiate the most advantageous terms for the partitioning. He must strive somehow to make Columbus his ally in this, for he would soon be as much a power to be reckoned with as the Sovereigns of Spain. When he returned in triumph, offering up a kingdom beyond the sea to Isabella and Ferdinand, they would be eating out of his hands, hanging on his every word. The admiral would be virtually a prince of the ocean-sea.

But Don Juan knew that the rights and privileges of a private citizen in and over vast and vague dominions, unless he had the

physical force of an army behind him or the spiritual seal of a
pope, could vanish in an instant if he lost the favor of the king and
queen.[12] He saw clearly the nature of this new-found power and
vulnerability, both of which he intended to exploit.

His first ploy, therefore, was to suggest that he could use his
influence on behalf of Columbus, if the need were to arise, to see
that his agreements with regard to the "discoveries" were hon-
ored. Columbus had drafted agreements with the Spanish sovereigns before setting out, making him a partner with the Crown
in his prospective discoveries. These agreements (referred to in
his diaries as "the Capitulation") had been finalized in his absence and copies of the documents submitted to the Portuguese
king. Don Juan said he had looked at these very closely. He
understood from his reading of them that the real credit for the
"conquest" belonged to Columbus.[13] He was keen to emphasize
that this was Columbus' personal conquest, implying that it was
well within the power of the admiral even now to bargain over
those lands with any foreign prince with whom he might come
to an agreement.[14]

Columbus was cautious. He had not yet seen the Capitulation,
he said. He knew nothing more than that the king and queen of
Spain had advised him not to encroach on Portuguese territory
during his journeys, not to go to San Jorge de Mina nor to any
other part of Guinea, and this had been announced in all the
ports of Andalusia before he set sail. This was his way of saying
that Spain and her agents fully respected the Portuguese sphere
of power and influence, and that the Portuguese were expected
to show equal respect for theirs. Columbus also seemed to imply
that he needed no one to act as protector or go-between in the
matter of any agreements he might enter with the Sovereigns of
Castile. To this Don Juan graciously responded that he was certain mediators would not be necessary in this matter.[15]

On the following Sunday and Monday the discussions between
the king and the admiral continued. It became clear that Don
Juan's real concern was not with the chain of islands Columbus
claimed to have discovered in the Gulf of the Ganges. Beyond
them, beyond the mainland of Asia (if indeed it were true that

Columbus had chanced, as he claimed, upon Asia by way of the west), to the south and southeast, lay another world. The king was certain of this. Africans, he said, had traveled to that world. It could be found just below the equinoctial line, roughly on the same parallel as the latitudes of his domain in Guinea. In fact, "boats had been found which started out from Guinea and navigated to the west with merchandise."[16] He was a fool not to have sent an expeditionary fleet into these waters in spite of persistent rumors and reports. But Portugal already had its hands full in Africa, and it was concentrating its exploratory energies on the eastern route to India.[17]

Columbus listened intently. The information about the Guinea boats was new to him. He had been to Guinea ten years before and had seen the fortress at San Jorge de Mina which Don Juan was then constructing.[18] Little was known of Guinea trade and navigation at that time, for the African world was vast and strange, and the Portuguese had but one consuming interest—gold—in the pursuit of which they had scratched a mere fraction of the Guinea coast. But why was Don Juan telling him all this, and in such a conspiratorial tone? What did he want?

"I want a line," the king said, "drawn across the map of the world from north to south, from pole to pole. This line should be drawn 370 leagues* west of the westernmost islands of the Cape Verde. Let it be the divider between the two Catholic kingdoms. Anything found west of the line goes to you and Spain. Anything found east of the line falls to me and Portugal."[19]

As he sat there, brooding on this proposition, Columbus could hear the rain, driven by fierce winds, wasting its fury along the plains of Paraiso. The clamor of the rain and the wind stirred in him strong memories of Africa. He remembered how, at San Jorge de Mina on the Guinea coast, the rain would sometimes come rushing through the trees, sweeping forward like a violent river that had burst its banks, but beaten from passion into impotence by the high brick walls of the Portuguese fort. He used to feel

---

* A league was usually calculated as four Roman miles. According to Pohl, Vespucci measured it as four and a half miles.

so lost in those days, dismissed as a dreamer, sustained only by a conviction, passionate as the wind, as persistent as rain, storming insistently the minds of those who thought his schemes "chimerical and foolish." He remembered his last audience with Don Juan before he had decided to try his luck in the Spanish court. The king had stared at him with a bored, tired face, his skin strangely puffed by some unknown sickness, his eyes mocking Columbus with disbelief. Now they sat man to man (or was it prince to prince?). Don Juan was actually seeking his help to bring about a new division and reapportionment of power and possessions in the Christian world. Yes, he would go along with the drawing of the line. Yes, he would present the case with all his new-found power and influence at the Spanish court. But surely not out of gratitude for Don Juan's earlier indifference to his exploratory schemes nor his later attempts (if the rumors were correct) to seize him and his ships as they set out across the western ocean. Columbus now saw his advantage. He could name his price. What that price was no one can tell, but before he left the court on Tuesday morning some bargain over the line must have been struck.

This line, as proposed by Don Juan on the strength of his intelligence from Guinea, was finally settled by the two great powers at the Treaty of Tordesillas a year later—on June 7, 1494.[28] This was years before incursions into South America by either Spain or Portugal. The later "discovery" of the continent placed Brazil east of the line, and so within Portugal's domain of influence (see Plate 1). This region of South America is washed by the North Equatorial current which joins the Canaries current off the Senegambia coast of Africa. This current pulls boats caught in its drift toward the shores of the New World with the irresistible magnetism of a gravitational field. It was along this current that the Portuguese captain, Alvares Cabral, driven by a storm off the coast of West Africa in 1500, was blown helplessly but swiftly to Brazil.[21]

One wonders why Columbus, so greedy for his own gain and glory, would, out of the goodness of his heart or a fondness for

Portugal, try to promote an agreement on this line, a line which, as far as Don Juan claimed, however skeptical his listener, could put a potentially rich slice of land into the rival camp. What did he stand to gain except to attract to himself the suspicions of the Spanish? When he raised the matter on behalf of Don Juan at the Spanish court he did so, it seems, with such imprudent force that it led to some contention between himself and King Ferdinand.[22] History does not record the details of that quarrel, but it would be interesting to speculate on the line of argument Columbus used to persuade the Spanish to agree to the drawing of the line. There was no basis, he probably said, for Don Juan's belief that land lay east of the line proposed. Spain, therefore, stood to lose little or nothing and to gain the peace and unity of the Catholic world by conceding Don Juan a slice of his hypothetical dominion. To assume that Columbus acted as Portugal's advocate in return for the courtesies he had enjoyed in the valley of Paraiso would be to ignore the history of the man and his extraordinary avarice.

Even those historians who would canonize Christopher Columbus have all agreed he was inordinately greedy. He demanded of Spain one third, one eighth and one tenth of everything found in the New World. "Thus, if the gains amounted to 2,400 dollars for a ship, Columbus would expect to receive first 800 dollars for the third; next 300 dollars for his eighth; and last, 240 dollars for his tenth, making in all 1,340 dollars, receiving more than the Crown."[23]

Knowing what a hard bargain the Genoese adventurer had struck with Spain over his potential discoveries, King Ferdinand must have wondered what really went on in the Portuguese court. It was later to appear in charges leveled against Columbus that the storm that drove him into Lisbon was either exaggerated or fabricated, and that he had made for Portugal deliberately in order to intrigue with Don Juan.[24] Columbus, Ferdinand knew, was no stranger to the Portuguese court; he had been trying to further his schemes there for nearly fourteen years. He had sailed to Guinea in 1483 on a Portuguese ship. His relationship with Portugal had only soured because its kings Alfonso and Don Juan were both slow to finance his enterprise. The same, however, could have been said of the Spanish sovereigns.[25]

Isabella at first was not suspicious of her favorite. She attributed his curious advocacy of the Portuguese case to what she thought was his political naïveté. The very month he sailed again for the Caribbean on his second voyage she wrote, warning him: "In this affair of Portugal no determination has been taken with those who are here [Don Juan's ambassadors]; although I believe that the king will come to terms therein, I would wish you to think the contrary, in order that you may not on that account fail or neglect to act prudently and with due caution, so that you may not be deceived in any manner whatever."[26]

Only after Columbus' tardy response to her request for charts of navigation, and for the precise number and proposed names of the islands he claimed to have discovered off Asia, did she begin to wonder whether he was as open and straightforward as he seemed.[27]

Two months after the signing of the Treaty of Tordesillas, about which the Spanish king had strong misgivings, King Ferdinand wrote Columbus asking him to come home immediately and help them sort out disputes with Portugal arising over the settlement of this extraordinary boundary line. Columbus was in Cuba (which he claimed at that time was the mainland in spite of native pronouncements to the contrary) when a mail boat arrived, carrying the king's letter. Columbus replied promptly, saying he could not go home, for he was too gravely ill to move.[28] "Whether you are to go on this business or not," wrote Ferdinand, "write to us very fully all that you know about this matter."[29]

The matter, however, cooled when Don Juan died of dropsy a year later. His death came as a relief to the Spanish who, in spite of the agreement (and the continuance of their obligation to his successors) were none too eager to fix with an irrevocable finality and precision the limits of their domains within the ocean-sea. Few Spanish maps, in fact, show a recognition of this line.[30]

Columbus was slow to act on what Don Juan had told him about the Guinea route which led to the continent in the south. Circumstances made it difficult for him to investigate this matter on his

second voyage. One of the reasons may have been his own dis-
arming argument that Portugal stood to gain—and Spain stood to
lose—little or nothing by the drawing of the demarcation line.
One can only speculate that part of his secret deal with Don Juan
was that he should have a piece of the pie if and when the land
was found, so that west of the line he would have his coffers filled
by Isabella and Ferdinand, and east of the line by Don Juan.

This kind of double-dealing came as second nature to his fellow
countryman, Amerigo Vespucci, whom Frederick Pohl tells us
"paid homage to both courts and changed flags when it suited
his advantage."[31] Columbus had some secret understanding with
Vespucci, and in a letter to his son, Diego Columbus, there is a
strong hint of this. Columbus in this letter, dated 1505, asks his
son to contact Vespucci as he is about to appear before the Spanish court but to do so "secretly that there may be no suspicion."
In the same letter Columbus speaks of "payment that has been
made to me and is being made" but is afraid to detail this payment, saying, "I will give the information yonder because it is
impossible to give it in writing." If he referred to the usual pay-
ments due him for his excursions and discoveries in the Indies,
the terms of these were well-known, published and protected by
letters-patent or legal articles. Why then the secrecy? Why was
it impossible to commit the matter to writing? Why the great
fear of arousing suspicion? Also, how do we explain the strange
relationship to Vespucci, to whom he refers in this letter as if he
were a messenger or agent in his pay: "see what he can do to
profit me there [at the court] and strive to have him do it for he
will do everything."[32]

This and other pieces of evidence seem to indicate that Columbus was deliberately holding back on South America. His strange
insistence to King Ferdinand that Cuba was a continent (although
he wrote Luis de Santagel, Chancellor of Aragon months earlier
declaring that the natives, who lived there for centuries, were
certain it was an island)[33] and his equally strange insistence that
South America was an island, after the most cursory and superficial examination, may be seen in this light.[34] He had committed
himself, it seems, to keeping the Spanish away from the southern

continent, perhaps to facilitate his deal with the Portuguese. No
wonder Ferdinand and Isabella grew suspicious and allowed
Bobadilla to seize Columbus and his brother and drag them back,
naked and in disgrace, to Spain.

Whatever Columbus may have personally known or felt or
plotted, his argument (nothing but water to the east of the demarcation line) was the best to counter Spanish suspicions and
objections to the pact. It was the worst argument, however, to
present to the court if he wanted to secure immediate promotion
of further explorations to the south. If the theme of the first voyage had been "discovery and exploration," the theme of the second
was "colonization and consolidation." The order went out. Take
two thousand Spaniards with you! Plant a colony! Build a church!
Build a city! Let us have forts, farms, towns! Above all, pursue
vigorously the search for gold whenever a break from ordinary
labors will permit![35]

The building of the new city of Isabella, the struggle to subdue
and convert the natives of the Caribbean (who had massacred
the first settlement of Spaniards and demolished their fort), occupied most of Columbus' time until his return from his second
voyage in 1496. While in Española,* however, something happened that confirmed and complemented what Don Juan had
said. The Indians gave proof that they were trading with black
people. They brought to the Spanish concrete evidence of this
trade. "The Indians of this Española said there had come to Española a black people who have the tops of their spears made of
a metal which they call *gua-nin*, of which he [Columbus] had sent
samples to the Sovereigns to have them assayed, when it was
found that of 32 parts, 18 were of gold, 6 of silver and 8 of
copper."[36]

The origin of the word *guanin* may be tracked down in the
Mande languages of West Africa, through Mandingo, Kabunga,
Toronka, Kankanka, Bambara, Mande and Vei. In Vei, we have
the form of the word *ka-ni* which, transliterated into native pho-
netics, would give us *gua-nin*. In Columbus' journal gold is given

* Present-day Haiti and the Dominican Republic.

as *coa-na*, while *gua-nin* is recorded as an island where there is
much gold. Fray Bartolomé de las Casas, the Spanish scholar who
traveled with Columbus, and who was often appalled by his linguistic blunders, even in the use of Castilian Spanish, wrote in
the margin of the journal, correcting Columbus, "This guanin is
no island but that gold which according to the Indians had an
odor for which they valued it much." Similarly, in *Raccolta*, the
Italian account of the voyage, one reads "there were pieces of
gua-nin as large as the caravel's poop."[37]

The African spears presented by the Española Indians, which
corroborated Don Juan's statement about the Guinea boats, were
just one in a number of new factors pushing Columbus toward
an exploration of the route from Guinea. His brother Bartholomew
arrived in Española in command of three caravels on June 24,
1494.[38] The admiral had not seen his brother for many years, and
Bartholomew knew more, Las Casas tells us, than Christopher
himself, of the intelligence coming out of the Portuguese-African
world.[39] Bartholomew had worked as a cartographer in Lisbon.
While there, he had drawn numerous maps for mariners, and he
witnessed yearly the return of ships which had been navigating
to the western lands of Africa by way of the ocean. "Enlightened
and moved by the tales told him by those who returned, as one
might say, from another world, and himself more versed in maritime affairs, he communicated to his elder brother his reasons and
arguments, proving to him that in sailing away from the southern
part of Africa and directing his course straight upon the ocean-sea
he would surely arrive at continental land."[40]

He confirmed what Don Juan had told Columbus the previous
year. When Columbus returned to the Spanish court in 1496 he
found everywhere a spirited discussion of these continental lands
"said to lie to the south of the lands he had discovered and which
the King of Portugal seemed to think lay within his own domain."[41]
Jaime Ferrer, "a jeweller and trader in precious stones," also a
distinguished geographer who had done extensive traveling in
Africa and had been called in by the Spanish sovereigns to head
the commission fixing the Tordessillas line, wrote letters to Isa-

bella, who commanded him to get in touch with Columbus and
tell him all he had heard about this new continent.[42] Ferrer said
he had picked up his knowledge from Ethiopians and Arabs. He
had had "many conversations in the Levant, in Alcaine and
Domas," and from these he had gathered that "within the equinoctial regions there are great and precious things, such as fine
stones and gold and spices and drugs . . . the inhabitants are black
or tawny . . . when your Lordship [Columbus] finds such a people
an abundance of the said things shall not be lacking." His letter
ends with the strange rider (which goes beyond mere graciousness and implies that he knew some of this information had already been conveyed to Columbus) "of all this matter, your
Lordship knows more when sleeping than I do waking."[43]

The king and queen were excited. They saw whole new kingdoms opening up. Colonization of a ragbag of islands was not
enough. Columbus' mission would not be complete, they said, until
these continental lands had been "discovered" and brought under
the banner of Spain.[44]

Thus the scene was set for the exploration of the route the
African mariners had taken to the New World. Columbus sailed
with six ships on May 30, 1498. He issued instructions to three
of them to proceed to Española directly while "he ordered the
course laid to the way of the south-west, which is the route leading
from these islands to the south because then he would be on a
parallel with the lands of the Sierra of Loa [Sierra Leone] and
the Cape of Sancta Anna in Guinea, which is below the equinoctial
line . . . and after that he would navigate to the west, and from
there would go to this Española, in which route he would prove
the theory of the King Don Juan; and that he thought to investigate the report of the Indians of this Española who said that there
had come to Española from the south and south-east a black people who have the tops of their spears made of a metal which they
call *guanin* . . ."[45]

The journey by that route proved to be swift and the seas calm.
But it suited the Africans far more than the Europeans, who could
not bear the sun burning down upon the wild floating grasses of

the sea with the same intensity as upon the grasses of the West
African savannah lands. The heat tormented them almost to madness as they advanced through the Sargasso Sea. So ardent it was,
so penetrating, that Columbus "feared the ships would take fire
. . . the butts of wine and water swelled, breaking the hoops of the
casks, the wheat burned like fire: and the pork and salted meat
roasted and putrefied." Fortunately the rains came, without which,
according to Columbus, none of them, unaccustomed as they were
to such burning latitudes, would have escaped alive.[46]

Columbus ended up on a branch of the North Equatorial current which took him initially into a Caribbean island with three
great rocks which made him think of the Holy Trinity. He named
this island Trinidad. A little more to the south, however, he did
come in sight of the South American mainland (August 1, 1498).
Columbus, for some odd reason, would not land.[47]

On this third voyage he came upon more evidence of the contact between Guinea and the New World. From a settlement
along the South American coast on which his men landed on Tuesday, August 7, the natives brought "handkerchiefs of cotton very
symmetrically woven and worked in colors like those brought
from Guinea, from the rivers of Sierra Leone and of no difference."[48] Not only were they alike in style and color but also in
function. These handkerchiefs, he said, resembled *almayzars*—
Guinea headdresses and loincloths. "Each one is a cloth so woven
in colors that it appeared an *almayzar* with one tied on the head
and the other covering the rest."[49]

These were the earliest documented traces of the African presence. Within the first and second decades of the so-called "discovery," African settlements and artifacts were to be sighted by
the Spanish. When they were not reported as mere asides, they
were ignored or suppressed. But history is not easily buried. In
the oral traditions of the native Americans and the Guinea Africans, in the footnotes of the Spanish and Portuguese documents,
part of the story lies. Another part lies embalmed under the American and African earth. As this earth is now being lifted by archaeological picks and trowels, a new skeleton emerges of the history
of these adjacent worlds.

NOTES AND REFERENCES

For the evidence in this chapter the author draws to the reader's attention a 2,114-page study published in 1903. His interpretation, however, of the events documented in this study is original. John Boyd Thacher, in his three-volume work on Christopher Columbus —his life, his writings, his voyages—examines all the original documents known and available, in half a dozen languages. Although this work, the labor of a lifetime, is inspired by a blind adulation of Columbus, by a vision of the admiral's "saintly" character and motives, no other work on the man, of which there are many, can match it for its encyclopedic scope and detail. In the footnotes, however (which seem like another book compulsively writing itself), we begin to see the night-side or half-hidden face of history. There emerges, from under all the contradictions and cross-references, the sentences deliberately doctored or deleted in the conventional histories, the little-known deeds and statements of the admiral so nimbly glossed over, an illuminating pattern of consistency, through which we glimpse another image of the man and his time than the one his biographer strives to create.

1 John Boyd Thacher, *Christopher Columbus, His Life, His Work, His Remains*, New York, G. P. Putnam's Sons, 1903, Vol. 1, p. 665.
2 Ibid., p. 518.
3 Ibid., p. 664.
4 Idem.
5 Ibid., p. 537.
6 James Bailey, *The God-Kings and Titans*, New York, St. Martin's Press, 1973, p. 40. Also, J. V. Luce, "Ancient Explorers" in Gordon Ashe (ed.) *The Quest for America*, New York, Praeger Publishers, 1971, pp. 91–92.
7 Thacher, op. cit., p. 533.
8 Ibid., p. 666. This extraordinary incident is recorded by Friar Bartolomé de las Casas, the first historian of the Indies, as well as by the Portuguese historian Garcia de Resende.
9 Idem.
10 Ibid., p. 665.

11 Ibid., p. 667.

12 Thacher, op. cit., Vol. 2, p. 84. "As Columbus required the countenance of the Princes to hold his discovery, so these Princes required the seal of the Roman pontiff not absolutely to possess but to maintain in peace their sovereignty in the New World."

13 Thacher, op. cit., Vol. 1, p. 665.

14 This argument was later reflected in Columbus' *Book of Privileges*, in which he claimed "it was in the power of the said Admiral, after God, our Lord, to give them to any Prince with whom he might come to an agreement." See Thacher, op. cit., Vol. 3.

15 Thacher, op. cit., Vol. 1, p. 666.

16 Thacher, op. cit., Vol. 2, p. 379.

17 Bartholomew Diaz, Patron of the King of Portugal's ship, who intercepted Columbus in the harbor of Rastelo inside the river of Lisbon on March 5, 1493, was the first to push his way southward along the Atlantic coastline of Africa till he turned the southern extremity of the Old World. He did this in 1486, winning for Portugal a southern route to Old India. See Thacher, Vol. 1, p. 664.

18 Thacher, Vol. 1, p. 282.

19 Thacher, Vol. 2, p. 379. References to these discussions are made in Columbus' Journal of the Third Voyage. Columbus' son Ferdinand deliberately omits in the *Historie* (as do other works using this source as an authority) passages in the journal related to these discussions between his father and the Portuguese king on the Tordessillas line. He also omits reference to "the views held by King Don Juan of Portugal as to there being great lands within the line and to the south-west." Columbus' son was aware that this could later be presented as evidence of the prior discovery of the American continent.

20 For the full text in Spanish of the Treaty of Tordesillas, see Thacher, Vol. 2, pp. 165–186.

21 The expedition made by Pedro Alvares Cabral, who sailed from Lisbon for Calicut, March 9, 1500, with thirteen ships, found itself unexpectedly driven from the African coastline by

a storm onto the shores of Brazil. Cabral gave to this region the name of "Terra de Santa Cruz." He returned to Lisbon at the end of July 1501. See Thacher, Vol. 2, p. 444.

22 Ibid., p. 379.

23 Thacher, op. cit., p. 541.

24 In a letter sent to the Nurse of Prince Don Juan of Castile in 1500, Columbus notes that when "after losing my sails, I was driven into Lisbon by a tempest, I was falsely accused of having gone there to the King in order to give him the Indies." See Thacher, Vol. 2, p. 435.

25 Ibid., p. 698.

26 Letter of Queen Isabella to Columbus dated September 5, 1493. See Thacher, op. cit., Vol. 2, p. 554.

27 Idem.

28 Thacher, Vol. 2, p. 377. In his Journal of the Third Voyage, Columbus mentions how the Sovereigns sent for him that he should be present at the meetings in regard to the partition and that he could not go, on account of the grave illness which he had incurred in the discovery of Cuba, "which he always regarded as the mainland even until the present time as he could not circumnavigate it." This sentence was suppressed by Ferdinand Columbus in the *Historie*, and one is left to wonder whether Columbus was making a pretense about Cuba being a continent in order to forestall any further exploration south at this stage until the matter of the Tordesillas line (which he had helped to promote on behalf of the Portuguese) was cleared up. It is strange that Columbus should insist in his letter to King Ferdinand that Cuba was the continent, when in earlier correspondence, discovered among the papers of Luis de Santagel, Chancellor of the Exchequer of Aragon, Columbus had written, "I have learnt from some Indians whom I have seized that this land was certainly an island." For this reference, see note 33.

29 Letters of the sovereigns of Spain dated from Barcelona, May 24th, 1493, Thacher, Vol. 2, p. 556.

30 Ibid., p. 200. "The Spaniards seemed loath to put the line into their maps."

31 Frederick Pohl, *Amerigo Vespucci, Pilot Major*, New York, Octagon, 1966.

32 Thacher, op. cit., Vol. 3, p. 399.

33 R. H. Major, *Selected Letters of Columbus*, London, The Hakluyt Society, 1870, p. 3.

34 Thacher, Vol 2, p. 371.

35 Thacher, op. cit., Vol. 3, p. 96.

36 Thacher, op. cit., Vol. 2, p. 380.

37 Leo Weiner, *Africa and the Discovery of America*, Chicago, Innes & Sons, 1922, Vol. 1.

38 Thacher, Vol. 2, p. 344.

39 Las Casas, *Historia*, Lib. i, cap. xxix. See Thacher, Vol. 2, p. 341.

40 Antonio Gallo, *De Navigatione Columbi*. See Thacher, Vol. 2, p. 340.

41 Thacher, Vol. 2, p. 363.

42 Ibid., p. 365.

43 Letter dated August 5, 1495. See Thacher, Vol. 2, p. 369.

44 Ibid., p. 363.

45 Ibid., p. 380.

46 Ibid., p. 381.

47 Ibid., p. 371. Although some of his men landed on the South American coast on August 5, 1498, and Columbus held ceremonies of possession (as was the normal protocol in these matters) he himself did not put his foot on the southern continent. He immediately, hastily and mysteriously pronounced it an island.

48 Ibid., p. 392.

49 Ibid., p. 393.

2

THE VISIBLE
WITNESSES

*It is in contradiction to the most elementary logic and to
all artistic experience that an Indian could depict in a mas-
terly way the head of a Negro without missing a single racial characteristic, unless he had actually seen such a person. The types of people depicted must have lived in
America . . . The Negroid element is well proven by the
large Olmec stone monuments as well as the terracotta items
and therefore cannot be excluded from the pre-Columbian
history of the Americas.*

—ALEXANDER VON WUTHENAU,
*The Art of Terracotta Pottery in Pre-Columbian
South and Central America*

There is a narrow neck of land between the two Americas, which
in a way both joins and splits them. From this point, the Isthmus
of Darien, one could—if one flew above the clouds with the wing-
span and vision of the condor—look down upon the two great
seas that divide the world, the waters of the Pacific and Atlantic
oceans.

From such a point, though at a much lower altitude and with
only a fraction of the range and binocular vision of the condor,
the Spanish explorer Vasco Nuñez de Balboa stood on the summit
of the Sierra de Quarequa, looking down upon the Mar del Sur,
or Sea of the South, billowing far below him.

It was the twenty-fifth day of September 1513.

It had been a long and dangerous march through the forests of

the isthmus to this lonely peak in Darien. Below him at last lay
the great sea of which the son of Comogre, the Indian *cacique*,
had spoken. On this sea, according to what the young man had
said, boats as big as the brigantines sailed, from a land richer in
gold than any the Spanish had so far seen. (Strange, how the Indians always seemed to be pointing a finger southward, whisper-
ing, "Gold! gold! gold!" into the greedy, expectant ears of the
Spaniards. When they sailed in the direction of that finger, under
the mesmeric spell of that chant, there was still another Indian,
his finger beckoning ever farther southward, with the same en-
chanting whisper, "Gold! gold! gold!" Were these savages trying
to make fools of them?) The thought occurred to Balboa, but it
blew at the back of his mind faintly. In the forefront was the
warm, bright vision of golden sands beyond the Mar del Sur.

He recalled the morning his companions had sat on the porch
of the great long house of Comogre. They were still in a partial
stupor from the festivities of the previous day. Comogre had entertained them lavishly and had presented Balboa with four thousand ounces of golden ornaments. The Spanish were dazzled by
this generosity, but furious arguments broke out among them
when Balboa ordered everything to be weighed so that the king's
Exchequer could have its fifth part before any division of the
spoils. The men hovered darkly over the weighing scales like crows
over a battlefield.

Suddenly in the midst of the commotion, in strode the eldest
son of Comogre. He was obviously incensed by the vulgar fuss
and noise. The spectacle of these foreigners wrangling on the
porch of his father's palace disgusted him. To the amazement of
everyone, he leaped at the scales and knocked them over with his
fist, scattering gold all over the porch.

They were fighting over trifles, he told them contemptuously.
If they were so greedy for gold, why, over those mountains—he
pointed in the direction of the inevitable south—there was another sea. On it sailed boats as big as theirs, from a land where
they would find more gold than they could ever weigh.

The Spaniards in Balboa's company were so delighted by news
of this sea and the land beyond and the gold, that it blunted any

sense of insult they might have felt at this impetuous outburst of the chief's son. His words ran through the Spanish settlements in Darien like a brushfire. Balboa himself was so overwhelmed by the glittering prospect that he decided forthwith to remove all obstacles in the way of his pursuit of it. In a rash, daring action that was later to cost him his head but shower him for a moment in glory, he usurped the government of Darien, drove out the governor Nicuesa, imprisoned the chief justice Encisco, and marched at the head of his own army into the forests of the isthmus. He thus stole a march on Pedro Arias, whom the Spanish had officially sent out to check on the rumor of the new land and sea. "Partly by force, partly by conciliation and by pacifying the native kings in the area with presents," Balboa made it across the mountains.

As he stood on the summit of Quarequa at last, he sank to his knees and gave thanks to God. He ordered his companions to build a wooden cross and plant it on the spot where he had knelt. He then went down the southern slope of Quarequa, and making his way to the shore of the bay, ran like a madman with a banner straight into the sea, declaring that he had taken possession of it in the name of Jesus Christ and King Ferdinand.[1]

Inspired by this discovery of the southern sea, Balboa and his men decided to push further south along the isthmus. Under the shadow of Quarequa, they came upon an Indian settlement where, to their astonishment, they found a number of war captives who were plainly and unmistakably African. These were tall black men of military bearing who were waging war with the natives from some settlement in the neighborhood. "Balboa asked the Indians whence they got them but they could not tell, nor did they know more than this, that men of this color were living nearby and they were constantly waging war with them. These were the first Negroes that had been seen in the Indies."[2]

Peter Martyr, the first historian of America, reports on this remarkable meeting between the Spanish explorers and the blacks of Darien. "The Spaniards," wrote Martyr, "found Negroes in this province. They only live one day's march from Quarequa and they

are fierce . . . It is thought that Negro pirates from Ethiopia established themselves after the wreck of their ships in these mountains. The natives of Quarequa carry on incessant war with these
Negroes. Massacre or slavery is the alternate fortune of these
peoples."[3]

Martyr uses the word Ethiopia as a general term for Africa. He
is not suggesting a specific country in Africa as the origin of these
mysterious Africans sighted by the Spanish. He could not conjecture on their exact country of origin or tribal identity, but he certainly knew from his own acquaintance with Africa, as a diplomat
to Egypt from the Spanish court, that there was nothing far-
fetched about African boats being washed up as wrecks on the
other side of the ocean's coast. His comment also makes it clear
that the African settlement was large enough to enable its members to wage wars of aggression or defense within the hostile
environment in which they found themselves.

An encounter with New World negroes was also reported off
Colombia. Fray Gregoria Garcia, a priest of the Dominican order
who spent nine years in Peru in the early sixteenth century, pinpoints an island off Cartagena, Colombia, as the place where the
Spanish first encountered blacks in the New World. Once again,
as in the Balboa incident in Darien, the blacks were found as
captives of war among the Indians. In a book silenced by the
Spanish Inquisition, Garcia wrote, "Here were found slaves* of the
lord—Negroes—who were the first our people saw in the Indies."[4]

Darien and Colombia were easily accessible to African shipwrecked mariners. These places lie within the terminal area of
currents that move with great power and swiftness from Africa
to America. These currents may be likened to marine conveyor
belts. Once you enter them you are transported (even against your
will, even with no navigational skill) from one bank of the ocean

---

* The word used by Garcia, "*esclavos*," means slaves, but it is important to
point out here that this party of blacks who were caught away from their
settlement in Quarequa were not "slaves" in the loaded post-Columbian
American sense. They were war captives. The blacks also killed and made
war captives of Indians they caught in these raids along the Isthmus, as
Peter Martyr points out. That was the fortune of war, then as now.

to the other. We shall deal with them and all the problems of the Atlantic sea voyage in Chapter 4, but it is important to point out here how many small, isolated black communities have been found on the American seaboard at the terminal points of these currents. Alphonse de Quatrefages, professor of anthropology in the Museum of Natural History in Paris, noted in his study *The Human Species* (published in 1905) that "black populations have been found in America in very small numbers and as isolated tribes in the midst of very different nations. Such are the Charruas of Brazil, the black Caribees of Saint Vincent in the Gulf of Mexico, the Jamassi of Florida . . . Such again is the tribe of which Balboa saw some representatives in his passage of the Isthmus of Darien in 1513. Yet it would seem, from the expressions made use of by Gomara, that these were true Negroes. This type was well known to the Spaniards . . ."[5]

De Quatrefages shows how the location of these African New World communities coincides with the terminal points of Africa-to-America currents or sea roads. "We only find these black men in America in those places washed by the Kouro-Siwo [a Pacific current known as the black stream] and the Equatorial current of the Atlantic or its divisions. A glance at the maps of Captain Kerhallet will at once show the rarity and distribution of these tribes. It is evident that the more or less pure black elements have been brought from Africa through some accident at sea; they have there mixed with the local races, and have formed those small isolated groups which are distinguished by their color from the surrounding tribes."[6]

These Spanish sightings of Africans in the New World and the later discovery by anthropologists of distinctive black settlements along the American seaboard (outside of the mainstream of the post-Columbian slave complex) constitute only one strand of the evidence of pre-Columbian contact between Africa and America. An overwhelming body of new evidence is now emerging from several disciplines, evidence that could not be verified and interpreted before, in the light of the infancy of archaeology and the great age of racial and intellectual prejudice. The most remarkable examples of this evidence are the realistic portraitures of

Negro-Africans in clay, gold and stone unearthed in pre-Columbian strata in Central and South America.

It has only been within the last decade, however, that this evidence has begun to filter down to the general public. When in
1862 a colossal granite head of a Negro was found in the Canton
of Tuxtla, near the place where the most ancient of pre-Columbian
statuettes were discovered, the historian Orozco y Berra declared
in his *History of the Conquest of Mexico* that there was bound
to be an important and intimate relationship between Mexicans
and Africans in the pre-Columbian past.[7] In his time, however,
the Negroid heads could not be conclusively dated. We now
know, without the shadow of a doubt, through the most modern
methods of dating, that some of the Negroid stone heads found
among the Olmecs and in other parts of Mexico and Central
America are from as early as 800 to 700 B.C. Clearly American
history has to be reconstructed to account for this irrefutable
piece of archaeological data. Explanations, not excuses, have got
to be found. The implications of these discoveries can no longer
be dismissed or ignored. The time has come to disperse the cloud
of silence and scepticism that has settled over this subject for a
century.

A break in that cloud came about seven years ago with the work
of Alexander von Wuthenau. Fired by a passionate conviction that
America was an inseparable part of the mainstream of world culture before 1492 and excited by the vitality and sophistication of
pre-Columbian art (so long neglected in the great art museums
of the world), this art historian and lecturer carried out intensive
diggings and investigations in Mexico. Out of his dedicated com-
mitment emerged a wealth of visible witnesses to the pre-Columbian presence of Africans and others in the Americas. His book
*The Art of Terracotta Pottery in Pre-Columbian South and Cen-
tral America*[8] broke new ground. It shattered conventional assumptions in the field of American art as well as history. But its
favorable reception has only become possible because there has
been a genuine change, however gradual, however slight, in the
climate of prejudice that has long inhibited any serious scholarly
inquiry into this matter.

Two recent conferences of American anthropologists have contributed to this change. These were the International Congress of Americanists, held in Barcelona in 1964, at which a French anthropologist said that the only things missing in connection with the Negroid terra cottas of ancient America as final proof of the African presence, were Negroid skeletons, which have since been reported in early pre-Christian as well as medieval layers;[9] and the Society for American Archaeology, which held a symposium at Santa Fe, New Mexico, in May 1968 to discuss the problems of pre-Columbian contact between the continents and concluded: *"Surely there cannot now be any question but that there were visitors to the New World from the Old in historic or even prehistoric time before 1492."*[10]

What Von Wuthenau has done is to open a door upon the photo gallery of the Americas. For, lacking the camera, the ancient and medieval Americans sought to capture for all time, in the art of realistic portraiture through the medium of clay, the significant figures of their respective generations. Africans move through all their major periods, from the time of the Olmec culture around 800 B.C., when they arise in massive stone sculptures, through the medieval Mexico of the Mayas, when they appear not only in terra-cotta portraits but on golden pectorals and on pipes, down to the late post-Classic period, time of the Conquest, when they begin to disappear as they disappeared all over the world until today, reemerging once more as significant figures.

A head from the post-Classic period stares at us across five centuries with a lifelike power and directness (see Plate 5). This is clearly the type of African who came here in 1310 in the expeditionary fleet of Abubakari the Second of Mali. These men made a tremendous visual impression upon the Mixtecs, last of the great pre-Columbian potters, for this is one of their finest clay sculptures. It was found in Oaxaca in Mexico. Its realism is striking. No detail is vague, crudely wrought or uncertain. No stylistic accident can account for the undisputed Negro-ness of the features. From the full, vivid lips, the darkened grain of the skin, the prognathic bone formation of the cheeks, the wide nostrils, the generously fleshed nose, down to the ceremonial earring and the cotton cap Cadamosto noted on warrior boatmen on the Gambia, the American artist has deftly caught the face of this African.

The court tradition of Mali and documents in Cairo tell of an African king, Abubakari the Second, setting out on the Atlantic in 1311. He commandeered a fleet of large boats, well stocked with food and water, and embarked from the Senegambia coast, the western borders of this West African empire, entering the Canaries current, "a river in the middle of the sea" as the captain of a preceding fleet (of which only one boat returned) described it.[11] Neither of the two Mandingo fleets came back to Mali to tell their story, but around this same time evidence of contact between West Africans and Mexicans appears in strata in America in an overwhelming combination of artifacts and cultural parallels. A black-haired, black-bearded figure in white robes, one of the representations of Quetzalcoatl, modeled on a dark-skinned outsider, appears in paintings in the valley of Mexico (see Postscript), while the Aztecs begin to worship a Negroid figure mistaken for their god Tezcatlipoca because he had the right ceremonial color. Negroid skeletons are found in this time stratum in the Caribbean (see Chapter 6). "A notable tale is recorded in the Peruvian traditions . . . of how black men coming from the east had been able to penetrate the Andes Mountains."[12] Figures, like the one described above, return to prominence in American clay. We shall deal with this in subsequent chapters, but it is important to bear in mind that the Negroid terra cottas are scattered over several periods and bear witness, in conjunction with other evidence, that this was just one of several contacts between the two continents, joined throughout pre-Columbian history by a long but easily accessible and mobile waterway.

Onto this waterway Africans sometimes stumbled accidentally. This may account for some of the Negroid heads in Plate 2, which represent Africans appearing on the plateau of Mexico and other parts of Mesoamerica just before and after Christ. Here we see native American artists struggling in clay two thousand years ago to come to terms realistically with the alien physiognomy of the African. This struggle is not always successful. Prognathism

or some other distinct Negro-African feature is sometimes deliberately overemphasized for effect, producing vivid but grotesque
evocations. Nonetheless, the dense, close curl and kink of Negroid
hair, the goatee beard, so uncommon to the hairless American
Indian chin, and the heavy ear pendants, a popular West African
feature, come through quite clearly. With respect to the latter,
Cadamosto, the Portuguese explorer who visited the Senegambian
border of Mali in 1450, notes "these people all have their ears
pierced round with holes in which they wear various ear rings,
one behind the other."

There may be some stylistic distortion in the Negroid head from
the Mandingo contact period in Plate 6 (bottom row). The chin
juts out with an exaggerated and primitive power. Strangely
enough, it was regarded by the American Indians as a sacred face.
It was venerated later by the Aztecs, simply because it was black,
as their god Tezcatlipoca.[13] Black gods and *gods with Negroid
features* (for black is sometimes just a ceremonial color) may be
found among the American Indians. Another black god is the
god of jewelers, Naualpilli. The Negroid features of this god were
sculpted in green stone by the Mexicans, while his kinky hair was
cast in pure gold.[14] There is also the god of traveling merchants,
of whom we shall later speak, Ek-chu-ah, who enters Mayan
mythology in the wake of the Mandingo (see Plate 18).

It is hard for many to imagine the Negro-African figure being
venerated as a god among the American Indians. He has always
been represented as the lowliest of the low, at least since the era
of conquest and slavery. His humiliation as a world figure begins,
in fact, with the coming of Columbus.* It was in the very decade
of his "discoveries" that the black and white Moors were laid low.
The image of the Negro-African as a backward, slow and unin-
ventive being is still with us. Not only his manhood and his freedom but even the memory of his cultural and technological
achievements before the day of his humiliation seem to have been
erased from the consciousness of history. Even in the thinking

---

* Columbus himself was the first to initiate slavery in the Americas, even
against the wishes of the Spanish Sovereigns.

of Leo Wiener, M. D. W. Jeffreys and James Bailey, white scholars who have all sought to prove the Negro-African presence in pre-Columbian America, the black man still figures as an inferior.

Bailey, in his book *The God-Kings and Titans*, disclaims any indigenous base for African cultures before the Arabs and Romans. "That African culture, prior to the Arab and Roman gold-trade was an independent African invention . . . is nonsense."[15] He sees them in ancient America simply as mercenary soldiers of the Phoenicians. Leo Wiener, the Harvard philologist, assumes that the great Mali empire of medieval West Africa owed all its refinements, even its animist ritual and magic, to the Arab-Islamic civilization. The Mandingo came to America before Columbus, he declares, but carrying another man's cultural baggage. He sees the Negro-African as simply a conductor of Islamic cultural electricity.[16] M. D. W. Jeffreys, the South African anthropologist, refers to the Negro in one of his articles as "a West African item,"[17] and while he presents forceful arguments for his pre-Columbian presence, suggests that he came here as a porter and paddler for the Arabs. For all these men, therefore, the image of the Negro-African has not changed. They remain victims of the myth created and sustained for half a millenium, while appearing to strive manfully to dispel it. For them, before and after Columbus, the Negro is still a beggar in the wilderness of history, a porter, a paddler, a menial, a mercenary—the eternal and immutable slave.

If this had indeed been the case, why should the Olmecs erect huge monuments to him which dwarf all other human figures in the Americas? Why should some of the Negroid representations be venerated among the Maya and Aztecs as deities? Why should the finest of American potters sculpt such vivid and powerful portraits of this contemptible man? Can we image modern black artists in Mozambique building colossal monuments to the Portuguese soldiers who clashed with the freedom-fighters of Cabral? Or the South African whites, for that matter, erecting altars and temples to the garbage-collectors or street-cleaners of Pretoria? These contradictions do not appear as the glaring absurdities they really are unless a shift in consciousness occurs. Such a shift is required if we are to reconstruct the history of America and Africa during those periods in which these worlds and cultures are seen to collide and converge. We cannot see very far if we enter an ancient time with contemporary blinkers, even if our pathways into the past are illuminated by a hundred torches lit by the most recent archaeological discoveries. What is needed far more than new facts is a fundamentally new vision of history.

In this new vision the Atlantic is an open sea long before Columbus. But accidental drift voyages by African men, except in those cases where they brought fruit or grain with them alien to America (and this happened in prehistory at least twice) would in themselves have a very minimal effect, if any. Planned expeditions, however, or expeditions intended for other destinations in Africa which were blown off-course, would be a different matter. They would bring not only a substantial but a select group of aliens to American shores. This may account for the presence of Negroid women in pre-Columbian America (see Plate 3). These women, of course, did not rule out interbreeding between the Africans and the natives, as terra cottas showing American Indians with a Negroid strain attest, but their coming managed to prevent a clean obliteration of the evidence of an African presence through its total absorption into the genetic pool of the American and to preserve through the generations several distinctive racial traits.

One of these women from the early pre-Classic period bears a striking resemblance to the ebony head of the Egyptian queen Tiy, the Negroid mother of Tutankhamen. This racial type— Negro-Egyptian—with its peculiar coiffure, facial geography and expression, appears in the Mexican heartland around 800–700 B.C.

The most remarkable representations of Negroes in America are those that appear at this time. So realistic are these representations that even the most conservative Americanists have found it difficult to deny their Negroid identity, but they have been found in such incredibly early strata and as an integral part of such an early American culture that some investigators have been forced to ignore their embarrassing existence. No other archaeological discovery in the history of this hemisphere has presented such a puzzle. The questions they raise are as momentous as those once raised by the ancient observatory at Stonehenge and still hovering over the mysterious giants of Easter Island.

There is no denying the great antiquity of these Negroid figures. The archaeological contexts in which they have been found have been radio-carbon dated.[18] Carbon 14 can only be wrong one hundred years either way (if we are dating materials less than 7000 years old) and indisputably clear carbon-14 datings have been procured for organic materials associated with the culture and people who produced these Negroid figures. There is no denying their Negro-ness either. The ancient Americans who sculpted them have been shown to be absolute masters of realistic portraiture, and did not arrive at these distinctive features through accidental stylization. The features are not only Negro-African in type but individual in their facial particulars, canceling out the possibility of ritual stereotypes of an unknown race produced by some quirk of the sculptor's imagination.

The people who were host to these Negro-African figures are known as the Olmecs. At the sacred center of the Olmec culture— La Venta—about eighteen miles inland from the Gulf of Mexico which flows into the Atlantic, there stood four colossal Negroid heads, six to nine feet high, weighing up to forty tons each. They stood in large squares or plazas in front of the most colorful temple-platforms, the sides and floors of which were of red, yellow and purple.[19] They stood twelve to twenty times larger than the faces of living men. They were like gods among the Olmecs. In this center of La Venta there were great altars. One of these (known as the third altar) was made out of one of the Negroid heads, flattened on top for that purpose. A speaking tube was found to go in at the ear and out at the mouth so that the figure could function as a talking oracle,[20] a detail we shall see later to be of considerable significance in identifying the area of the Old World from which these Africans came.

The construction of these Negroid figures is a fact of staggering proportions. Imagine forty tons of basalt block mined from stone quarries eighty miles away and transported to the holy center of La Venta—not in pieces but in one massive chunk—for the Negroid heads seem to be sculpted out of gigantic balls, not jointed shelves or built-up layers of stone. Hundreds of these balls making perfect spheres are still found today in Central America, suggesting that this was the way the stone may have been found by the Olmecs, huge basalt bubbles wrought by freak volcanic or meteoric activity.[21] This would have facilitated rolling them across vast tracts of land. Other investigators, however, have suggested that crude stone was transported from quarries eighty miles downriver on rafts.[22] It was not only at La Venta that these extraordinary heads were found. In all, eleven colossal Negroid heads appear in the Olmec heartland—four at La Venta, five at San Lorenzo and two at Tres Zapotes in southern Vera Cruz.[23]

The Olmecs who lived in the jungled country of the Gulf Coast and built these powerful monuments to the Negro were obsessed with the figure of the jaguar. The jaguar motif appears on hundreds of clay, stone and jade figures that survive their culture. Half-jaguar, half-human monsters with small fat baby faces and snarling mouths, sexless and smooth with the obesity of eunuchs, haunt and stamp this culture with a signature both unique and foreign. "This feline," says Frederick Peterson in his book *Ancient Mexico*, "evidently proceeds from tropical regions and was imported into Mexico." Peterson also mentions investigations into the skeletons of the ancient Mexicans. He pinpoints a "a substratum with Negroid characteristics that intermingled with the magicians."[24] In September 1974 the Polish craniologist Dr. Andrzej Wiercinski disclosed to the Forty-first Congress of Americanists held in Mexico, that "some of the skulls from Tlatilco, Cerro de las Mesas and Monte Albán [all pre-Christian sites in Mexico] show, to a different degree, a clear prevalence of the total Negroid pattern."[25] In February 1975 a Smithsonian Institution team reported the find of two Negroid male skeletons in a grave in the U.S. Virgin Islands. This grave had been used and abandoned by the Caribs long before the coming of Columbus. Soil from the earth layers in which the skeletons were found was dated to A.D. 1250. A study of the teeth showed a type of "dental mutilation characteristic of early African cultures," and clamped around the wrist of one of the skeletons was a clay vessel of pre-Columbian Indian design.[26]

Skeletons have also been found in pre-Columbian layers in the valley of the Pecos River, which, flowing through Texas and New Mexico, empties via the Rio Grande into the Gulf of Mexico. Professor Hooton, a physical anthropologist, reporting on these finds, said of the skeletons: "The Pecos skulls resemble most closely crania of Negro groups coming from those parts of Africa where Negroes commonly have some perceptible infusion of Hamitic blood."[27]

Finds like these, in addition to the stone heads and Negroid clay masks of the same period (like the Negroid "Silenus" mask in the bottom row of Plate 6) force us to consider afresh the extraordinary parallels between ancient America and Africa in this period, dismissed before as mere coincidences. Is it not strange that it is in this very period when the Negro-African begins to appear in Mexico and to affect significantly the Olmec culture that the first pyramids, mummies, trepannated skulls, stelae and hieroglyphs begin to appear in America? Is it not strange that it is during this very period that a Negro-African dynasty gains ascendancy in Egypt and black Pharaohs (Negro-Nubians) don the plumed serpent crown of Upper and Lower Egypt? No mummies, no pyramids, appear in this hemisphere during the heyday of these things in the Egyptian world, but suddenly they spring up in full flower at the same point in time as the Negro-Nubians usher in an Egyptian cultural renaissance, restoring these features that had long lapsed in Egypt and for which there are no evolutionary precedents in America (see Chapters 8 and 9).

Egypt was passing through a very unstable period, and unusual movements of fleets and armies reflected this uncertainty. Egyptian fleets, as well as Phoenician fleets in the pay of the black Nubian rulers of Egypt, were traversing the Mediterranean (the Phoenicians moving even into the North Atlantic to points as far north as Cornwall in the quest for supplies of tin). Metal supplies had been severely curtailed by the Assyrian control and blockade of Asian sea routes, and they were sorely needed for the weaponry of the Nubian-Egyptian armies.[28] Ships on this metal run, moving in the vicinity of the North African coast, could very easily have been caught in a storm and swept off-course by the North Atlantic currents. Such an accident (which has happened in many documented instances) could account for the startling appearance in the Olmec heartland of Negroes with elements of Egyptian culture. One branch of the North Equatorial current would have taken them from the North African or West African coast right into the Gulf of Mexico. (See map of Atlantic currents, Plate 10.)

But what impact could a boatload or even a fleet of Negro-Egyptians have had on the Gulf of Mexico? These men would have been, in numerical terms, a drop of water in the human ocean of Mexico. It is estimated that the populations surrounding La Venta must have been quite substantial, at the time of Negro-Egyptian contact, to have made the building of this great ritual center possible. The first Egyptian-type pyramid, which appears at La Venta in this period, is 240 by 420 feet at the base and 110 feet high. To construct temple platforms, burial chambers and all, took 800,000 man-hours and involved a labor force of at least 18,000.[29] This does not include administrators and priests. How could a score or even a hundred shipwrecked mariners from the Old World have a significant culture-transforming effect on so many people? This argument, advanced by some anti-diffusionists, who contend that a few aliens cannot, without military power, significantly affect a native population of substantial size, is pure nonsense. Cabello de Balboa cites a group of seventeen Negroes shipwrecked in Ecuador in the early sixteenth century who in short order became governors of an entire province of American Indians.[30]

The influence of Negro-Africans on Olmec culture (which we shall discuss in detail in subsequent chapters) was considerable. Even more profound was the impact of Olmec culture upon all future civilizations in Mesoamerica. As Michael Coe, the distinguished authority on Mexico, has pointed out, "There is not the slightest doubt that all later civilizations in Mesoamerica, whether Mexican or Maya, rest ultimately on an Olmec base."[31]

NOTES AND REFERENCES

1 For a historical outline of incidents dramatized in the opening pages of this chaper, see Arthur James Weise, *Discoveries of*

America to 1525, New York, and London, G. P. Putnam's Sons, 1884, pp. 225–228.

2 Lopez de Gomara, *Historia de Mexico, Anvers*, 1554.

3 F. A. MacNutt (ed. and trans.), *De Orbo Novo: The Eight Decades of Peter Martyr d'Anghera*, New York, 1912.

4 Alexander von Wuthenau, *The Art of Terracotta Pottery in Pre-Columbian South and Central America*, New York, Crown Publishers, 1969, p. 167.

5 Alphonse de Quatrefages, *The Human Species*, New York, Appleton and Co., 1905, p. 200.

6 Ibid, pp. 201–202.

7 M. Orozco y Berra, *Historia Antigua y de la Conquista de Mexico*, Mexico, 1880, Vol. 1, p. 109.

8 See Note 4 above. An earlier edition in German was published by Holle Verlag, Baden-Baden, 1965.

9 Von Wuthenau, op. cit., p. 96.

10 Herbert Baker, "Commentary: Section III" in Riley, Kelley, Pennington and Rands (eds.) *Man Across the Sea*, Austin, University of Texas Press, 1971, p. 438.

11 Ibn Fadl Allah al Omari, *Masalik el Absar Fir Mamelik el Amsar*, traduit par Gaudefroy, Paris, 1927, pp. 61–63. See also Mohammed Habibullah's translation from the Arabic text quoted in Basil Davidson, *The Lost Cities of Africa*, Boston, Little Brown, 1970, pp. 74, 75, and J. Spencer Trimingham's version of the Abubakari expedition in *A History of Islam in West Africa*, London, Oxford University Press, 1962, p. 67.

12 Harold Lawrence "African Explorers in the New World," *The Crisis*, June–July, 1962, pp. 321–332. Heritage Program Reprint, p. 11.

13 Von Wuthenau, op. cit., p. 178.

14 Ibid., p. 96. Naualpilli is mentioned in the Florentine Codex. R. G. Granados quotes the listing in the register of Mexican antiquities of the Archivo de Indios. See representation on page 168 of Von Wuthenau and Plate 18 of this volume.

15 James Bailey, *The God-Kings and the Titans*, New York, St. Martin's Press, 1973, p. 189.

16 Leo Weiner, *Africa and the Discovery of America*, Philadelphia, Innes and Sons, 1920–22, Vols. 1–3.

17 M. D. W. Jeffreys, "Arabs Discover America before Columbus," in *The Muslim's Digest*, June 1953, p. 69. In this article Jeffreys remarks: "The colocasia, the yam, the Negro and the non-barking dog are all West African *items*, and if these are found in the Americas before Columbus *someone* must have taken them there before him" (italics added).

18 Philip Drucker, Robert F. Heizer and Robert J. Squier, "Radio-carbon Dates from La Venta, Tabasco," *Science*, Vol. 126 (July 12, 1957), pp. 72–73.

19 Michael Coe, *Mexico*, New York, Praeger Publishers, 1962, p. 88.

20 Constance Irwin, *Fair Gods and Stone Faces*, New York, St. Martin's Press, 1963, p. 166.

21 There are hundreds of giant basalt balls, almost perfectly spherical, to be found in Central and South America. One of these, in Costa Rica (weighing 16 tons), is reproduced in James Bailey, *The God-Kings and the Titans*, p. 9.

22 Coe, op. cit., p. 89.

23 Bailey, op. cit., p. 51.

24 Frederick Peterson, *Ancient Mexico*, New York, G. P. Putnam's Sons, 1959.

25 Alexander von Wuthenau, *Unexpected Faces in Ancient America*, New York, Crown Publishers, 1975, p. 136.

26 The Washington *Post*, February 29, 1975, page A 17 (Associated Press Report). See also Ivan Van Sertima, "Archaeology's Discovery of an African Presence in America," *The New York Times*, Op-Ed Page, December 4, 1975, p. 41.

27 E. A. Hooton, *Apes, Men and Morons*, New York, G. P. Putnam's Sons, 1937, p. 183.

28 For details of alliances and maritime commerce of the period, see Chapter 8 of this volume. For Negro mariners and capabilities for ocean voyages, see Chapter 4.

29 Coe, op. cit., p. 88.

30 Stephen Jett in Riley, Kelley, Pennington and Rands (eds.)

Man Across the Sea, Austin, University of Texas Press, 1971, p. 16. Jett gives as his source for this statement M. Cabello de Balboa, *Obras*, Vol. 1, Quito, 1945, p. 133.

31 Coe, op. cit.

3

THE MARINER PRINCE OF MALI

We are vessels of speech, we are the repositories which harbor secrets many centuries old . . . without us the names of kings would vanish from oblivion, we are the memory of mankind; by the spoken word we bring to life the deeds and exploits of kings for younger generations.

History holds no mystery for us; we teach to the vulgar just as much as we want to teach them, for it is we who keep the keys to the twelve doors of Mali . . .

I teach the kings of their ancestors so that the lives of the ancients might serve them as an example, for the world is old but the future springs from the past.

—THE WORDS OF THE MALI GRIOT MAMADOU KOUYATÉ, QUOTED IN D. T. NIANE, *Sundiata: An Epic of Old Mali* A.D. 1217–1237

The following is a reconstruction of an event in the medieval empire of Mali, based on Arab historical and travel documents and the oral tradition of the Mali griots—author's note.

That morning the king was in a somber mood. Everyone within the palace courtyard sensed it, and as he came through a door in a corner of the palace with the great bow of the Mali kings shining in his hands, a chill fell over the assembly. His golden skullcap was askew, and the daggerlike edges of the brocaded band looked blunted. He had obviously spent the night nodding and dozing in full royal regalia, for under the velvety red tunic of *mutanfas* the silk was heavily crinkled. Word was passed down

through the crowd, waiting under the trees outside the gates, that
this was no propitious day to air trivial complaints or broach matters too contentious for quick settlement. The king walked slowly
to his *pempi*, with his face down. Even the stringed music of the
gold and silver *guimbris*, which usually brought a softness to his
stern, bearded face, sounded tuneless against his expression.

Beside him walked his griot, Kouyaté, the court historian, stop-
ping when the king stopped, affecting a grave frown to blend with
the temper of his master's mood. Behind them trailed a train of
three hundred armed servants.

The king moved heavily to the *pempi*, a three-tiered pavilion
which had been set up under a great silk-cotton tree dominating
the palace yard. He stopped before the silk-carpeted steps of the
pavilion, and for a moment appeared almost frozen in thought,
so that the long train of servants, reflecting his stride, became
dutifully immobile. For the first time that morning he lifted his
head and looked around. It was a restless, hurried look that took
in everything and nothing. He stared for a moment at the white
sun of the savannahs burning behind the webs of the great tree
under which Sundiata, the founder of the empire, once sat. Then,
like a preacher ascending his pulpit, he climbed the steps.

The moment he was seated on the cushions of the *pempi*, under
the shade of the royal umbrella, surmounted by its golden bird,
there was a roll of drums, and trumpets and bugles sounded. Three
pages ran out to summon his deputy and the military commanders
of the regions. These dignitaries entered and sat down. There also
entered into the king's presence two horses. They were without
mounts, yet saddled and bridled, cantering with a beautiful control, as though ridden by spirits. Beside them trotted two sacred
goats whom the magicians believed protected their sovereign from
the evil eye.[1]

It was the year 1310, in the city of Niani, on the left bank of the
Sankarini. Abubakari the Second, grandson of a daughter of Sundiata, was holding court.

One of the military commanders opened the day's business.
Things were not going so well for Mali in the siege of Jenne. It
was a small city, set in the backwaters of the Bani River, a tribu-

tary of the Niger, about three hundred miles southwest of Timbuktu. But it had repulsed everything the Malian forces had hurled against it.

The news did little to lift Abubakari's spirits. He had lost all heart to take Jenne. It was a beautiful city, he was told, distinguished by its waterways and the design of its buildings. There were scholars within its walls as learned as the wisest men of Timbuktu, doctors who performed more advanced and delicate operations (such as the removal of cataracts) than any then known in the Arab world or Europe. It would be a feather in any conqueror's cap to take Jenne. Gaw and Mamadu before him had tried and failed. Jenne was protected by treacherous swamps and approachable only by twisting canals and streams.[2] Pour more troops into the battle, the commander advised, but the king shook his head. Leave Jenne alone, he said; it is no Taghaza, Takedda or Kangaba, it has neither salt, copper nor gold. But he spoke against the counsel of his deputy and commanders without conviction. The truth was he was tired of this war.

Since ascending the throne of Mali he had had but one ambition. It was to use all his power and wealth to realize a dream that had haunted him all through his childhood. Sakura, the slave turned king, the upstart and usurper, had broken the legitimate line of succession of the Mali kings, but during his fifteen years of illicit rule he had extended Mali down along the Gambia River to the sea. Abubakari had heard many tales of that sea. It was known in his boyhood as the world's end.

It was also said that the world began and ended in the water. Water stood at the end of the conquered world for Alexander, who, pushing at last to the sea, charged the waves with his horses, crying his heart out at the thought that there were no more lands, no more armies or cities to conquer. Water mocked Alexander, upon whom all the Mali kings from Sundiata down had modeled themselves. Water fascinated Abubakari the Second—spacious, mobile, brooding bodies of water. Water was like stored grain at Niani, for it took a full day for the servants to fill the royal jars in the river Kala and return with them to the palace. The boy Abu sometimes thought it strange that his ancestors had built a

palace so far from the water's edge. Abu had once traveled in a
great canoe down the somber waters of the Sankarini. He mar-
veled at the way the boatmen used their paddles to listen to the
drumming of fishes and the whisper of currents and the canoe
sped as though it were sliding down a steep floor when the
paddlers paused. He wondered dreamily where all the running
bright brown water went, as boys are wont to wonder over what
strange far-off lands go drifting clouds.

He had heard that the Senegal and other rivers in his kingdom
ran beyond the land into a great sea. Men were more terrified of
that sea than of the vast, blinding plains of the Sahara. The Arabs
called it "the green sea of darkness." Few had been known to
enter upon it. Fewer still had been known to return. It was said
that there was a powerful current, like the hand of a violent god,
not far from the land's end, which beckoned boats into its fingers
and threw them out at the uttermost edges of the world, where
they fell with the sea into a black hole. But during Sakura's reign
diplomats had come from the court of Morocco who said that this
was all nonsense. Brand new ideas about worlds beyond this sea
were circulating in North Africa.[3] The works of Abu Zaid, Masudi,
Idrisi, Istakhri and Albufeda had trickled down to the university
at Timbuktu. Scholars had come more recently, in the time of
Gaw and Mamadu, saying strange things—that the waters that
washed the western end of Mali were not the end of the world
at all, that the world had no end, for it was built like a bottle
gourd. If you put your finger at any point of a gourd and tried
to trace a line across it, his griot told him, you would come at the
end of the line to the point where you started, beginning again at
the point where it seemed you had come to an end. So it was
with the world. Thus would a man return to the very spot from
which he had set out, if he could march or sail across the circle
of the gourd-shaped world.

But there were those—the most closed and conservative of the
clerics—who felt that the new thinkers in North Africa were pre-
sumptuous, romantic, insane. How could they believe that men
were walking upside down in unknown lands at the bottom of

the gourd-shaped world? He was glad that Kouyaté, like Balla
Fasséké, Sundiata's griot, had too lively and questing a spirit to
allow these reactionaries to rein in his imagination, had lived too
close to the Mandingo magicians to forget that he himself was a
vital force among the forces and not a mere victim of a pre-
arranged destiny. Kankan Musa, his brother, took the Muslim
clerics more seriously but he, Abu, had always been in secret conflict with them. He had worn the robes of a Muslim when he was
inaugurated as emperor over the twelve kings of Mali, but he
was no more a Muslim than were the feathered and masked magicians of his court. He had even encouraged them to perform their
rites ostentatiously on Muslim festival days.[4]

True, he appreciated his association with Islam, the superficial
but diplomatically important link through this international religion between his and the Arab courts. But Mali had gone its own
way and would continue to do so. Little did he owe to the Arab
Muslims by way of the rituals of his culture, the appearance of
his court, or the legal-political structure of his government.

He was vital to them, as they to him. Even Europe depended
on the gold the Arabs got from him for their currency and jewels.
The first coins to circulate in Europe since Roman times were
minted from his gold.[5] Thousands of Arab and African caravans
every year passed through Timbuktu and Niani and the invincible
little city of Jenne, keeping the line of exchange and communication open between his dominions and Cairo. He had given, as
had his ancestors before, most generously to the Muslim teachers
and scribes at Timbuktu. But he would never allow them to take
their ideology too far. Diplomacy was diplomacy, trade was trade,
but culture and religion were inseparable strands of a native and
sacred tradition. It was the lifeblood of the people. He understood why, on closer reflection, Sundiata had built his palace at
Niani. It was close to the life of the cultivators, the life of the
people on the land. Sometimes the kings of Mali had shifted their
capital, but never away from the heartland of the peasants, where
they could lose the feel of the earth from which they sprang.[6] He
had found it amusing when he heard how the gold diggers of

Bambouk had withdrawn from trade with the Muslims when they
tried to slip their alien god in among the Arabian silks and amulets and perfumes.

He knew when he ascended the throne that many a Muslim de-
votee in the circles of the court would scoff at his transoceanic
scheme. Several Mali kings, after they had taken their conquests
to the limits their power would allow, had but one conventional
ambition. His brother, Kankan Musa, was already talking about
it. If Kankan Musa ever succeeded him, he would choose that
way to make his mark upon the world: to lead a massive train
of caravans, like the tribes of Israel on the move, across the desert
to Mecca. It was less his brother's Muslim faith, Abu knew, than
the desire to impress the Arabs, their greatest allies and rivals,
with Mali's great wealth and power.

Abu wanted to do something different, something new, something for which there was no precedent. Something too that would
keep his spirit quick and young with a lifelong excitement. He
was bored by petty wars, which meant so little in terms of new
territory, now that Mali had extended itself down to the deserts
of the north and the jungles of the south, as far east as the copper
mines of Takedda, and as far west as the great and mysterious
waters of the western sea. He was master of the largest empire
in the world—larger, said the Arabs, than the Holy Roman Empire, large as all the civilized states of Europe. Where would be
the Alexandrine joy that Sundiata—or his adversary, Sumanguru
the sorcerer—felt when they started out on their great campaigns?
And he was bored by the thought of a pilgrimage, even if it involved mile-long trains of camels and people,[7] as Kankan liked
to dream his would. He was bored by pious duties and by pious
men. They repeated themselves endlessly. Some of the muezzins
of the mosques reminded him of crickets singing at sundown in
the darkening savannahs.

He could not conceal a certain hostility and contempt. Koranic
recitals fell like an icy breath upon the warm, turbulent spirit of
the Bambaras. Muslims were terrified of real life, he felt, terrified
of the senses, terrified of the primitive power of sex. They were
alarmed to see his grown-up daughters swim stark naked in the

Kala, while they entombed their women up to their eyes in cloth.

He surrounded himself with people of like mind. Scholars of Timbuktu who entertained theories of a gourd-shaped world and dreamed of lands beyond the waters, as men now dream of life on lands beyond the stars. The king gave all his attention to these men, so much so that affairs of state began to suffer, and even his griot tactfully reminded him of Kalabi Dauman, the ancestor of those who preferred adventure to the responsibilities of government.

The king turned his head away. Mali was strong enough, and its tribute-paying estates independent and loyal enough at this stage, to sustain good and easy government. He would lose no time in the endless tasks of administration. He would spare no pains to build a fleet. Let it be known throughout Mali and beyond, by all those who fished and sailed in lakes and rivers and off the sea's great coasts, and who knew about boats and the water and currents and winds and direction-finding by the map of the stars, and about all such nautical things, that they were needed at the court. Let the Bozo come forward and the Somono, to whom Sundiata had given "the monopoly of the water,"[8] and the boatmen of the Niger and the Gambia and the Senegal. And let messengers go even unto Lake Chad, beyond the copper mines of Takedda, where it was said that men still built boats on the principles of the ancient Egyptians.[9]

Night and day, it was the talk of the court. The king himself was sometimes confounded by the conflicting tales and theories of his advisers. Some said it was pointless to call on the experience of the river people. The sea to the west was no river. It did not behave like an inland lake or stream. One would have to build something truly massive to meet its monstrous moods. River craft would simply be dashed to pieces. Others said big ships sank more easily on stormy water than small ones. They set up too much resistance to the winds and waves.

One man came forward from a fishing village on the western border of Mali. He lived on the edge of the sea, he said. There were seasons when it was still and smooth as a lake of glass, and the problem was not the winds and the waves at all, but the great

calms. A big ship could sit on the water for days like a stone. Small
boats like his had traveled on the ocean, and once, caught in a
storm, he had drifted for a few days until he came to an island.
The king listened to this with great excitement, but the old man
finished his story by saying that the island was small and poor,
as barren as a sandbank, and that no one lived there. An Arab
captain, who had come up the Niger River to Timbuktu and had
heard of the king's great interest, said there was truth in the old
man's tale, that he had heard of similar islands visited by North
African sailors, but that they also were small and poor, and the
people who lived on some of them were simple-minded folk.[10]
But these, he assured the king, were not the lands of the great
ocean. They merely stood on its edge. If one sailed on and on,
perhaps one would then come to a vast new world on the other
side.

Great discussions arose as to what kind of ship should be built.
Some of his advisers said it should most certainly carry a sail.
Others, that they should not depend on the sail, for they could be
stalled for days on the sea when the winds dropped. The ship
should be like the *dua la mtepe* the Bantu and Arabs of East
Africa were using on the Indian ocean, which could shift from
sail to oar, and oar to sail, so that it would have the double advantage of wind and muscle power.[11] All that was needed, said one
scholar, was the initial thrust. Birds were observed to fly for thousands of miles without getting tired. This was because they traveled on a moving stream or current in the air and could sleep
with open wings, drifting with no muscular power across the lands
of the world. He believed there were such streams and currents
in the ocean.

Abubakari listened to all this but took no chances. There would
be no single design, no one kind of boat. He would give his bless-
ing to all that seemed practical. He was not going to gamble on
one man's theory and ignore the rest. He saw the configuration
of his fleet like the political configuration of Mali. At its helm
stood he, the central and unifying authority; under him, the most
diverse and incongruous crew of elements on the Sudanic deck
of the world. His fleet would be a mirror of his ship of state.

A broad plain was chosen along the Senegambia seacoast of Mali for the great boat-building operations. Troops were withdrawn from the east, where they were skirmishing with the Songhai, and from other minor campaigns, to focus their energies on this, the most ambitious of all campaigns. Great trees from the inland forests were felled and floated down the rivers to the border coast. Smiths, carpenters, captains of provision boats along the Niger, caravan guides, who used the compass and nautical instruments to plot their paths across "the sandy sea" of the Sahara, magicians and diviners, thinkers from Timbuktu, grain and gold merchants, potters and porters, weavers and jewelers, were all assembled in that place. While the building of the boats progressed, a number of megaliths were erected, crude stone observatories, such as ancient seafaring nations used for astronomical calculations, the ruins of which survive today as indicators of the science of that time and the activities of that place.[12]

The king specified that each boat built for the ocean voyagers should be accompanied by or attached to a supply boat, which stored gold and other items of trade, along with dried meat and grain and preserved fruit in huge ceramic jars to last its company in the master boat for at least two years, four times as long as the stocks of the trans-Saharan caravans from Cairo to the Sudan. Two hundred master boats were built, and two hundred supply boats.[13] As the task neared completion Abubakari left his palace at Niani and encamped on the seacoast to watch the final stages of the operation. It was the scene an Egyptian pharaoh must have witnessed during the erection of a pyramid. He felt pride at the thought that he was probably the only king in the world at that time who was wealthy enough and enough at peace within his borders to divert such a vast labor force from its military and agrarian duties to gratify his royal whim. He would go beyond Sundiata after all, beyond the wildest territorial ambitions of the Mali kings, even beyond Alexander, "the mighty king of gold and silver whose sun shone over half the world." He called the captains of the boats together and issued this order: "Do not return until you have reached the end of the ocean, or when you have exhausted your food and water."[14]

"They went away and their absence was long, none came back and their absence continued."[15] The king could not find peace. He was obsessed by the arrow he had hurled across the spaces of the ocean. What lands would it strike? Where would it fall from its flight to the end of the unknown world? He could think of nothing else. He found no joy in his food, his wives or his children, no comfort in music or the discourse of his griot. He yawned and made impatient signs during important discussions of affairs of state. He called in the soothsayers. They could see nothing. "It is too soon, Sultan," the old men said. But early that morning, before he entered the palace yard to hold audience at the court, he had had a dream from which he woke trembling. In this dream he saw hundreds of blackbirds drifting lazily across the sky. One of them in the tail of the flock began to fall. It fell clear out of the sky and hit him like a gourd, which then cracked and spilled white froth and salt sea-water. The other birds turned to a cloud in the distance and dissolved.

He confided this dream to Kouyaté, who said it was an omen, and he would soon hear news. Was it good news or bad news? The king pressed him. Kouyaté was cautious. The drift of the birds was good news, the fall of the tail was bad. It could be seen both ways, he said.

In the midst of the discussion about Jenne, a commotion was heard outside the gates. The king, aroused by an obscure flicker of his instincts, half rose from the *pempi*. A murmur ran through the court. It was soon conveyed to Abubakari that a captain of one of the ships was waiting outside the gates to have audience. Let him take precedence, said the king, curtly dismissing the business at hand, whereupon a man came forward dressed in ritually poor garments and a dirty skullcap, holding his trousers knee-high as he appoached the king's platform. He shuffled forward in an attitude of reverent humility, knocking the ground with his elbows, then as he came within a few yards of the *pempi*, stood up with bowed head, waiting for permission to speak.

The king forgot himself. He descended the *pempi* in one step. The captain of the boat, fearing his wrath, began to speak.

"Sultan, we sailed for a long while until we came to what seemed to be a river with a strong current flowing in the open sea. My ship was last. The others sailed on, but as they came to that place they were pulled out to sea and disappeared."

"All is lost, then," said the king.

"I do not know, sire. I do not know what became of them. The waters there were strong and swift, and I was afraid. I turned where I was and did not enter that current."[16]

The king stared at him for a long while. The captain took a handful of dust and threw it nervously over his head and back like a bather splashing himself with water. The king returned to his *pempi* without a word. He clapped his hands and dismissed the court.

This news made Abubakari the Second more fixed in his obsession. Some said it made him mad. He abandoned Niani and journeyed with a greater part of his court to the plain at the western edge of Mali, where the first fleet had been fitted out and had disembarked. Like the pyramid builders of dynastic Egypt he began to reorganize his whole empire around a single massive project. Word was sent out to the provincial governors and passed down to the Kun-tigi, the political chiefs of the villages, that all gold, all grain, after due deduction for official services, should be sent on to his camp on the Senegambian plain. A vast army of craftsmen, dwarfing the planners and workers of the first expedition, were assembled on that plain. Caravans which came into Niani in that period found the army, the royal family and its vast retinue, the drummers and the buglers and the medicine men, all gone. Paired men and women were being chosen for the new expedition, and fears were expressed that the king in his madness would sacrific hundreds of his subjects to the devils of the dark sea.

Abubakari the Second never looked back. He never returned to the court at Niani. This time he had a special boat built for himself, with a *pempi* on the poop deck shaded by the bird-emblazoned parasol. He would commandeer the new expedition himself, keeping in touch with the captains of the fleet by means of the talking drum. Thus, in 1311 he conferred the power of the regency on his brother, Kankan Musa, on the understanding that

Kankan was to assume the throne if, after a reasonable lapse of time, the king did not return.[17] Then one day, dressed in a flowing white robe and a jeweled turban, he took leave of Mali and set out with his fleet down the Senegal, heading west across the Atlantic, never to return. He took his griot and half his history with him.

NOTES AND REFERENCES

1 Court ceremonial and royal regalia described in the opening pages of this chapter are based on detailed observations of the Mali king and his court recorded by the Moroccan traveler Ibn Battuta, who visited Mali in 1352. See Ibn Battuta, *Travels in Asia and Africa 1325–1354* (trans. and selected) M. A. R. Gibb, New York, Augustus Kelley, 1969, pp. 326–330.
2 For a description of Jenne and the struggles of the mighty empire of Mali to control this beautiful but intractable little city, see Daniel Chu and Elliott Skinner, *A Glorious Age in Africa*, New York, Doubleday, 1965, pp. 51–78.
3 Harold Lawrence, "African Explorers in the New World," *The Crisis*, 25, June–July, 1962, pp. 321–332. Heritage Program Reprint pp. 1–16.
4 Ibn Battuta, op. cit.
5 E. W. Bovill, *The Golden Trade of the Moors*, London, Oxford University Press, 1968.
6 J. Spencer Trimingham, *A History of Islam in West Africa*, London, Oxford University Press, 1962.
7 Daniel Chu and Elliott Skinner, op. cit., p. 64. The pilgrimage of 1324 is estimated to have involved some 60,000 people. "By the time the caravan was assembled it had become possibly the biggest moving crowd that Africa had ever seen . . . They assembled some 80–100 camel-loads of gold-dust, each load weighing 300 pounds." In *A History of Islam in West Africa*, Trimingham points out that the lavish generosity of Abuba-kari's brother and successor, on his visit to Cairo, led to the devaluation of gold in the world for twelve years.

8 D. T. Niane, *Sundiata: An Epic of Old Mali*, trans. from the Mande by G. D. Pickett, London, Longmans, 1965, p. 79.

9 See Chapter 4 of this volume and Thor Heyerdahl in Gordon Ashe (ed.) *The Quest for America*, New York, Praeger Publishers, 1973.

10 These islands on the edge of the Atlantic coast of Africa are given Arabic names and included in a Geography of the World published by a Franciscan friar in 1350. For this reference, see Sir Clements Markham, *The Book of Knowledge*, London, 1912, p. 28.

11 See Chapter 4 of this volume.

12 Bovill, op. cit., p. 53. Bovill notes that "In the Senegal and Gambia there exists a number of megalithic sites in the form of stone circles. Other megalithic sites have been found further east within the borders of modern Mali."

13 Ibn Fadl Allah al Omari, *Masalik el Absar fir Mamalik el Amsar*, traduit par Gaudefroy, Paris, 1927, pp. 61–63.

14 Idem.

15 Idem.

16 Idem.

17 In several popular histories of the Mali empire, the abdication of Abubakari the Second and the assumption of power by his brother, Kankan Musa, is erroneously dated 1307 (see Lawrence, Chu & Skinner etc.). Kankan Musa did not ascend the throne until 1312, and played the role of regent for several months before concluding that his brother, who left in 1311, would not return. See Trimingham op. cit. for the most accurate and reliable dates and genealogical charts.

4

AFRICANS ACROSS THE SEA

Perhaps Heyerdahl's greatest contribution has been to show by example that long voyages in "primitive" craft were not impossible. This may have been necessary for some Americanists; it was not for those who know the sea.

—CLINTON EDWARDS, *Man Across the Sea*

Once you are on the West Africa run the interesting alternatives should be noticed; the better your ship, the more easily you will cross to America on purpose, the worse your ship, the more easily you will cross by mistake.

—JAMES BAILEY, *The God-Kings and the Titans*

In the proper season it was quite feasible to cross the Atlantic near the equator from Africa to South America in small, open boats.

—FREDERICK POHL, *Amerigo Vespucci, Pilot Major*

Alvise da Cadamosto stood on the poop deck, looking out on the far blue banks of the Gambia, as his caravel sailed into the river. The Gambia was broad and bright at its mouth, streaming silently back into the Atlantic, from whence they had come. The Portuguese pilot felt his pulse quicken as he saw the jungled banks fade into mist like a distant range of mountains. He liked to think of himself as a pioneer, although unknown to him, Phoenician sailors had circled Africa since 600 B.C. and Hanno, a century

later, had taken the Carthaginians beyond the Gambia, even as
far as Sherbro Sound or the Bight of Benin.[1]

Farther up the Gambia, they dropped anchor and lowered the
rowing boats. Cadamosto went down into one of these, which
soon entered a stream branching from the main waterway. It was
like a canal between the trees, which now began to close in on
them, their submerged roots lifting and sinking in the swell. Suddenly this stream widened, and they saw in the distance what
looked at first like a drifting island of black men. Cadamosto
shouted to his crew to swing around and head back with all haste
to the ships. Bearing down upon them were three large boats.
They were of the type the Portuguese called *zopoli*, dugouts made
from enormous trees hollowed out. Like the ship's boats they were
propelled by oars, but they were much larger. "There were twenty-
five to thirty negroes in each."

Everyone strained at his oar with a mounting terror. This was
a dreaded region of the Gambia country. To come within bowshot of these men meant certain death. The tips of their arrows
sent poisons darting to the heart as fast as the pace of blood.
Cadamosto was glad he had ordered the retreat the very instant
he had sighted them. The race back to the ships was close. His
men "did not return so rapidly, however, but that these boats
were close behind, within a bowshot of them, when they reached
the ships, for they are very swift. When the men had boarded
their ships, they began to gesticulate and to make signs for the
African boats to draw near. These slowed down and approached
no nearer . . ."

Attempts to persuade the boatmen that they had come in peace,
and that they meant no harm, failed. The Africans held back,
guarded and suspicious. They were as fascinated, however, by the
strangers as they by them. They studied the Portuguese quietly
at a safe distance, then, at a signal from their captains, turned and
departed.

The next day, as the caravels penetrated farther up the Gambia,
there issued from another stream another company of black men.
They approached the Portuguese in a flotilla of huge boats. Cada-

mosto, in the leading ship, split the African flotilla into two sections, thrusting into the midst of them.

"They numbered seventeen," he wrote of this encounter, "of considerable size. Checking their course and lifting up their oars, their crews lay gazing . . . We estimated on examination that there might be about one hundred and fifty at the most; they appeared very well-built, exceedingly black, and all clothed in white cotton shirts: some of them wore small white caps on their heads, very like the German style, except that on each side they had a white wing with a feather in the middle of the cap, as though to distinguish the fighting men.

"A Negro stood in the prow of each boat, with a round shield, apparently of leather, on his arm. They made no movement towards us, nor we to them. Then they perceived the other two vessels coming up behind me and advanced towards them. On reaching them, without any other salute, they threw down their oars, and began to shoot off their arrows . . ."[2]

This encounter between the Portuguese and the boatmen on the Gambia occurred in 1455. It is the only account of West African river boats documented by Europeans before the coming of Columbus. But Africa was largely unknown to them, even to the pioneering Portuguese. Recent investigations into African watercraft show that some West African tribes specialized in fishing and boat-building, that they ferried goods in huge water-buses across their waterways as we ferry them in trucks on our roads. The boats seen by Cadamosto on the Gambia were very large and swift and built on the principle of the galley, using oars instead of paddles, but we would hardly think of them as the type of craft we would use to venture across an ocean. Some basic protection from the elements and the rudiments of a sail would at least be found on fishing craft.

A. C. Haddon and James Hornell cite "fairly sophisticated watercraft" in use in pre-European West Africa.[3] The anthropologist P. Malzy has drawn attention to sewn boats large enough to carry twelve tons of cargo across the Niger. These huge provision boats were made by the Bozo, a West African people who live by fishing.[4] In the "talking book" of the thirteenth century, which records the oral tradition of the Mali empire during the reign of its founder, Sundiata, we learn of the vast fishing fleet of the Somono, also a people of the Niger, who covered that river with their boats so that Sundiata's infantrymen, returning to Niani from their victory over the Sosso, would not wet their feet.[5] Richard Hull, in his book *Munyakare: African Civilization Before the Baturee*, notes the medieval prosperity enjoyed by Western Sudanic markets "thanks to the security maintained by armies and riverine navies of first Mali and later Songhay. Huge boats laden with grain, ivory, and other commodities could travel swiftly and safely along the Niger."[6] The Niger, of course, is a thousand miles from the Atlantic. It was the eastern border of the medieval Mali empire. But it provides easy communication with the Gulf of Guinea, and its headwaters originate in the same highlands as those of Senegal, thus facilitating a link-up with other African fisherfolk and riverine traders all the way to the North Atlantic.

Fishermen and traders of West Africa traveled not only on inland lakes and rivers but along the Atlantic coast. Caught in a strong gale or sucked into a powerful current, they could easily find themselves adrift. How would these fishermen or traders, with provisions to last them only a few days at most, survive a journey lasting at least two months? How would these boats, intended only for inland transport or off-coast fishing, fare on the great ocean?

Before one sets out to answer these questions it is necessary to examine the prevailing myths about ancient boats and the sea which traditional historians and scholars have promoted and perpetuated. These myths, created by men who did not even trouble to inquire into the basic facts of navigation and oceanography, made it difficult in the past, make it difficult even today, for the popular imagination to conceive of transoceanic crossings before Columbus.

It is generally admitted that the first people to inhabit America were Mongols from Asia who came to this continent via the Bering Straits some forty thousand years ago (the earliest date suggested by the most recent research). They came as Ice Age primitives, with the barest rudiments of Asian culture, across a land bridge made possible by the weight of advancing ice sheets that buckled the earth's surface, reducing the sea level by three hundred feet. This bridge was a plain one thousand miles long. As the ice re-treated, the plain sank into the sea, reappearing about twenty-five thousand years ago to form once more a passage for wanderers from Asia.[7]

After this second glacial epoch, America is assumed to have lived in total isolation from the rest of the world and to have de-veloped all its cultures independently until Columbus came. This latter assumption is a myth that has only been seriously challenged —seriously enough to force second thoughts on conservative Americanists—within the last few years.

The absence of a land bridge since the last glacial epoch has accounted for the resistance of scholars to any consideration of contact in the post-glacial epoch. The sea stood in their imagina-tion more forbidding than ten Saharas, an impassable wilderness of wind and wave, mocking any movement between the two hemi-spheres. For more than a millenium after Christ, few Europeans dared sail into this vast sea, beyond the legendary pillars of Her-cules. How then could other peoples, especially Africans, con-ceived of as naked barbarians with a boatless culture, venture the crossing?

Professor Stephen Jett, a geographer, in a recent book, *Man Across the Sea*, has highlighted the prevailing attitudes among Europeans and Americans toward pre-Columbian crossings of the ocean. "Western scholars," says Jett, "particularly Americans (who are imbued from an early age with the doctrine of the discovery of America by Columbus) have tended to assume: first, that the West (including Southwest Asia) has always been the leader in technological progress and that, as a corollary, other areas of the world did not have equal or superior sailing craft or navigational knowledge; and second, that European ships of the fifteenth cen-tury, which made transoceanic voyages only with difficulty, must have been superior to those of a thousand or two thousand years earlier. Hence, polygenesists have contended that the watercraft of pre-Columbian times could have crossed the oceans only acci-

dentally and by miraculous good fortune and that, therefore, there
could have been no significant influence on ancient America from
beyond the seas."[8]

It is to combat these and other assumptions that I shall outline
what is known about pre-Columbian watercraft in Africa, and
the factors—winds, currents, natural Africa-to-America routes,
basic survival kits, seafood and fresh-water sources—favoring and
facilitating the Atlantic crossing.

But first, we should dismiss the popular notion that the ships
of Columbus represented an advance over earlier ships, thus
making the Atlantic passage open, whereas before it had been an
impassable barrier. The navigational knowledge of the fifteenth-
century Spaniards was elementary indeed. Eight or nine pilots
guided the Santa Cruz and the Niña, the caravels of Columbus,
on his 1493–1496 expedition (Second Voyage), and according to
Columbus himself, they were like blind men: "Although there
were eight or nine pilots on board the two vessels, yet none of
them knew where they were." On another occasion, he wrote in
his journal, "Our ignorant pilots, when they have lost sight of land
for several days know not where they are. They would not be able
to find the countries again which I have discovered."[9] The Spaniards knew nothing about longitude, and Columbus had to strike
out for the latitude of Japan, hoping thereby to chance upon India.

The major inventions in maritime navigation that were to trans-
form European shipping during the Renaissance had been made
before Christ and were completely lost to Europe during the
Dark Ages. The system of latitudinal and longitudinal coordinates,
used as early as 100 B.C. in China,[10] had not, even as late as the
Conquest period, been acquired by Europe, whose navigators
could not read longitude until the eighteenth century.[11] The lateen
sail hoisted on the Spanish and Portuguese caravels came from
the Arabs. The astrolabe (an instrument to determine latitude by
the sun's altitude), although originally invented by the ancient
Greeks, diffused to fifteenth-century Europe after passing through
centuries of development by the Arabs.[12]

Other popular notions that must be dismissed are that Africa
had no knowledge of the sea, never had mariners, never made

boats, nurtured a landlocked race; that her empires ended at the edge of the desert, unwashed by the world's seas. Africans were navigating the Atlantic before Christ. They had moved up the North Atlantic to Ireland, capturing part of that country in a very early period. Sewmas McManus in *The Story of the Irish Race* records that "In their possession of Ireland the Firbourges were disturbed by the descent and depredations of African sea-rovers, the Fomorians, who had a main stronghold on Torrey Island off the northwest coast."[13] Everyone accepts, of course, that this myth of Africa being a continent of landlubbers was not true of the North. The shipping of the ancient Egyptians is well-documented. Archaeology is rich in its evidence of these ships (painting, graffiti, sculpture, reliefs on temple walls, ancient texts, even shipyard accounts, and most recently the wrecks themselves).

The Norwegian writer and explorer Thor Heyerdahl has made more than an academic study of these ships. He has put the shipbuilding ideas and designs of the ancient Egyptians to a practical test and proven that their most primitive boats—the papyrus reed boats that were built before their wooden ships—could have made it across the Atlantic from Africa to America. What is extremely interesting about his experiment is not only the demonstration of the seaworthiness and ocean-going capabilities of the reed boat, but the fact that some of the far more sophisticated and elaborate boats with rigid wooden frames, built along the same papyriform design, would not have been able to make it. The famous Cheops boat, discovered in 1954 in the Cheops pyramid in Egypt, for example, is the oldest preserved vessel in the world. Built around 2,600 B.C., it is very impressive-looking—146½ feet long and nearly 20 feet wide. It tries to imitate in wood the ocean-going lines and curves of the papyrus boat, but is more like a huge, spectacular toy. It would have disintegrated quickly under the violent slaps of the ocean.

Heyerdahl wondered why the builders of the Cheops boat tried so hard to imitate in rigid cedar the ocean-going lines of the pliant papyrus boat if papyrus was useless on the ocean. Scientists had scoffed at the idea that an ancient papyrus vessel could make it on the Atlantic. They had demonstrated in the laboratory, with

loose sections of papyrus reed, that this material becomes water-
logged and loses all carrying capacities in less than a fortnight.
They had also put the reed in stagnant sea-water in laboratory
tanks to show that the cellular core of the reed quickly starts to
deteriorate. All this struck Heyerdahl as meaningless. The real
conditions, he felt, would disprove them all. Could one conclude
that the *Queen Mary* would not float because a piece of its iron
body sank like a stone in a laboratory tank?

Flying in the face of these negative experiments, he organized
the building of a papyrus boat near the Cheops ship at Gizeh in
Egypt. He used the paintings and reliefs of boats in Egyptian
burial chambers as his models. He bought twelve tons of sun-dried
papyrus reeds, about ten to twelve feet long, from Lake Tana in
Ethiopia and hired two experienced boat-builders, along with an
interpreter, from Lake Chad in central Africa. This area is not
far from Takedda, the copper mines of medieval Mali. It is close
to Egypt, and large boats of robust construction, similar to those
used by the Egyptians, are still in common use. With Buduma
tribesmen under the direction of Abdullah Djibrine, a papyrus
expert from Lake Chad, a replica of the ancient papyrus boat was
built. Heyerdahl called this the *Ra*, the word for sun in ancient
Egypt as well as in parts of America and on all the islands of
Polynesia.

The *Ra I* set out from Safi, on the Atlantic coast of North Africa,
on May 25, 1969. It sailed to within a few days of the New World
before it got into serious trouble. The Heyerdahl expedition had
made one mistake. In the Egyptian model a rope ran down from
the curved tip of the stern to the afterdeck. It was thought that
this rope was only there to maintain the curve of the stern. In
fact the stern, through this rope, acted as a spring supporting the
pliant afterdeck. The ill-advised removal of this rope caused the
afterdeck to sag, and the boat listed dangerously as it neared
Barbados. A smaller model, *Ra II*, built on the identical Egyptian
pattern by a native American tribe, the Aymara, who profited from
this trial and error, made it across the Atlantic from Africa successfully.[14]

What Heyerdahl had proven, in effect, was that the most ancient of Egyptian ships, predecessors of even more sophisticated models, could have crossed the Atlantic. He demonstrated also, through the shipbuilding labors of the Buduma tribesmen, that these navigational skills had been largely preserved among riverine and lacustrine Africans even to the present day. The papyrus boat, however, is but a modest curtain raiser on the vast theater of ancient Egyptian shipping.

Even in the very early predynastic times the Egyptians were building plank boats as well as papyrus boats. These plank boats were sewn together, and the joints caulked with fiber. It was an extension of the method first used for the papyrus boats. By the dynastic period, they could boast of boats as long as three-car trains. It is recorded that the black African Pharaoh Sneferu,* at the close of the Third Dynasty, in one year made sixty ships that were 100 feet long and in the following year built three with a bow-to-stern measurement of 170 feet.[15]

The Egyptians got their timber for boat-building from Lebanon and from Byblos (major Phoenician ports), because Egyptian timber suitable for the purpose was the wood of the sycamore tree which was so needed for its fig-fruit that it could not be cut down for boats. without special permission. "From the earliest times Egypt had carried on trade with the Phoenician capital of Gebal (Byblos). This was the land from which the Egyptians obtained wine, certain oils for funerary use, and cedarwood from the Lebanon ranges for construction of ships, masts and flagstaves, for coffins and choice furniture of every type. In exchange for such products the Egyptians made deliveries of gold, fine metalwork and writing materials—especially the precious Egyptian papyrus. Intercourse was carried on by traders in caravans, but even more so by sea in Egyptian trading vessels so characteristic of the service in which they were engaged that they were designated 'Byblos travellers.' Byblos itself was greatly influenced by Egyptian commerce and culture, even if it was not actually an Egyptian colony . . . Egyptian ornamentation and script were

* The mixed racial composition of the Egyptians and the role of black Africa and black Africans in ancient Egypt is discussed in Chapter 7.

employed by Phoenician craftsmen in the decoration of metalwork and in other applied arts, while the Egyptians in turn borrowed certain of the Phoenician technical processes for working
metals."[16]

Egyptian boats were always welcome in the port of Byblos, for
the Egyptians would present gifts of alabaster vases, jewels and
amulets to the king in return for resin and planks of timber. The
Egyptians sometimes bought boats from the Phoenicians of Lebanon, though they often built their own from the timber imported
from Phoenicia. In a subsequent chapter I shall discuss the relationship between the Phoenicians and the Nubian-controlled
Egyptians in the 800–700 B.C. period, but it is important to emphasize at this point the long-standing maritime bond between
these two states—Egypt and the island complex of Phoenicia—
and the fact that a high percentage of Egyptian cargoes was carried in Phoenician bottoms (even though the Phoenician was the
paid mercenary and the Egyptian the master-employer and patron, in most cases). What has been claimed to be a Phoenician
figure (probably a merchant-captain) was found standing engraved on a stele beside the Negroid stone figures at La Venta.
The maritime relationship between these two states must therefore be examined. Why should Negro-Africans in Egyptian-type
helmets be found in juxtaposition with Phoenicians in an archaeological site, dated circa 800 B.C. along the Atlantic seaboard?

This juxtaposition is not an incongruous one at all. Egyptian
mariners were a very mixed bunch indeed. During the Eighteenth
Dynasty, it is recorded that Egyptian crews were comprised of
native Egyptians, Asiatics (mostly from Palestine, Syria, and
Libya), other foreign mercenaries and Nubians. In the Nineteenth
Dynasty, there was a fine royal navy consisting of merchant ships
sailed by their own crews and skippers but carrying trained ma-
rines. Mention is made of "a Division of Sheriden, Meshwesh and
Negroes."[17]

The Phoenician element in Egyptian shipping is not to be ignored, but it should not be exaggerated either. Some writers have
made lengendary navigators and maritime supermen out of these
people. It is true that Egyptians did not rove the Mediterranean

from one end to the other like the nomadic Phoenicians, but boats
and the sea were as important to the Egyptians as caravans and
the land. In fact we owe a great deal of what we now know about
ancient ships to the huge ritual boats that were buried with some
of the Pharaohs. The walls of tombs and temples abound with
paintings of them, from the sixty-oared predynastic boats found
on inscriptions in the tomb of the Pharaoh Menes at Abydos to
the fresco of a squadron of five ships belonging to the fleet of
Queen Hatshepsut in the temple of Deir el-Bahri. We can watch
the evolution of the Egyptian ship over a span of three millenia.[18]
The Egyptians were the great innovators of maritime science. The
Phoenicians were probably among the boldest and the best sea
pilots of their time but not equals, surely, of the Egyptian ship
architects and engineers. The Phoenicians copied the Egyptian
warship, developed by 1194 B.C., and from them it passed on to
the Greeks and Romans.

The ships of the Far East also came heavily under the influence
of Egyptian navigation. Among these influences we may mention
"the papyrus and reed boat, the steering oar, quarter rudders, both
the sheer and tripod mast, the square sail twice as high as wide,
the boom at the foot of the sail, spoon-shaped hulls, transverse
beams projecting through the hull sides and the central mat-
covered cabin."[19] There is also the persistent influence of ancient
Egyptian models on boats of the Upper Nile in the Sudan (the
black South). Sewn-plank boats closely resembling the Egyptian
boat of King Sahure (circa 2,600 B.C.) still sail on the Nile.

We have pointed to Egyptian influence on the shipping of the
Far East. Egyptian ships also visited the Somali coast of Africa
(Punt). In East Africa, however, shipping, though of great antiquity, owes less to early Egyptian than to a much later Arab
influence in the Indian Ocean. It would be of interest to look at
the ships of these maritime African peasants—the Swahili—for
it appears that some of them, while trading on the Indian Ocean,
through storm in the monsoon season, drifted or were blown into
the Kouro-Siwo, a current known as "the black stream." This is a
Pacific current, at the terminal point of which, on the Pacific coast

of North America, a tiny isolated African community, the "black Californians," has been found. Accidents of this nature must have been very rare indeed, and the likelihood of survival very slim. An accidental voyage from Asia to America is far more complicated, immeasurably longer and torturous, than the Africa-to-America drift voyage. It would appear, however, according to Bancroft and De Quatrefages, that it did sometimes happen.[20]

On the East African coast, along the shores of the Indian Ocean, lies the Bantu-Islamic civilization of the Swahili. These Africans were trading with India and China many centuries before Columbus. In the thirteenth century it is recorded that the Swahili transshipped an elephant to the court of the Emperor of China as a gift. One of their early trading vessels, the *mtepe*, is shown in Plate 11. It was used in Indian Ocean trade for many centuries. Some of these vessels weigh as much as seventy tons and are much larger than the one shown in the illustration, which is from a model in the Fort Jesus Museum at Mombasa. They are secured by palm-fiber lashings and are completely without nails or other metal clinchings.[21]

A considerable range of sailing ships was used by the Swahili for trade, fishing and the ferrying of farmers along the East African coast. Hundreds of Swahili ships (quite apart from the Arab *dhows* that came in from the Persian Gulf in the November–December months) plied between ports such as Tanga, Bagamoyo, Kilwa (in what is now Tanzania), Kipini, Kilifi and Mombasa (to name just a few of the Kenyan ports). Some of these vessels did not use the compass or navigate by the stars, since they kept close to the familiar coastline and ventured forth only by day, but others sailed into the ocean to India and China, south toward the island of Madagascar and beyond, or took a northwesterly route to the shores of Arabia and the Persian Gulf.

There were interesting variants of the Swahili *mtepe*—a smaller craft known as the *dua la mtepe* which alternated between the use of oars and sail so that the ship was not at the mercy of the wind and current, and could, except in a violent storm, maintain course and speed against them both. When the wind was in the

sailor's favor he unfurled the sail, but when it was not he disman-
tled it and rowed.[22]

This dual feature, the capacity to shift from sail to oar and oar
to sail, from wind power to muscle power and back, proved in-
valuable in the absence of engines on the open sea, and was common to many vessels—those of ancient Egypt, the Arab world,
and the East African coast. But it was not an attribute of the Spanish caravel, the type of ship in which Columbus made his historic
voyage. Columbus was taken off course for days by contrary currents. Evidence of this comes from several letters, such as the one
he wrote to King Ferdinand and Queen Isabella from Jamaica as
late as the Fourth Voyage, July 7, 1503: "I was carried away by
the current for many days."

The total dependence on the wind could also lead to complete
stasis. Here again, the letters written by Columbus substantiate
this. "The vessels of India [America] do not sail except with the
wind abaft. This is done not because they are badly built or
clumsy, but because the strong currents in these parts, together
with the wind, make it impracticable for them to sail with the
bowline for in one day they would lose as much way as they might
have made in seven. For a similar reason I could not use the caravels, even though they were Portuguese lateens. This is the reason
for their not sailing except with a favorable wind and they will remain in port, waiting for one, seven or eight months at a time, nor
is this particularly strange for the same often occurs in Spain."[23]

Due to this kind of paralysis in windless seasons and spaces, a
Spanish caravel of the fifteenth century could actually take longer
to complete the Africa-to-America journey than the simplest African boat. Thus Vespucci, in a Spanish caravel using sail power,
took sixty-four days to make it from the Cape Verde islands off
West Africa to the South American coast, while Hannes Lindemann, a German medical doctor in an African dugout using current
power, accomplished the crossing in 1955 in fifty-two days.

The invention of the sail was a crucial event in the story of
seamanship, occurring six thousand years before the introduction
of the steamship engine, yet "wind propulsion by sail, setting such
rigorous limits upon the direction in which a ship could move,

and enforcing, by the nature of the winds, a very low average speed between ports, is a far from satisfactory way of achieving motion over great tracts of ocean."[24]

It will be contended, however, that even if the caravel was not as agile and maneuverable as some of the simpler craft cited, it was a better gamble on the ocean because of its size, which could withstand the buffeting of the wind and waves. There were Arab ships of greater size and tonnage in pre-Columbian times[25] (to be discussed in Chapter 12), but though African boats were considerably smaller, since they were largely designed for river traffic and coastal fishing, it should be pointed out that "seaworthiness is not proportionate to size: to the contrary, the larger the size, the greater the stresses set up by wind and wave as they encounter the inertia of the heavy craft and thus the greater the possibility of breaking up. A fairly small craft, if it is well constructed, is more likely to survive a long sea voyage, especially if it is of flexible construction, as are lashed log-rafts and sewn-plank boats."[26] Several mariners have made this point. J. Merrien in his Lonely Voyagers notes that "the notion that a small boat cannot go far afield is a complete fallacy,"[27] while C. A. Borden in Sea Quest asserts, "Again and again it has been proven that seaworthiness has little to do with size."[28]

In boats much smaller than the thirty-man zopoli which attacked Cadamosto, in an African dugout without sails and without the muscle power that could propel the zopoli in the absence of favorable winds or currents, Hannes Lindemann made the Atlantic crossing from Africa to America to show that such a journey could be made in such a boat. To prove this point, that river boats can make it on the ocean, again and again Atlantic crossings have been made by small boats of every description. "At least two rafts, two dugout canoes, two dories propelled only by oars, several dories fitted with sails, conventional sailboats as small as five feet, eleven inches in length, and unconventional boats including kayaks, folding boats and amphibian jeeps have been successfully floated across the ocean."[29] The mariner Merrien lists 120 intentional modern solo and two-man long ocean voyages.

These crossings of the Atlantic to America and the Caribbean from points in Africa and Europe have been made not only in boats inferior to the heavily manned watercraft of Africans found on the Gambia before 1500, but also in some cases with little or no provisions, thereby establishing that even if by some mishap of storm or treacherous current, African fishermen or riverine traders were cast out into the Atlantic, they could have survived the ocean voyage. Fishermen and riverine traders, as a rule, take some provisions with them. But Dr. Alain Bombard rode a life raft, *L'Hérétique*, from Casablanca in North Africa via the Canaries to Barbados in 1952 without any food or water, with only a cloth net for small sea fauna, a fishing line with hook for tunny, and two spears—a small one for sea perch and a large one for bigger fish. He survived his sixty-five-day voyage in perfect health.[30] Lindemann, the tester of the African dugout, only took along, in addition to Bombard's fishing kit, an implement to squeeze liquids from fish to make sure of a drinking supply, in case no rain fell on the ocean.

"If adequate water is available, a man can survive for 50 days or longer without food and, contrary to popular opinion, sea water can be used as a supplementary water source as can fish juices. At least in some latitudes and at some seasons, rainstorms and the ocean would provide adequate fresh water and food, especially to people familiar with the sea; such was Heyerdahl's experience in the Kon-Tiki . . . There is a nineteenth century record of 9 Japanese surviving an accidental drift of 11 months and landing on Oahu, and Brooks refers to two accidental voyages from Japan to North American waters, of 17 and 18 months respectively, with 3 of the crew surviving in each case."[31]

In view of the foregoing, the question of accidental drift voyages of Africans to America (apart from the intentional and well-provisioned voyages of the Mandingo in the fourteenth century and the voyages by the Songhay in the latter half of the fifteenth), needs the most serious examination. Accidental African voyagers would have been likely to make their landfalls within the same wind and current band, striking points in the region of the Gulf of Mexico, the Caribbean or the northeastern corner of South

America. As Alexander Marchant has pointed out, "once cast into the mid-Atlantic, it is almost impossible to avoid the South American coast." It is not surprising, therefore, that Alvares Cabral, caught in the pull of currents off the Guinea coast, drifted westward across the Atlantic and "discovered" Brazil in 1500. The Portuguese were to learn then officially that nearly 200 miles of territory lay within the Tordessillas line, that after about 1500 miles from the Cape Verde islands off West Africa there was the continental land mass which their king, Don Juan, had confidently claimed, on the strength of African testimony, existed.

The famous explorer Alexander von Humboldt, in his *Examen Critique*, explains what happened to Cabral. "Pedro Alvares Cabral, whom Dom Manuel sent on the track of Vasco da Gama to the Indies, wishing to avoid the calms of the Gulf of Guinea . . . landed unexpectedly on the shores of Brazil . . . the intimate knowledge that we have today of the multiplicity of these currents or pelagic streams of different temperatures which traverse the great longitudinal valley of the Atlantic offers an easy explanation for the extraordinary drift towards the west which the little squadron of Cabral experienced."[32]

A lot more is known today about these currents from Africa to America than was known in Humboldt's time. Two main currents—the Guinea current and the Canaries current—are relevant to our study. The following information, so vital to an understanding of how the ocean provides its own pilots and propellers, is illustrated in Plate 10.

"The Guinea Current" according to Karl Schwerin "flows eastward along the Guinea Coast, with frequent cycles out to sea where it joins the South Equatorial Current. The northern portion of the South Equatorial Current joins the North Equatorial Current in mid-Atlantic (between 25 and 50 degrees West Longitude, depending on the season . . .) This current originates along a likely part of Africa and although it runs the wrong way it communicates frequently and naturally with the South Equatorial Current which runs in the right direction. Furthermore, there are relatively fast-flowing currents, so in spite of the increased distance, time of transit would be comparable to that along the Canaries Current.

"The Canaries Current flows southward along the coast of Africa to Cap Blanc or Cape Verde (depending on the season) where it splits. One branch continues south along the coast. The other branch flows into the Atlantic and becomes the North Equatorial Current. *This strikes the American coast in a broad band from the Guianas through the Antilles.* The strongest part of the current runs along the coast of Venezuela from Trinidad to the Guajira Peninsula. This is one of the areas of South America where we have evidence of early horticulture. *This current also leaves the African continent in a most propitious region, along the coast of Senegal and Gambia*" (italics added).[33]

The coast of Senegal and Gambia was a propitious region indeed, for this was the Atlantic border of medieval Mali. It was out of the Senegal River into the Atlantic that the fleets of Abubakari the Second sailed for the western lands. Long journeys across charterless wastes were not new to the Mandingo. They knew that the desert, like the great sea, had its signposts in the sky, and they called the Sahara "the sandy sea." They navigated it as though it were a sea, using nautical instruments and astronomical computations to guide them. *Toffut-al-Alabi*, an Arab text quoted by E. W. Bovill in *The Golden Trade of the Moors* states that "The Negroes travel in the desert as it were upon the sea, having guides to pilot them by the stars." The compass too was used by both Arab and African merchants in the Sudan who had to cross the desert in their caravans. "Of nautical instruments the Sharif was a keen buyer. His interest in them seems to have sprung from their proved value in the desert . . . merchants travelling to the Sudan were forced to use nautical instruments." Paul Imbert, a French sailor, making his journey across the desert by caravan, remarks in a letter to a friend, "To steer their course they [heads of the caravans][34] make their observation from the rising and setting of the sun, and the stars and compass direct them. They always take care to have someone in the caravan who understands these matters."

If West Africans were using the compass and astronomical computations for desert travel, it hardly makes sense that they would venture out intentionally on the unknown sea without these aids to guide them. It would make little sense too if the Emperor of Mali, Abubakari the Second, during whose reign (1307–1311) Timbuktu had already become a seat of learning, had equipped an expeditionary fleet without drawing on the storehouse of knowledge available to him and which he, with the enormous wealth of Wangara, Bambouk and Bouré, was philantrophically financing. The skill of the Arabs in seafaring, after all, was known the world over, and although their secrets were jealously guarded from commercial rivals, as were Mali's secrets regarding the source of its envied gold,[35] this nautical knowledge would have been readily available to such a generous patron of scholarship at Timbuktu.

At Timbuktu, which was approachable by both land and water, visited by both caravans and boats, the black emperors kept "a magnificent and well-furnished court . . . Here were a great store of doctors, judges, priests, and learned men that were bountifully maintained at the King's cost . . . and hither were brought divers manuscripts of written books out of Barbary, which are sold for more money than any other merchandise."[36]

Because of all these factors the court tradition of Mali should be taken seriously. This tradition, which was dramatized in the previous chapter, has come down to us through al-Qalqashandi and the Masalik-al-Abasar, the works of the scholar al-Umari, an Arab of Damascus who spent his early life in the service of the Sultan of Egypt. He quotes the words of the then governor of Cairo, Ibn Amri Hajib, who questioned Kankan Musa on this matter.[37] In fact much of what is known of the memorable pilgrimage to Mecca in 1324 comes from the works of al-Umari. Like the Meccan pilgrimage, Abubakari's expedition was done in a grand style, involving perhaps as many vessels as the caravans of Kankan Musa thirteen years later, but leaving only ripples on a very far shore, an enigmatic chain of artifacts and influences, which, like resuscitated mummies, are beginning at last to haunt us with questions.

NOTES AND REFERENCES

1 J. V. Luce, "Ancient Explorers" in Geoffrey Ashe (ed.) *The Quest for America*, Praeger Publishers, New York, 1971.
2 G. R. Crone, *The Voyages of Cadamosto*, London, Hakluyt Society, 1937, pp. 57–59.
3 A. C. Haddon and J. Hornell, *Canoes of Oceania*, Honolulu, Bishop Museum, Special Publications, no. 27–29.
4 P. Malzy, *"Les Bozos du Niger et leurs modes de pêche,"* Bull. de l'Institut Francais d'Afrique Noire, 8, 1946, pp. 100–132.
5 D. T. Niane, *Sundiata: An Epic of Old Mali*, trans. from the Mande by G. D. Pickett, London, Longmans, 1965, p. 79.
6 Richard Hull, *Munyakare: African Civilization Before the Baturee*, New York, John Wiley & Sons, 1972, p. 59.
7 Morris, Greenleaf and Ferrell, *America: A History of the People*, New York, Rand McNally, 1971. See Introduction.
8 Stephen C. Jett, "Diffusion versus Independent Development," in Riley, Kelley, Pennington and Rands (eds.) *Man Across the Sea*, Austin, University of Texas Press, 1971, p. 7. This is, in my opinion, the most distinguished and informative essay in the symposium, touching with admirable concision on all the main problems of pre-Columbian contact between the Old World and the New.
9 Arthur James Weise, *Discoveries of America to 1525*, New York, G. P. Putnam's Sons, 1884, p. 159.
10 See H. F. Tozer, *A History of Ancient Geography*, New York, 1964, pp. 167, 172, 343; also J. Needham, *Science and Civilization in China*, Cambridge, England, 1959, pp. 498, 537. Needham claims the Chinese were the pioneers in the use of magnetic polarity for direction finding, and that they invented the compass before the Arabs; but the diffusion to Europe of this invention through the Arabs cannot be disputed.
11 Weise, op. cit., pp. 66–68.
12 G. F. Hourani, *Arab Seafaring in the Indian Ocean in Ancient and Early Medieval Times*, Princeton, N.J., Princeton University Press, 1951.

13 Sewmas McManus, *The Story of the Irish Race*, revised edition, New York, Devin Adair, 1944.

14 Thor Heyerdahl, "Isolationist or Diffusionist?" in Geoffrey Ashe (ed.) *The Quest for America*, Praeger Publishers, New York, 1971.

15 James Bailey, *The God-Kings and the Titans*, New York, St. Martin's Press, 1973, p. 87.

16 George Steindorff and Keith C. Seele, *When Egypt Ruled the East*, Chicago, University of Chicago Press, 1957, p. 21.

17 Pierre Montet, *Everyday Life in Egypt in the Days of Rameses the Great*, London, Arnold, 1958.

18 Eric Marx, "Egyptian Shipping," *Mariner's Mirror*, 33, 1947, pp. 139–169.

19 G. Elliot Smith, "Ships as Evidence of the Migration of Early Cultures," *Journal of the Manchester Egyptian and Oriental Society*, 1916, pp. 63–102.

20 Donald Mackenzie, *Myths of Pre-Columbian America*, London, Gresham Publishing Co., 1924, p. 117. The "Black Current" or "Black Stream" (Kuro Siwo) flows steadily in a northerly direction along the eastern coast of Japan, and then sweeps in a curve towards the west coast of North America. "The January monsoons from the north east," writes Bancroft (*The Wanderings of People*, pp. 4, 5), "are apt to blow any unlucky coaster which happens to be out straight into the Kuro Siwo." The vessels are drifted either to the Sandwich Islands or to North America, "where they scatter along the coast from Alaska to California." For de Quatrefages' comment on the black Californians, see *The Human Species*, New York, Appleton, 1905, p. 202.

21 Basil Davidson, *The African Genius*, Boston, Little Brown, 1969, p. 213.

22 A. H. J. Prins, *The Swahili Speaking Peoples of Zanzibar and the East African Coast*, London, International African Institute, 1967, pp. 66–68, 52–55, 74–75.

23 Weise, op. cit., footnote on p. 180.

24 Douglas Philips-Birt, *A History of Seamanship*, New York

Doubleday, 1971, p. 23. See also H. B. Culver and G. Grant, *A Book of Old Ships*, Garden City, New York, 1935. On p. 78 of that work, the following remark on the Columbian caravels is made: "They went to windward slowly, or not at all."

25 Jett in Riley et al. (eds.) *Man Across the Sea*, p. 9.

26 Ibid., p. 10.

27 J. Merrien, *Lonely Voyagers*, trans. J. H. Hawkins, New York, 1954. For this reference, see Stephen Jett in Riley et al. (eds.) *Man Across the Sea*.

28 C. A. Borden, *Sea Quest*, Philadelphia, Macrae Smith, 1967.

29 Alice Kehoe, "Small Boats on the North Atlantic," in Riley et al. (eds.) *Man Across the Sea*, p. 275.

30 Ibid., p. 276.

31 Jett, op. cit., p. 14.

32 See *Cabral's Voyage to Brazil and India*, London, Hakluyt Society, 1937, p. 49.

33 Karl H. Schwerin, *Winds Across the Atlantic*, Mesoamerican Studies, No. 6, University Museum, Southern Illinois University, 1970, p. 12. See also Thor Heyerdahl, "Feasible Ocean Routes to America in Pre-Columbian Times," *American Antiquity*, 28, 1964, pp. 482–488.

34 E. W. Bovill, *The Golden Trade of the Moors*, New York, Oxford University Press, 1968, p. 119. Also titled *Caravans of the Old Sahara*.

35 Bovill, op. cit. "The source of West African gold," Bovill states, "was a remarkably well-kept secret. It puzzled almost all outsiders for over 2000 years, and for half of that time their efforts to discover where the gold came from were as unremitting as they were unsuccessful."

36 Margaret Shinnie, *Ancient African Kingdoms*, New York, New American Library, 1970.

37 For an English translation of this oral tradition, see Basil Davidson, *The Lost Cities of Africa*, Boston, and Toronto, Little Brown, 1970 (revised edition), pp. 74, 75.

5

AMONG THE QUETZALCOATLS

The Quetzalcoatl of the Mexican valley documents was never blond (or fair) as stated by the friars, but virtually always pictured as black-bearded, and in illustrations had his face painted black.

—BASIL HEDRICK, "QUETZALCOATL: EUROPEAN OR INDI-
GENE?" IN *Man Across the Sea*

*"Yellow as the straw his beard is"—is in flat contradic-
tion to other descriptions of Quetzalcoatl that refer specifically to his black hair or black beard; from which several
scholars have inferred that the nameless Aztec poet, em-
ploying poetic license, bleached the black beard of Quetzalcoatl to present him as a sun symbol.*

—CONSTANCE IRWIN, *Fair Gods and Stone Faces*

It was the sound of the drums that filled the shore with watchers. It came from far over the water like the playful thunder of gods on a calm, bright day. When they looked out to sea, at first they saw nothing. Then several dark forms appeared, boats drifting out of the east toward them like a shoal of sea dragons.

The year was 1311. The strangest things had begun to happen. The diviners had said there would be another messenger coming from the lands of the sun god in that year.

The vessel that bore him was the first to approach the shore. They saw him standing like a king under a canopy that had been mounted on a stepped dais in the center of the boat. He was clothed from head to foot in long flowing white robes. He looked

like a true child of the sun burned dark by its rays. His black hair
and beard stood out against the whiteness of his vestment. Surrounding this white, bearded figure was a great company of boats.
The men all looked marvelously black, as if they had been bathed
in the sacred fire. Surely they had come from a land burning in
the white heart of the sun.

Against the blue canopy under which he stood they could see
quite clearly the outlines of a great golden bird, the serpent-
slaying eagle, they thought, that was an ensign of Quetzalcoatl.
Truly this was he come back again, as he had promised, "by way
of the sea where the sun rises" and with many white-capped,
white-robed companions. It was exactly six cycles since he had
disappeared from among the Toltecs at Tula.

Thus must Abubakari the Second have appeared to natives in
the American heartland when his fleet drifted into that world in
1311. As a white, bearded figure, coming from the east, the land
of the sun, in boats. In like manner did Cortez appear exactly four
cycles later (1519), figuring in the imagination of the Mexican
king, Montezuma, as another Quetzalcoatl or messenger of the
sun king. Quetzalcoatl, as a solid figure of American history (the
son of Mixcoatl, chieftain of the Toltecs), goes back to the tenth
century (980–999). As a mythical configuration (plumed serpent, rain god, etc.) he goes back many centuries before that.
Enormous confusion surrounds this complex figure. How could
he have appeared and reappeared on the Atlantic seaboard, at
times far separated, assuming different forms? How could he have
been both native and foreigner, man and god, black and white?

No one definition can embrace Quetzalcoatl. He had several
representations or aspects. He was the feathered serpent king and
rainmaker god in central America. *Quetzal* (bird or plume) and
coatl (serpent) signified a connection between bird and snake.
The snake was supposed to be a kind of evil dragon guarding the
well of life. He contained or imprisoned the life-giving moisture.
An eternal conflict existed between him and the great bird who
nested in the tree of life and would wrestle with and devour the
snake, thus releasing the rains, the fertilizing waters necessary

for men and crops. The origin of this serpent-devouring bird lies in Africa. The plumed serpent myth and all its highly arbitrary abstractions and interconnections (such as the winged disc motif) evolved through ancient Egypt's contact with black Africa and because of special political circumstances in the Egyptian dynastic period.

Donald Mackenzie, in his book *Myths of Pre-Columbian America*, has shown how this happened.[1] He has demonstrated what very real circumstances in Africa and Egypt led to the very abstract relationships between birds and serpents. The bird and serpent were incorporated at an early period into the mythology of the ancient Egyptians, but Africa provided the concrete stage for what was later to become a mythical combat between bird and serpent.

There is only one bird in the world, Mackenzie points out, that is a persistent and successful hunter of serpents. This is the well-known secretary bird of Africa.[2] "In general appearance," writes a naturalist, "it looks like a modified eagle mounted on stilts and may exceed four feet in height." It is heavy and powerful, with webbed feet and sharp talons.

The naturalist Verreaux gives the following description of the bird and of its method of attacking snakes. "As nature exhibits foresight in all she does, she has given to each animal its means of preservation. Thus the Secretary Bird has been modelled on a plan appropriate to its mode of life and it is therefore for this purpose that, owing to the length of the legs and tarsi, its piercing eye is able to discover at a long distance the prey which, in anticipation of its appearance, is stretched on the sand or among the thick grass. The elegant and majestic form of the bird becomes even more graceful; it now brings into action all its cunning in order to surprise the snake which it is going to attack; therefore it approaches with the greatest caution. The elevation of the feathers of the neck and the back of the head shows when the moment for attack has arrived. It throws itself with such force on the reptile that very often the latter does not survive the first blow."[3]

To avoid being bitten, if the first attack is not successful, the bird uses its wings as a kind of shield, flapping them vigorously; its powerful feet are the chief weapons of offense. No other bird has been so well-equipped by nature for battling with snakes. Eagles and vulcans have powerful talons and beaks, but they do not possess the long legs of the secretary bird, which are absolutely necessary to ensure success when a serpent is attacked.[4]

Stories regarding this strange African bird were prevalent in ancient Egypt. The priests and seamen who visited Punt (in what is now Somaliland) became familiar with its habits. Mackenzie shows how the secretary bird of Africa suggested that form of the Egyptian myth of Horus in which the god as the falcon hawk attacks the serpent form of Set, the slayer of Osiris. The Set serpent took refuge in a hole in the ground, and above this hole was set a pole surmounted by the falcon head of Horus.[5]

In the winged disc symbol of the sun god in ancient Egypt, "we may trace the influence of stories about the secretary-bird brought from Africa; as the winged disc the god Horus pursues Set and his companions in their various forms, including their serpent forms."[6] This winged disc symbol is made up of the religious symbols of Lower and Upper Egypt. Since these two divisions of ancient Egypt came to be joined through conquest, the winged disc became a political symbol of unity in the Nile Valley, representing the merger of the two parts. The disc represents the sun. The wings are those of the falcon god, Horus, the chief deity of the dynastic Egyptians, who united Upper and Lower Egypt by conquest. The two serpents that entwine the disc and extend their bodies above the wings are the serpent goddesses of the two ancient divisions of Egypt, namely Nekhebit and Uazit (known by the Greeks as Buto). Occasionally these serpents were crowned with the diadems of Upper and Lower Egypt.[7]

This bird and serpent motif in the winged disc symbol traveled in ancient times to America. We find not only clear evidence of the Egyptian prototype in the winged disc of ancient Mexico and Polynesia, but we find it used in the same way. The ancient Egyptians placed the image of the winged disc "over the entrances to the inner chambers of a temple, as well as over its gates, and on stela and other objects. Sometimes the symbol was simply the

winged disc without the serpents . . . In pre-Columbian America
the winged disc was placed on temple door lintels as in Egypt . . .
The Polynesian form of the winged disc is of special interest because it shows in the disc the head of the bird-devouring serpent—
the secretary bird of Africa with which seafarers had become familiar . . ."[8]

Professor Elliott Smith has shown how Egyptians influenced
symbolic gateways in Asia. The winged disc of Egypt on the gates
"represent the means of communication between the living and
the dead and symbolically the portal by which the dead acquired
a rebirth into a new form of existence."[9] The megalithic gateway
of the sun at Tiahuanaco in South America is one of several American gateways distinguished by the Egyptian winged disc symbol.
It not only carries this symbol over the gate but a frieze depicting
three rows of birdmen attendants. The origin of birdmen and of
gods with bird heads in black Africa and their later diffusion to
dynastic Egypt will be discussed when we come to deal with
Negro-African influence on ancient Egypt, and the Negro and
Egyptian influence on the Olmec heartland (see Chapters 7, 8,
and 9).

But now let us return from the ancient symbols of Quetzalcoatl
to Quetzalcoatl as man in the medieval Mexican world. The name
was given to the native son of an American king, Mixcoatl, as
well as to a number of extraordinary figures or cultural innovators
from outside, at least one of whom appeared on the eastern Atlantic seaboard with a fleet of boats, and after an indeterminate stay,
set out again on the Atlantic with the intention of returning home.
Quetzalcoatl was also the name given as a honorific title to two
high priests of Tenochtitlan in Mexico "in memory of the God
of Civilization and Learning . . . archetype of the priestly ideal."[10]
Tenochtitlan was founded by the Aztecs in 1325, and the deci-
sion to found a city in that place was based upon a legendary
battle between an eagle and a serpent there.

The confusion between the native Mexican (son of Mixcoatl)
and the alien figure appearing on the eastern seaboard has presented historical problems, but certain facts are now clear. The
Quetzalcoatl who came from outside and was reputed to have

landed in America in a company of boats was a tall, bearded man. He was clad in long *white* garments, probably carried a royal mace or ball of some kind in his hands, and wore a turban, conical crown or similar headdress.

The main source of confusion over his appearance has been the use of the word *white* in some oral traditions. This word has been completely misinterpreted by many scholars and has led to the most fanciful notions that it was a European who innovated civilization and religious reform in America. The myth and ritual, the pattern of religious expression in America, differ sharply from that of Europe. The Catholic friars finding the cross in America (the cross is also found in pre-Christian Africa and had nothing to do there with Christ)[11] pounced on the term "white, bearded figure" and claimed that Quetzalcoatl was St. Thomas or St. Brendan.[12] In 1949 P. M. Hanson even made claims for Quetzalcoatl as a reincarnated Jesus Christ.[13] As Basil Hedrick points out, "*The Quetzalcoatl of the Mexican valley documents was never blond (or fair) as stated by the friars, but virtually always pictured as black-bearded, and in illustrations had his face painted black.*"[14]

The truth is, *white* is a purely European convention when used as an *exclusive* referent for skin color and race. *White* in American Indian terms did not mean (in pre-Columbian times) Caucasian. Quetzalcoatl did not have Northern European features. Native Americans spoke of him at times as being white in a symbolic sense, in the way Muslims may speak of Mohammed as a handful of white light in Allah's palm. A black or brown Negroid-Hamitic man, as Abubakari was, appearing out of the east in long flowing white Muslim robes would be called white. White may also be used, as a referent to skin, for pale Asiatics like the Japanese. Moncacht-Apé relates in a narrative published in 1725 that when a band of "white, bearded figures" haunting the Pacific coast in a post-Columbian period were hunted down they were found to be Japanese.[15] Even in this instance the term "white" used as a literal referent for the skin of the Japanese was a post-Columbian linguistic influence.

Mackenzie has discussed all the tales of white, bearded men who were alleged to have appeared in America. He presents a number of Quetzalcoatl representations that are indisputably based on an Asiatic figure. A Quetzalcoatl from the west (the Pacific) does not cancel out a Quetzalcoatl from the east (the Atlantic). The Asiatic Quetzacoatl is found in the world of the Incas, the black Quetzalcoatl in Mexico and the Yucatan. Thor Heyerdahl, however, has argued strongly for the pre-Columbian appearance of a Caucasoid figure to explain the so-called "white" god of civilization with which Quetzalcoatl is sometimes identified. His arguments are ingenious, but when he presents sculptures of "the white Quetzalcoatl" they all speak very clearly against his case. They are all native or Asiatic, or black-faced or nonhuman.[16] None are European in facial contour. This is not to deny that there may have been a few Europeans in America before Columbus. There is a real case, for example, for the pre-Columbian presence of the Vikings in the northernmost part of the American continent (circa A.D. 1000). The most brutally critical appraisal of the literature on this subject (a vast library) by Brigitta Wallace concedes "incontrovertible archaeological proof" in the Norse site "L'Anse aux Meadows" in Newfoundland,[17] even though the Newport Tower may be questionable and the Vinland Map a fake.

What, however, is the significance of this early contact in the cultural history of the American? The Vikings brought no new plant, influenced no art, introduced no ritual, left no identifiable trace of their blood in the native American. Like waves, they broke for a moment on alien sands and then receded. The same may not be said of the African. He is not enshrined, perhaps, in an architectural monument, but his face broods over the Olmecs, his skeleton lies beside the ancient Mexican magicians, a strain of his cultivated cotton is found married to an American "wild" ancestor, his blood runs even in the veins of the Lacandons, the most secluded of the Maya tribes. It is one thing, therefore, to concede a European pre-Columbian presence. It is another thing to claim that Europeans, be they northern Vikings or Southern Viracochas, brought "civilization" to the Americans before Columbus. This flies in the face of all the known cultural facts. The myths, the rituals, the magico-religious systems of native America stand out in sharp contrast to those found anywhere in Europe. What is more, the agricultural system and the calendar (a "white" Quetzalcoatl is alleged to have introduced elements of both) bear no relationship to ancient or medieval crop-science and time-keeping among European peoples.

There is a disturbing and persistent attempt (and it may be quite unconscious, so involuntary has become the racial reflex) to create a white superman to account for all civilization and all major achievements of non-Caucasoid peoples. In this connection I would like to take issue with Erich von Däniken who, in his *Chariot of the Gods?*, invents a divine species from outer space to account for the building of both the Egyptian pyramids and the gigantic stone figures of Easter Island. Quetzalcoatl, in some of his representations, does wear solar ear discs, but this is be-cause of his association with the sun-god complex. Von Däniken finds representations of birdmen in Egypt and America, but these have nothing to do with outer space. The first birdmen appear in the rock art of Africans in the Tassili mountains of the Sahara, centuries before they appear in the tomb art of dynastic Egypt and in the art of ancient America (see Chapter 7). It is true, of course, that the huge figures of Easter Island represent no known human race, but are a race of lengendary giants. The prototype of the superhuman giant, however, may be found on this earth and within the same sun-god complex. The Egyptian god, Horus, attained, according to J. H. Breasted, "a stature of eight cubits" (nearly fourteen feet).[18] Camels have been found etched on the rocks of the desert plateau of Marcahuasi in South America.[19] Because there were no camels in South America, von Däniken assumes spacemen etched them there. A native American camel existed in prehistoric times, as finds in Gypsum Cave, Nevada, show.[20] But even if this were not the prehistoric camel, is it not more logical to assume that Africans, who were very familiar with the camel, drew these animals? Is it harder to believe in Africans crossing the Atlantic, a distance of 1500 miles, than in artists from outer space, etching camels in Marcahuasi, fifteen light years away from their home star?

Hedrick, who has done the most recent research on the subject

of Quetzalcoatl, has tried to link the appearance of the native
Quetzalcoatl in the north with the later appearance of Kukulcan
(the feathered serpent figure) in the south. He gives a late tenth-
century date (A.D. 999) for the disappearance of Quetzalcoatl
from the Toltec capital of Tula and a date of circa 1020 for
his appearance as Kukulcan in the Yucatan.[21] Hedrick believes
the man Quetzalcoatl and Kukulcan were one and the same, and
dismisses any consideration of him as an alien from another hemisphere. He believes he was an indigenous Mexican, being dark-
skinned, as opposed to a fair European outsider. He succeeds in
effectively dismissing the myth of a white pre-Columbian visitor
as the origin of Quetzalcoatl. But in his attempt to do this, he
limits the issue to a simple either/or proposition. Thus his article
on Quetzalcoatl is entitled "Quetzalcoatl: European or Indigene?"
The possibility of Quetzalcoatl being a dark-skinned outsider, such
as an African or Arab-African, which would fit in with the relevant
descriptions and cultural data, does not enter into his considera-
tions at all.

The tenth-century dates that Hedrick gives fit in well with his
thesis. I would not contest a native Quetzalcoatl. Mixcoatl's son
came to be known as Quetzalcoatl simply because he was the high
priest of that god. But while Quetzalcoatl's first appearance as a
man may be traced to a native figure, Quetzalcoatl grew into a
complex myth and emerged as a god of cultural innovation and
civilization because of a series of reappearances, actual and expected, in American history. As the Jews waited for the appearance of a Messiah, so did the Americans await the "cyclical" return
of the legendary Quetzalcoatl. Such an expectation led them to
assume that Cortez was a Quetzalcoatl when he appeared in
Mexico in 1519, precisely four cycles after the appearance of
Abubakari the Second in 1311. (A cycle is fifty-two years by
American Indian time.) Abubakari the Second himself, as I mentioned earlier, appeared exactly six cycles after the disappearance
of Quetzalcoatl by way of the sea from among the Toltecs (A.D.
999).

How developed was the Quetzalcoatl cult and its rituals when
the Mandingo came? This is hard to say, but it must have taken

on a broad general pattern to which details from outside were
later added. We can be certain it did have some embryonic form
before the coming of the Mandingo. The pyramid of Cholula
dedicated to Quetzalcoatl predates the Mandingo journeys by
many centuries. The plumed serpent *motif* in ancient Mexico
goes back to a much earlier contact. We can be equally certain
that the feathered serpent *cult* in medieval Mali fused with that
in medieval Mexico. The ritual correspondences between the two
cults are so close that they pass beyond the stage of mere cultural
convergence to the point where "the incidence of coincidence"
clearly suggests a medieval marriage and fusion.

The Mexican Quetzalcoatl was the "Fine Feathered Snake." He
was also "the symbol of water or moisture produced by rain, which
after a long drought, awakens vegetation to new life." The high
priests also spoke of Kukulcan, his counterpart in South America,
as "the feather snake which goes into the water," and these figures
in both cases became identified with the rain god. The rain ceremonial dedicated to the rain god is represented by the image of
Quetzalcoatl, and to him is ascribed the invention and conscien-
tious execution of penance and chastisements. In the figure of
Quetzalcoatl, the rain god was combined with the rain magician
who, with his prayer and his practices, ensured to his people the
rain needed for their crops.[22] From this, Quetzalcoatl evolved as
a god from whom prosperity could rain. In medieval Mali the
equivalent of Quetzalcoatl is the Dasiri of the Bambara, the tribe
of the Mandingo from which Abubakari came.

The Dasiri is the protector of the village, the beneficent spirit
whose sacred animal is a snake, who is addressed with the words
"Preserve us from evil doers . . . above all give us rain, without
which the harvest is impossible."[23] The feast of the Dasiri takes
place at the beginning of the year, like that of Quetzalcoatl. The
worship of the Dasiri is closely associated with the activity of
the Mandingo *kuare*. This *kuare* or *kore* is a semisecret sect whose
initiates perform certain dances and sacrifices under a tree where
the spirit is supposed to live.

The most striking of these are the self-flaggelating dances
(dances of penance and chastisement) in which the dancers wrap

themselves in thorns or lacerate their breasts and armpits. Some beat themselves with long flexible scourges.[24] In the Quetzalcoatl ceremonial the same self-chastisement and the use of thorn-pricking occurs. In both the Mexican Quetzalcoatl and the Mandingo Dasiri worship, these thorn-prickings and whippings were designed to bring blood out in drops. This blood dropping or blood-letting symbolized the falling of raindrops.

Again, Quetcalcoatl is later represented with a beard, so alien to the native American chin. In Dasiri worship the house chiefs are all old men, and the religious priest who presides over them is bearded. In the Mexican ritual the presiding priest of the Quetzal-coatl cult adopted an artificial beard.[25] The artificial beard, as such, was an earlier influence.

As the Dasiri and *kore* festivals take place annually, the god or spirit becomes the measurer of time. Similarly, Quetzalcoatl is considered to be the inventor of the calendar, some aspects of which have been shown to correspond closely to an Egyptian calendar introduced as late as 747 B.C. (see Chapter 9). There is also an ancient calendar found in Chiapas, described by Bishop Francisco Nuñez Vega, that mentions seven *"negritos"* representing the seven planets and in detail refers to the naming of their twenty-day calendar.[26]

Quetzalcoatl is associated with a tree. The Dasiri and *kore* are inseparable from a tree. The Dasiri is supposed to live on a specific tree, which is sacred.[27] In like manner Quetzalcoatl is represented as a hummingbird kneeling on the top of a tree.[28] The Dasiri is also worshiped on an altar of a conical or truncated form, which supports a clay bowl.[29] The bowl, which receives libations, is placed under a tree or on the first branches of the tree. This same tree is represented in America.

D. G. Brinton, in his *Primer of Mayan Hieroglyphics*, describes this tree, a central design in the *Chilan Balam*, or Sacred Book, of Mani. This work reveals the Mayan design of the Cosmos, known as the Tableau of the Bacabs or the Plate of the Bacabs, an exact representation of the Bambara altar and of the bowl on the lower branches of the tree, with a celestial vase catching the rain from the cloud-mass.

"This design," according to Brinton "is surrounded by thirteen heads which signify the thirteen *ahau katuns*, or greater cycles of years . . . the number 13 in American mythology symbolizes the 13 possible directions of space. The border of 13 heads expresses the totality of Space and Time; and the design itself symbolizes life within Space and Time. This is shown as follows: At the bottom of the field lies a cubical block, which represents the earth, always conceived of in this shape in Mayan mythology . . . Above the earth-cube, altar of the gods, supported by four legs, which rest upon the four quarters of the mundane plane, is the celestial vase, which contains the heavenly waters, the rains and the showers . . . above it hang the heavy rain clouds ready to fill it; within it grows the Tree of Life spreading its branches far upward, on their extremities the flowers or fruit of life, the soul or immortal principle of man."[30]

Apart from the central design in the Plate of the Bacabs, within which are the altar, bowl, cloud-mass, tree and god, corresponding to the Mandingo altar, bowl, cloud-mass, tree and god of the Dasiri, there are other designs that are also remarkably similar to those found in Mandingo territory. Thus the thirteen heads in the Plate represent the division of the Zodiac into thirteen parts, and this zodiacal division into thirteen has been found in thirteen-headed zodiacal designs on calabashes in West Africa. It is a curious fact that a similar division into thirteen is recorded only among West Africans and Americans[31] (with the sole exception of a little-known people, the Kirghizes).

Secret signs and glyphs are inscribed within geometric designs on the Plate of the Bacabs. Leo Wiener has presented evidence to show that these signs and glyphs correspond closely to, and may have their origin in, Arabic and Sudanic *gadwals*. *Gadwal* is a technical term in sorcery. It is a talisman or charm and consists of a sign or inscription written or drawn on a piece of paper within quadrangular or polygonal designs, squares, parallelograms or even circles. These signs or inscriptions are supposed to possess magical powers. They usually consist of letters or numerals, magic words, the names of gods, the angels and demons, as well as the planets, the days of the week, and the elements, and sometimes even pieces from the Koran like the *fatiha* (the first chapter). The applications of these magical designs are manifold. Frequently the paper on which one is drawn is burned "to smoke someone with its smoke" or the writing is washed off and drunk. The underlying notion behind the *gadwals* is that secret relationships exist between the various components of the *gadwal*, and positive results may be achieved by the most propitious arrangement of these components.[32]

These talismanic signs written or drawn in columns, which have their origin in the Arab world and are found in the West African Sudan, show a strong resemblance to Central American glyphs. The most interesting of the Sudanic rock inscriptions photographed by Desplagnes have columns of glyphs, most of which begin with the form of spiders. The design of these spiders makes them identical to the ones on American burial mounds given by Holmes in *Art in Shell of the Ancient Americans*.[33] The amazing thing about these spiders, both the African and the American, is that they carry a cross in their center. This is not the Christian type of cross but is the simplest representation of the fourfold division of the *gadwal*. It is an ornamentation that is in constant use in the Western Sudan. It forms the central design of circular objects, and is done in square patterns with looped ends, exactly as in bird *gadwals* found in pre-Columbian American Moundbuilder *gorgets* (burial mounds) and is worked in dotted-line forms upon knobs. In the moundbuilder *gorgets* are found not only the spider with its *gadwals* but the looped-end *gadwal*, with a cross in the center, all placed within a circle (see Plate 15). These are among the most striking of the objects in the mounds.[34]

Another notable correspondence between the cultures of Mexico and Mali may be found in "the priestly cap of the Magi." This is a conical hat with a neck-flap which was a distinctive headgear of kings and priests in ancient Persia. It was passed on from Persia to the Arabs and perpetuated among the magicians of West Africa. It reappears in America as a crown worn by the black-bearded Quetzalcoatl. Its shape is not its only distinctive feature. It was the representation of the visible heaven, and so was painted to represent stars.[35]

Leo Wiener has traced the Arabic name for this starred hat through the Mande language, and the same name for the hat is found in Mexico. Arabic: *qu-bil-a*; Mande: *ko-fil-a*; in Mexico: *co-pill-i*). All are pronounced roughly the same, the same word in fact following the phonological rules of transformation in its passage through the three language areas. Standing by itself, this could be a simple coincidence. The details of the cap, however, seem conclusive.

Clavigero, in *The History of Mexico*, describes the hat. "The crown," he says, "which was called by the Mexicans *copilli*, was a sort of small mitre, the forepart of which was raised up and terminated in a point, and the part behind was lowered down and hung over the neck."[36] "And the *copilli*," says E. Seler in the *Codex Borgia*, "was a headdress frequently made of an ocelot skin, so as to represent a lot of dots, that is, the stars of the magician's cap."[37] That this kingly and priestly cap of the Magi, with its conical shape and star decoration, should have been preserved in America in its identical form and should also have kept almost the same name which was current for it among the Mandingo, strongly suggests that the cap represented the influence of the fourteenth-century African visitors.

Quetzalcoatl ritual was largely rainmaking ritual. Controlling the weather and ensuring an adequate fall of rain were among the primary tasks of the cult's priests and magicians. The rainmaker was thus an important person in both African and American cultures. There are instances of rainmakers entering foreign provinces during a time of drought and acquiring instant control over a people because they brought rain. The first Mandingo king to become a Muslim convert was persuaded to enter the new faith by a Mohammedan whose prayers in a time of great drought coincided with the fall of rain.[38] The Mohammedan, of course, was no rainmaker in the classical sense, but luckily he entered the king's court at a most propitious moment for his propaganda mission.

Often a special class of magicians existed in African societies for the sole purpose of regulating the heavenly water supply. In some African societies the rainmaker was known as the shepherd of heaven and held the office of both political and providential king. The Mandingo kings, in spite of their later Muslim orientation, never lost their ritual link with the land and the weather. They were princes of the magicians, animists first, Muslims a poor second, as the epic of Sundiata, the founder of the Mali empire, clearly shows. They always kept their royal capital in the agricultural provinces, close to the cultivators who preserved this mystical connection between the king and the crops.[39]

A number of general features in rainmaking ritual may be highlighted in a comparative outline of weather magic in African and American cultures. The discovery of the skeletons of ancient magicians of Mexico with strong Negroid characteristics, as reported by Frederick Peterson, suggests that here was a fertile area of influence. The "black figure" predominates in American magic, and while it was convenient to think this blackness was exclusively symbolic when one believed there was no contact between the cultures on opposite sides of the Atlantic basin, we are now left to ponder the nature and extent of that influence, some of which could have been as early as the African and Egyptian presence in the Olmec heartland (800–700 B.C.), some as late as the Mandingo contact period (1310–1311) during the critical years of the founding of modern Mexico. The evidence seems to suggest that these "black magicians" brought a number of new ideas. This would account for vague basic parallels between the two systems, parallels which may have proceeded *without contact* from a common idea, developing *through contact* into a complex of identical traits.

Rainmaking ritual in both Central America and West Africa, for example, included dancing with water-filled perforated pipes in the mouth and blowing the water through the perforation at the sky, throwing water from a vessel held high in the air so that the falling spray descended on the drought-stricken land or the suppliant crowd, squirting water in a fine stream from the mouth onto a field, and watering the graves of twins, who were thought in both cultures to have some mysterious connection with the weather. The rainmakers in both culture-areas made use of black rainstones, and in their sacrifices slaughtered black animals.

This was also the case in South America, which the Africans visited either before or after filtering through into Mexico. A Peruvian oral tradition tells of black men coming to them across the Andes. To procure rain the Peruvian Indians sacrificed black sheep in a field. The Africans of West Africa sacrificed black sheep, black fowl, the blood of black oxen and black cattle. Lest it be thought that these are natural choices, suggested simply by the color of rain clouds, it should be pointed out that the Chinese did the opposite. To ensure a good harvest of their five cereals, they offered to the gods *white* wild boars, white oxen and white sheep in sacrifice.[40]

It is a curious fact that before Columbus set out on his Third Voyage to pursue "the Guinea route" as Don Juan had outlined it to him, he sent some of his men into Santiago, one of the Cape Verde islands off Africa, to look for "a herd of black cattle."[41] (The ritual value of these animals must have been high, and one may surmise that Columbus contemplated them as a gift to the American Indians. The search, however, which lasted several days, was not successful.) Black clothes also were chosen by the West African and Mexican rainmakers for their ceremonials. Rain was stopped in both cultures by the use of firesticks and firestones, sometimes by placing hot coals on the ground to burn the stubborn footfall of the rain.

Many other analogies of a general nature may be noted, but let us confine ourselves to one on the same level of specificity as the rainmaking rituals: the creation of effigies or magical images, often of enemies, in the belief that to injure or destroy the image is to effect a like injury or destruction upon the enemy himself. For thousands of years this was known to the sorcerers of Egypt, and was widely practiced in Africa. The North American Indians employed the same ritual of pricking or piercing the doll. For example, when an Ojebway Indian desired to work evil on anyone, he made a little wooden image of his enemy and ran a needle into its head and heart, or he shot an arrow into it, believing that wherever the needle pierced or the arrow struck the image, his foe would at the same instant be seized with a sharp pain in the corresponding part of his body. If he intended to kill the person outright, he burned or buried the image, uttering certain magic words as he did so.

The use of a person's private castoffs—such as hair, nails, a rag of his garment, or drops of his blood—for magic directed against him was also an African and American practice. The magician kneaded these relics into a lump of wax, which he molded and dressed in the likeness of the intended victim, who was then at the mercy of his tormentor. The idea was that if the image were exposed to fire, the person whom it represented would immediately fall into a burning fever; if it were stabbed with a knife, the victim would feel the pain of the wound. These practices are of great antiquity in Africa. An Egyptian wizard was prosecuted in 1200 B.C. for making effigies of men and women in wax, thereby causing paralysis of their limbs and other grievous bodily harm.[42]

Remarkable as these coincidences in image-magic may seem, they could not be advanced as evidence suggestive of contact if other hard evidence were not available. Such evidence, however, exists, and it is in the light of this that these rituals should be re-examined, particularly when it can be shown that the analogies in African and American magic go beyond single-trait resemblances to major clusters or complexes of traits.

NOTES AND REFERENCES

1 Donald Mackenzie, *Myths of Pre-Columbian America*, London, Gresham Publishing Co., 1924, pp. 44, 57.

2 Ibid., p. 45.

3 Ibid., pp. 45–46.

4 Idem.

5 Ernest Budge, *The Gods of the Egyptians*, London, Methuen & Co., 1904, Vol. 1, p. 481.

6 Mackenzie, op. cit., p. 62.

7 Idem.

8 Idem.

9 Mackenzie, p. 63, quoting G. Elliot-Smith in *The Journal of the Manchester Egyptian and Oriental Society*, 1916.

10 George Vaillant, *The Aztecs of Mexico*, Garden City, New York, 1941, p. 182.

11 For a discussion of the pre-Columbian cross in America and its correspondence with the Egyptian use of the cross on the Nile, see Constance Irwin, *Fair Gods and Stone Faces*, St. Martin's Press, 1963, p. 166; also, Mackenzie, op. cit., pp. 84, 85. "As in the Old World," Mackenzie writes, "the cross symbol was connected with the gods of the four points of the compass who controlled the elements, and therefore with the doctrines referred to in the previous chapter [winged-disc symbolism, metal-symbolism, color-schemes affecting mummified organs, cyclical change of royal garments, sequence of ages, etc.] including that of the four ages of the world which were coloured like the cardinal points. The Spaniards were so convinced, however, that the pre-Columbian cross was a Christian symbol that they examined Mexican mythology for traces of St. Thomas."

12 D. Daly, "Mexican Messiah" (An attempt to identify Quetzalcoatl with St. Brendan), *Popular Science*, 39, 1891, pp. 95–105.

13 P. M. Hanson, *Jesus Christ among the Ancient Americans*, Independence, Mo., 1949.

14 Basil Hedrick, "Quetzalcoatl: European or Indigene?," in Riley et al. (eds.) *Man Across the Sea*, Austin, University of Texas Press, pp. 255–265.

15 Alphonse de Quatrefages, *The Human Species*, London, 1905, pp. 205–206.

16 Thor Heyerdahl, "The Bearded Gods Speak," in Gordon Ashe (ed.) *The Quest for America*, pp. 199–238.

17 Brigitta Wallace, "Some Points of Controversy," in Ashe (ed.) *The Quest for America*, pp. 155–174.

18 J. B. Breasted, *A History of Egypt*, Lancaster, Pa., Scribner's, 1905.

19 Erich von Däniken, Michael Heron (trans.), *Chariot of the Gods?*, Bantam Books, 1974, 45th edition, p. 106.

20 William T. Corlett, *The Medicine Man of the American Indian*, Springfield, Ill., C. C. Thomas, 1935, p. 6.

21 Hedrick, op. cit., p. 260.

22 Leo Weiner, *Africa and the Discovery of America*, Philadelphia, Innes & Sons, 1922, Vol. 3, p. 259.

23 J. Henry, *Les Bambara*, Münster, 1910, p. 120. See also Weiner, op. cit., p. 261.

24 Ibid., p. 102. See alsoWeiner, op. cit., p. 261.

25 Ibid., p. 116 and Weiner, op. cit., p. 264.

26 Alexander von Wuthenau, *Unexpected Faces in Ancient America*, New York, Crown Publishers, 1975, p. 77.

27 Maurice Delafosse, *Haut-Sénégal-Niger*, Vol. 3, p. 168. See also Weiner, op. cit., p. 264.

28 Seler, *Codex Borgia*, Vol. 2, p. 66.

29 Delafosse, op. cit., p. 169.

30 D. G. Brinton, *A Primer of Mayan Hieroglyphics*, Philadelphia, 1895, p. 47.

31 Weiner, op. cit., p. 270.

32 Ibid., pp. 268, 269.

33 W. H. Holmes, "Art in Shell of the Ancient Americans" in *The Second Annual Report of the Bureau of Ethnology to the Secretary of the Smithsonian Institution, 1880–1881*, Washington, 1883.

34 Ibid., p. 286.

35 Weiner, op. cit., pp. 319–321.

36 The Abbe D. Francesco Saveria Clavigero, Charles Cullen (trans.), *The History of Mexico*, Philadelphia, 1804, Bk. 7, Section 8.

37 Seler, *Codex Borgia*, Vol. 3.

38 J. Spencer Trimingham, *A History of Islam in West Africa*, London, Oxford University Press, 1962, p. 62.

39 Ibid., p. 65.

40 (Kato and Hoshina, trans.) *Kogoshui*, New York, Barnes and Noble, 1973, p. 91.

41 John Boyd Thacher, *Christopher Columbus, His Life, His Work, His Remains*, New York, G. P. Putnam's Sons, 1903, Vol. 2, p. 379.

42 Sir James Frazer, "The Magic Art" in *The Golden Bough*, Vol. 1, London, Macmillan, 1922.

6

MANDINGO TRADERS IN MEDIEVAL MEXICO

*We observe the fusion of two forces, tradition and new-
ness, to produce the Aztec empire . . . This fusion was ac-
celerated by the arrival of a series of cultured immigrants
who brought with them ancient knowledge. The most interesting are those whom the chronicles name* Those Who
Returned . . .

—IGNACIO BERNAL, *Mexico Before Cortez*

From across the water in nearby Tenochtitlan, he could hear the
hollow scream of the conches and the roll of the temple drums.[1]
Fainter than those sounded from the sanctuaries of his own quarter, they lingered longer nevertheless, echoing in the valley of
Mexico and in the silent marketplace of Tlatelulco as voices in the
secret valleys of the ear echo with the whisper of morning dreams.
He shook himself and rose from the sleeping-mat.

A soft silver dust and mist had settled on the water, but the
sun sliced it with sharp, swift strokes, sweeping clean the floor
of the lake until he could see the silhouette of canoes. Paddles
were already slapping the water—fishermen returning from the
morning catch, traders unloading their merchandise onto the
island's little quays.

He had lived for more than a cycle in Tlatelulco. As a young
man he had spent long hours emblazoning boards for Aztec nobles
by affixing the native duck, chicken and heron feathers with his
ixtli knives.[2] Now he was an officer of the guild, inspecting the

quality of featherwork offered to the public by his caste. Many years had passed since the days of Quaquapitzuac,[3] in whose reign *pochteca* from the Hot Lands had come, some of whom had skins as black as the sheen of ocelots. Their arrival had changed his life. They had come bearing the feathers of the *quetzalli* bird. None of the work he had done before their coming could compare with the coats of arms he later wrought with the green, blue and red plumes of that magnificent southern bird. They had come also with the hides of a strange animal not seen before in Mexico, even in the stalls of the hunting tribe, the Otomi.[4] These black merchants from the Hot Lands sold vivid colored mantles of cotton cloth, the cloaks so richly dyed they seemed to copy the iridescent plumage of the birds, so various in design that the radial wheel of the sun, feathers and stylized shells, the skins of tigers, the forms of rabbits, snakes, fishes and butterflies mingled in the myriad of motifs with triangles, polygons, crosses, squares and crescents.[5] Together with these garments they brought into the marketplace golden ear pendants, "smoking" pipes, some with the heads of the traders carved on the bowls, exotic stones and shells.

They came at first in twos, and then in a small band. Their coming attracted attention, but this was less because of the extraordinariness of their appearance (foreigners, after all, were expected to look different) than the extraordinariness of their wares. Some of the luxuries they offered in the common marketplace had been enjoyed almost exclusively by the noblemen and kings of Mexico, who seemed to have had some earlier contract with them.[6] In the reign of Quaquapitzuac they had suddenly appeared, the spearhead of a larger migrating group. Out of what world they had originally come no one knew, but they trickled in from the direction of the south and the southeast. It seemed as if everyone were on the move at that time. All sorts of people were gravitating toward the lakes to form the nucleus of a new Mexico.

Because they were of no known race or tribe, their origins obscure, their habits nomadic, they were confused at first with some dark, wandering branch of the Chichimecs. But Chichimec was often just a vague, broad term for vagrant peoples,* especially peoples whose language appeared to be mixed. These strangers had, in their passage to Mexico from some settlement in the South, picked up Nahuatl, the lingua franca of the Aztecs, but they spoke it as a second tongue, for several of their words were clearly not of that language.

Chichimecs, however, they certainly were not. He had known some of those nomads from the desert plateau. He thought of their condition as barbaric and wretched. They wore loincloths of palm fiber in that time, their women stood in awe of the simple loom, they had never fired a single pot. Unable to scrape a living from the land, they gathered mesquite seeds and hunted rabbits.[7] These foreigners, on the other hand, wore feathered headdresses, polished and brilliant earrings, cloaks and loincloths of the finest woven cotton. Small white shells on their ankles rattled softly as they walked. The Chichimecs had never built temples or idols, had no high priests. They lived in caves and domed brush shelters.[8] They always ended up as misfits when they lingered in the town. But he had watched these black trader men from the tropical south. They had entered the valley of Mexico, armed and apprehensive, but with an air of authority.

It was hard to tell what they thought and did in private as he peered at the walls of their houses. Windowless, these houses cloaked in mystery, like the gardens of an inner court, the lives within. But the blacks had built a temple in the town as soon as they had formed a sizable *capulli*. In the forecourt of this temple they set up the wooden statue of a werewolf, who was their *nagual*. This statue fascinated him.

They called the god to whom it was built *Coyotli-nauatl*. It was fashioned in the form of both a coyote (the American werewolf) and a man. It was dressed in a coyote skin, but it stood slightly bent like an old man, its coyote head covered by a human mask. Its teeth were long and pointed, sheathed in gold. In one hand it carried a stick which was adorned with black stones, so it looked

---

* As Ignacio Bernal points out, "after some time the meaning of the word was enlarged to include . . . all the recent arrivals or those emigrants who led a nomadic life." (*Mexico Before Cortez*, p. 75)

like a heavily knobbed club. On this the god leaned. Its feet were dressed like those of the traders, with small white rattles on the ankles and sandals of *yecotl* leaves on its paws.[9]

He was not the only one of the featherworkers who was fascinated by these strangers. The attraction of men from the Hot Lands who provided them with exquisite new material for their trade was overwhelming. It was not long before they were drawn also to their *nagual* and began to join in their rituals and festivities. Even though he himself had never worshiped Coyotli-nauatl, these were the men with whom he eventually did most of his business, and they had become his good friends. He had been allowed to stand on the edge of the palisade as the masked men chanted and danced on the day of the festival.

Only yesterday it was, and he had gone to sleep on his mat with the image of braziers piled with resinous pinewood burning away the night. A few native women, their faces luminous and unmasked, had danced with the men. They were daughters of the featherworkers who had been taken to wife by the blacks. Thus had the gods and rituals of the native and the foreign, of the *pochteca* and *amanteca* slowly fused.[10]

Through it all—the comings and goings, the meeting and the mixing, the wedding of gods and of women—he had been there. The years of the strangers had flowed over him like all the strange rivers flowing in that long *katun* of years into the valley of Mexico. He felt the change like water running over a subterranean floor as he looked deeper into the past and the morning. The sun was sitting on the edge of the lake now, and the sky and the stream had merged, mirroring each other. Beyond, in the distance, he could see the tops of the volcanoes, smoking. But he could no longer tell whether the thin, drifting dust he saw over the volcano Popocatepetl was truly *native* volcanic smoke or the far-flung flowers and branches of a *foreign* cloud . . .

Of all the strange rivers flowing in that age of change and flux into the valley of Mexico, that of the Mandingo was the strangest. Into the bloodstream of how many American tribes this alien stream was soon to flow it is hard to tell, but in central America at least it entered that of the Otomi and the Lacandon. In the southern lands, the Hot Lands, from which it had traveled to the central valley, it had flowed into the Aravos tribe of the Orinoco (where that river flows through what is now Venezuela), the Argualos of Critara, the Porcijis and Matayas of Brazil. Balboa had seen some of its surviving elements in Darien, now Panama. Through the Chuanas of the Panamanian isthmus, it had moved in its steady northward sweep.[11]

It is with Mexico, however, that we are most concerned, for here we can see the confluence of cultures, not just the confluence of bloods. When we compare the cult of the werewolf (the coyote of the prairies) found among the *amanteca** with the cult of the werewolf (the hyena of the savannahs) found among the Bambara of medieval Mali, we see quite clearly that we are at the very head of that confluence.

The werewolf cult among the Bambara, the leading tribe of the Mandingo, was known as the *nama*, and the priests or headmen of the cult as the *nama-tigi* (heads of the nama) or the *aman-tigi* (heads of the faith). It is a "simple jump from *nama-tigi* or *aman-tigi* to *aman-teca*, for both *tigi* and *teca* mean "master," "chief," or "head man." The morphemes *tec/tequi*, in fact, pronounced roughly the same as the Mandingo *tig/tigi*, carry the same and related meanings through nouns, adjectives and verbs in a number of Mexican languages and in Nahuatl.[12] This is but one of many coincidences.

In the Mexican ritual the god of the *amanteca* is clothed in the werewolf's skin, although it wears a human mask on its head. This is identical with the Bambara ritual. In the Mexican ritual the god wields a stick knobbed with black stones. This imitates the stick wielded by the werewolf god of the Bambara, for that too is knobbed, though with fragments of sheep's horns. The Bambara ritual involves the feathered carcass of two great birds. In Mexico a pot is carried on the back of the god, with numerous feathers of a bird introduced from the tropical South by the *poch-*

---

* A mixed trader/featherworker caste in medieval Tlateluco, the market island across the lake from Mexico-Tenochtitlan.

teca—namely the quetzalli bird. In Mexico the god wore an anklet of small white rattles.[13] Rattles are used in the Bambara ritual— not just the ankle rattle of the cult dancers but the gourd rattle, favorite paraphernalia of the African magician.

In fact, in both Mexico and Mali, the gourd rattle becomes a sort of ventriloquist's dummy for the voice of the god. This gourd rattle is the chief instrument of both the West African and American "fetish-man." In it resides the speaking divinity or devil. The rattle has the same name in America as in Mali. The Arabic *mitra-qah*, passing through the Western Sudan in Bambara as *man-taraka*, appears in the American language Guarani as *mbaraca*, also in the American languages Arawak and Tupi as *maraca*. The association with magical ritual is also the same. Tupi not only has the word *maraca* (gourd rattle) but *maraca-inbara* (wizard, witch). The refrain of the Carib diviners using the gourd rattle in other ceremonies in the pre-Columbian Caribbean was also the same. "The imprecation of the Caribs consists in a series of songs and chants of which the refrain is *haure*. Similarly the Mandingo Negroes call their talking devil *Hore*."[14]

But now to return to the werewolf cults. The Mexican werewolf god is described by the historian Bernadino de Sahagun as having five male idols and two female ones, seven in all. In Mali these accompanying idols were symbolic of the seven-day week intro-duced by the Arabs, but the Mandingo modified this introduction by inserting two rest days (Monday and Thursday) to bring it back to their five-day week. These two days are dramatized in the Mexican ritual by the females, who, unlike the males, are not dressed like the werewolf.[15] Again, the festival of the werewolf god was celebrated in both cultures twice a year. In Mali the god is smeared in blood, usually chicken blood. In Mexico, where human sacrifice was habitual and only slightly mediated by the humanity of Quetzalcoatl, blood is provided in the first of the two festivals by humans.[16]

The correspondence, however, between Mandingo *nama* and Mexican coyote worship does not end there. A look at *naual* from the word coyotli-*naual*, the werewolf god in America, leads us into other areas of correspondence. D. G. Brinton, in his book

Nagualism, discusses the nature and meaning of *naual* and the many derivatives of the verbal root *na,* indicating that these words and the body of beliefs attached to them—nagualism—were brought into Mexico by foreign medicine men.

"Nahual means knowledge," wrote Brinton, "especially mystical knowledge, the knowledge of the hidden and secret things of nature . . . It is significant that neither the radical *na* nor any of its derivatives are found in the Huasteca dialect of the Mayan tongue, which was spoken about Tampico, far removed from other members of that stock. The inference is that in the southern dialects it was a borrowed stem.

"Nor in the Nahuatl language—although its very name is derived from it—does the radical *na* appear in its simplicity and true significance. To the Nahuas, also, it must have been a loan.

"It is true that de la Serna derives the Mexican *naualli,* a sorcerer, from the verb *nahuatlia,* to mask or disguise oneself, because a *naualli* is one who masks or disguises himself under the form of some lower animal, which is his *nagual,* but it is altogether likely that *nahualtia* derived its meaning from the custom of the medicine men to wear masks during their ceremonies.

"Therefore, if the term *nagual,* and many of its associates and derivatives, were at first borrowed from the Zapotec language, a necessary conclusion is that along with these terms came most of the superstitions, rites and beliefs to which they allude; which thus became grafted on the general tendency to such superstitions existing everywhere and at all times in the human mind.

"Along with the names of the days and the hieroglyphs which mark them . . . were carried most of the doctrines of the Nagualists, and the name by which in time they became known from central Mexico quite to Nicaragua and beyond.

"The mysterious words have now indeed lost much of their ancient significance . . . Among the Lacandons, of Mayan stock, who inhabit the forests of the upper waters of the Usumacinta river, at the present day the term *naguate* or *nagutlat* is said to be applied to anyone 'who is entitled to respect and obedience by age and merit' but in all possibility he is believed to possess superior and occult knowledge."[17]

It should be mentioned in this connection that serological surveys of the Lacandon Indians, the most secluded of Maya tribes, conducted in the nineteen-sixties by Dr. Alfonso de Garay, Director of the Genetic Program of the National Commission for Nuclear Energy in Mexico, indicated early and extensive contact between the Lacandons and Africans. Negroid characteristics have been found in their blood, although they have not been known to mix with outsiders in post-Columbian times. Dr. de Garay's report includes, among other things, "a reference to the sickle cell, a malaria resistant mutant gene usually found only in the blood of black people."[18]

Brinton, in his study of nagualism, has provided us with a series of *na* words in Maya and Maya dialects (like the Quiche dialect of the Yucatan), the Zapotec language and the Nahuatl language to show that some foreign group passing through these linguistically diverse but geographically close peoples introduced this series of words. Looking at the series we see that *na* is at the root of words in these languages meaning mystical knowledge, intelligence, prophecy, sorcery and magic. One example from each language group should be enough to illustrate this point. *Na-at* (intelligence, in Maya), *na-ual* (to prophesy, in Quiche), *na-a* (medicine man, in Zapotec) and *na-ual-li* (magician, in Nahuatl).

The same root *na* is at the base of a series of words with the same meanings in the Mande languages. One part of the series springs from the Arabic *na-ba* (to prophesy), *na-bi* (prophet), *na-bah* (intelligent), and appears in the West African Peul and Dyula languages as *na-biu*, in Soso as *an-na-bi*, and in Wolof as *na-bi-na*. Ideas behind these Arabic *naba/nabi* words, however, have fused and become confused with ideas of the native *nama* cult, so that we get *na-ba* in the Habbes-Gara language for "masked men," who are known as the *nama* in Malinke. In Malinke also we get *nama-koro*, which literally means "hyena wise men," which is an exact translation of the Nahuatl *Coyotli-naual*, meaning "coyote wise men," where the American coyote (werewolf of the prairies) is substituted for the African hyena (werewolf of the savannahs).[19]

There is one aspect of the African *nama* ritual that was not carried forward in the main coyote ritual, but nonetheless preserved in another ritual associated with a black god the Mexicans call Ek-chu-ah. Attributes of a beekeeper god found in the Mandingo *nama* worship seem to have fused with attributes of the Mandingo traders themselves to produce the complex figure of this strange god among the Mexicans. Ek-chu-ah was a god of traders or "traveling merchants" and was often confused with the coyote god, whom the *amanteca* worshiped.[20] He is black in all his representations and is also pictured as warlike, armed with a lance, and sometimes engaged in combat. This is to be expected, because the Mandingo trader had to be warlike and always on his guard against hostile, suspicious tribes as he explored new trade routes. In fact, it is as a captive of native tribes with whom he had waged wars of self-defense that the pre-Columbian African was first seen by the Spanish in the New World in the Isthmus of Darien (now Panama) and on an island off Cartagena, Colombia. A particularly African feature of this trader god, Ek-chu-ah, was the bale of merchandise he carried on his head. Professor Gonzalo Aguirre Beltran has pointed out, in his ethnohistory of the Negro in Mexico, that this habit of carrying heavy things on the head (and young children astride the hip) is an indisputable African influence upon the Mexican.[21]

Ek-chu-ah is also often distinguished by his age. He is usually featured in the Mexican codices as an old man with a toothless jaw or one solitary tooth and a drooping lower lip. He is also related to bee culture. This is demonstrated by his presence in the Codex Troano in the section on bees.[22] All these aspects of Ek-chu-ah link him unequivocally with the old beekeeping god found in *nama* worship among the Mandingo. In *nama* worship the god, represented as an old man, was sometimes put in a beehive (used as a tabernacle) while his devotees drank a honeyed drink and danced and howled around him. The medieval Mexicans celebrated the festival of Ek-chu-ah on the same day as the holiday of Hobnil, the god of the beekeepers, and during this feast they drank three bowls of honeyed wine.[23]

A Mandingo element from *nama* worship also accounted for the extraordinary nose of this black god among the Mexicans. The long nose of the Ek-chu-ah is due to the fact that the idol of the *nama*, called the *Kungolo Nama* ("head of the *nama*") is represented by a fantastic bird, that is, with a beak. That beak is carried forward in the long nose. The Ek-chu-ah thus becomes among the Mexicans "the lord of the nose."[24]

The relationship may now be seen very clearly between the *amanteca* of Mexico and the *amantigi* or *namatigi* of Mali. The worship of the werewolf totem, or *nagual*, underwent very few changes indeed in its transplantation from Mali to Mexico. As in all transplantations, local fauna and materials simply replaced the original (the hyena became the coyote, the stick knobbed with sheep's horns became the stick knobbed with black stones, the bright tropical birds of Africa had their feathers matched by the rich plumes of the South American quetzalli bird), but the basic complex of ideas and their unique organization remained behind as skeletal evidence of their African origin. Vague, general parallels in ritual behavior may evolve independently in remote cultures, but there is a complex cluster of elements here—not only symbols, images and ritual acts, but even linguistic labels and conceptual confusions—that could not have been repeated in their arbitrariness by virtue of a similar response to the same phenomena. The identicals are so staggering that one feels one is looking into a mirror at what both the Mexican and Mali magicians would call the shadow of the twin, the spirit of the double.

As for the merchant caste known as the *pochteca*, let us examine some of the items they brought into Mexico. While these—or most of them—were obviously made by them in their new settlements along the Atlantic seaboard and in South America, they were copied from Mandingo prototypes. The names carried forward in these items demonstrate this.

From Sahagun's account of the first foreign merchants we learn that they sold mantles (*chimalli*) and waistcloths (*maxtli*).[25] In the language of Maya, *chimalli* is translated as "shield, buckler." *Valpalchimalli*, a derivative of the word, is translated as "battle cloak." A study of the word in the Mexican languages establishes a relationship between buckler and cloak. In Maya, more than one idea is rooted in the word. In addition to "shield" and "cloak," there is *chim* and *chimil*, meaning "pouch." These oddly linked ideas of "pouch" and "cloak" are also contained in terms found in the Mande languages. They have an Arabic origin and came into the Mande languages through the Arab caravan trade. An Arabic term is *šimla* (plural, *šimāl*, pronounced "chimal"), meaning "a garment in which one wraps oneself" as well as "a bag or pouch put to the raceme of a palm tree in order that the fruit may not be shaken off, or held under the udder of the ewe or goat, when the udder is heavy with milk."[26]

Equally interesting is *maxtli*, which in the American language of Nahuatl means "a waistcloth to hide the nudity." This garment is tied around the private parts of women as an intimate adornment. It is shown to correspond with the Malinke word *masiti*, "adornment," Bambara *masiri*, "adornment, to make one's toilet" and Bambara *masirili*, "ornamentation, toilet." There is also the female loincloth, which in Mexico is *nagua*. This barely covered a woman's privates, falling from the waist to the middle of the thigh. It may be traced back to *nagba* in Mande, from *lagba* in Malinke and Dyula (intimate female cover-cloth) to *lagām* in Arabic, which is a "menstrual cloth."[27]

The very composition of the word for trader, *pochteca*, provides us with an interesting clue as to its origin. *Pochteca* is a compound of *poch* and *teca*. *Teca* may be traced to the Mande word *tigi*, as I have already shown. The *poch* in *pochteca* is traceable to the *pol* in Maya *polom* (merchant). This finds its counterpart in the language of the Soninke, another people in the medieval Mandingo world. Soninke gives us *folom* (rich man, merchant).[28] Fray Toribio de Motolinia in his memoirs refers to the Mexican marketplace as *tian-quiz-co*, which may have been derived from *tan-goz-mão*, a word for trader in West Africa. Even today in Central America *tianquiz* and *tiangue* are used coloquially for "marketplace."[29]

Since many of the trader words and trading items we have been discussing have Arabic roots, it would appear that Arabic cultural influence on the medieval Mandingo was pervasive and overwhelming. This is not the case. The Islamic influence on medieval Mali hardly touched the common people. Even the kings, from Sundiata down to the king of the Atlantic expeditions, Abu-bakari the Second, gave Islam little more than lip service. There were of course exceptions. Kankan Musa, Abubakari's half brother, took a vast horde of sixty thousand Mandingo across the deserts to Mecca, the Islamic heartland, in 1324. But Mali's administrative and political structure owed nothing to the Arabs. It was not a theocracy but grew out of a federation of native families. Mandingo animist ritual and magico-religious beliefs were not Arab-Islamic, although the Mandingo later took scraps of the Koran and transformed it to suit their purposes. Their magicians chanted the fifth chapter of the Koran, the *fatiha*, as if it were another of their magical incantations. Arab-Islamic influence on medieval Mali, therefore, was very peripheral, but its impact on trade and on traders cannot be denied. Nearly all travelling traders in West Africa became Muslims. It was the pragmatic thing to do, since nearly all foreign trade was with the Arabs. Hence the many Arabic words to be found in Mandingo trading items.[30]

Another Arabic influence may be found in the coats of arms of medieval Sudan. Most notable of these is the crescent on some Sudanic medieval armor. It is generally represented by one upward sign, but frequently it has three stars connected with it, or the crescent is repeated two or three times. This is a characteristic Muslim emblem. It is also found in medieval Mexico. The crescent accompanied at the bottom by three stars or crescents is found on many Mexican shields.[31] The Norwegian historian Svien-Magnus Grodys has pointed out that when warlords moved on to conquer and settle in new lands, they carried their coats of arms with them. He maintains that some of the American glyphs were carried by Old World warriors as the heraldic emblems of their noble families.[32] It has been shown that one of the main Mandingo *n'tenne* or insignia of distinction or nobility (the triple crescent) was the same as the Mexican, except that within these crescents the Mandingo sometimes inserted pictures of animals (their totems or *naguals*).[33] Since the Mexican featherworkers designed coats of arms, and were heavily influenced, as we have seen, by the Mandingo merchants, it is only to be expected that some of these designs would be carried over. Even the word for noble or "man of distinction" is preserved in an identical Carib word "*nitaino.*"[34]

Extraordinary animal skins also entered Mexico from the south, skins of animals unknown in the Americas. In a letter to the Spanish sovereigns written in 1505, known as the "Lettera Rarissima," Columbus mentions the presence of the lion in America.[35] No such animal prowled the prairies or forests of either north or south in the age of Columbus, though there is evidence for a prehistoric American lion. It has therefore been suggested that he made a mistake, though Columbus probably became acquainted with the appearance of the lion during his visit to West Africa in 1483. In any case he could not have seen it as a living beast in free motion or in captivity in the New World, but may have been led to this remark by the sight of its skin somewhere on display. Bernal Diaz, who was taken along with Cortez by the Mexican king Montezuma to see the marketplace of Tlatelulco in the first quarter of the sixteenth century, mentions, in his detailed list of merchandise, the skins of lions.[36] It is hard to believe that a man with the meticulous care and precision of Diaz was led into the same mistake. The lion's visage, its mane, its proportions are very distinctive. Diaz could not have confused it with the tiger, its close cousin, for he also makes mention of tigers.

Lions would have been unusual even in medieval Mali, a savannah empire, known as "The Bright Country" because it had no jungle. There were lions, however, to the south of the bright lands, and rare as they were, they were captured in hunting raids. Medieval African kings and powerful men took pride in lion skins. Sumanguru the sorcerer, king of the Sosso, whose defeat by Sundiata led to the foundation of the Mali empire in 1234, lined a room of his nine-story castle with the skins of many animals, including the lion.[37] It is conceivable that since the lion was not native to the Americas in historic times and lion skins were seen in the Columbian contact period, these may have been the well-cured skins of animals Africans had hunted down in their original homelands and transported either in the Mandingo (1310–1311) or Songhay (circa 1462–1492) contact period. These skins could be preserved for generations. Lion skins of great ritual value in

Africa have been passed down the line of African chiefs and kings.

We have been concentrating in this chapter on the evidence of Mandingo traders in Mexico, but it would be wrong to suppose that the Mandingo settled only there, and that it is only in Mexico that their influence may be demonstrated.

It seems that the landfalls of the 1310 and 1311 expeditions were in the Isthmus of Darien (now Panama) and the northeastern corner of South America. A vanguard of the party certainly entered Mexico, but settlement in Mexico extended slowly over the ensuing decade.* Reports of foreign groups trickling into Mexico occur all through the first quarter of the fourteenth century, which quarter ended (1325) with the legend of a battle between an eagle and a serpent and the choice of the site of the battle as the place to build Mexico-Tenochtitlan.[38] Among these foreign migratory groups is one which is reported to have brought agriculture and pottery to a hunter-and-gatherer tribe of the Chichimecs and to have helped in the design and erection of the first "windowless" houses on Lake Texcoco around 1327.[39] Texcoco was the starting place for the inland journey to the Hot Lands. These immigrants were known as "Those Who Returned" and were credited with fine gold and silverwork and with "ancient knowledge." They may have replaced a company of blacks who settled fourteen or fifteen years earlier (1310?–1311?) in Mexico, and then abruptly left in a vain attempt to return to their native home.

The Mandingo blacks practiced settled agriculture, and they must therefore have had fixed settlements in South and Central America. But their traders, by the very nature of the occupation, were nomadic, ever on the move. Passing through unfamiliar and sometimes hostile territory, they built temporary bases for their defense. Some of these bases, built on elevated mounds, strongly resemble West African stockades. A comparison of the Peul African stockade from F. Moore's *Travels into the Inland Parts of*

---

* The "traders" from black settlements in Darien and northeastern South America came north to Mexico much later (1407–1425). These were descendants of the fourteenth-century immigrants.

Africa with Le Moyne's drawing of a Florida stockade made in
the mid-sixteenth century (reproduced in De Bry's *De Commodis
et Insularum Ritibus Virginia*) is most striking. Both are circular,
built of heavy upright posts, have an identical gate entrance, contain rows of circular huts, and within both the stockades are two
fields.[40] It is important to point out in this connection that the
Peuls were part of the complex of peoples within the medieval
Mandingo empire, and that their presence in pre-Columbian
America has been further established by Jules Cauvet's discovery
of an amazing number of animal names shared between them and
the Guarani, an American tribe.[41]

There were several bases from which the African traders spread
in the two Americas: from the Caribbean in the Songhay period
(circa 1462–1492); from the northeastern South America in the
Mandingo period (1310 onward) into Peru; and from a base in
Darien moving along roads marked by the presence of burial
mounds into and beyond Mexico, as far north as Canada.[42]

These burial mounds provide further witnesses to their presence and the lines of their dispersal. Within them, among the
usual native items, are to be found pipes with West African heads
and totems (see Chapter 11), other Negroid figurines and *gadwals*, and blue and white shells. These shells have been found in
such quantity and so selectively "stored" (akin in typology to a
coin collection) as to suggest very strongly that they were used
as money, a practice familiar to West Africans but alien to the
pre-Columbian American, for whom shells had simply a ritual and
ornamental, not a monetary value.[43]

NOTES AND REFERENCES

1 Jacques Soustelle, Patrick O'Brian (trans.), *The Daily Life of
the Aztecs*, London, Weidenfeld & Nicholson, 1961, p. 162.

2 Bernardino de Sahagun, *Histoire générale des choses de la
Nouvelle-Espagne*, Paris, 1880, Bk. 1, Chapts. 18, 19, p. 587ff.
See also Leo Weiner, *Africa and the Discovery of America*,
Vol. 3, p. 245.

3 Sahagun, op. cit., Bk. 9, p. 547ff, places the coming of the pochteca to Mexico in the reign of Quaquapitzuac. This is an obscure king, and the precise years of his reign are not given,
but we can safely assume (as does Weiner) that the event
occurred in the first quarter of the fifteenth century. Jacques
Soustelle also agrees with this date for the appearance of tropical traders in Tlatelulco (then Xatelulco). He places the coming of the pochteca in 1407, the year the king Tlacateotl begins
his reign. The evidence presented for the identification of some
of these traders from the Hot Lands with West African blacks
is of a ritual, linguistic, serological, artifactual and oral-histori-
cal nature.

4 Soustelle, op. cit., p. 27.

5 Ibid., pp. 132, 133.

6 Michael Coe, *Mexico*, New York, Praeger Publishers, 1962, pp.
165, 166.

7 Ibid., p. 133.

8 Idem. Also, see Ignacio Bernal, *Mexico Before Cortez: Art,
History and Legend*, New York, Dolphin Bks., Doubleday,
1963, pp. 75–88, 89.

9 Weiner, op. cit., Vol. 3, p. 242.

10 Sahagun, op. cit., p. 587ff. See also Weiner, Vol. 3, p. 245. Sahagun writes, "The quarters of the amanteca and pochteca
were confused and the same happened to their gods."

11 Harold Lawrence, "African Explorers in the New World," in
The Crisis, June–July, 1962. Heritage Program Reprint, p. 8.

12 Weiner, op. cit., Vol. 3, pp. 228, 229.

13 Ibid., p. 242.

14 Ibid., p. 193.

15 Ibid., p. 251 (re: rest days, Mondays and Thursdays); Ibid.,
p. 242 (re: the two female idols).

16 The American sacrifice of human blood in this ceremony was
later modified and brought in line with the African surrogate
sacrifice, which never involved humans as sacrificial victims.
Quetzalcoatl himself (that is, one of his human representations) is reported to have broken with the ancient American

traditions and introduced surrogate sacrifices in place of human sacrifice. Recent explorations in the sacred well at Chichen, where a pure maiden is supposed to have been sacrificed each year, have brought to light hundreds of small wooden figures covered with latex. Some Mexican archaeologists think that these dolls were sacrificed symbolically in place of flesh-and-blood maidens. For the latter reference to the latex dolls, see Irene Nicholson, *The X in Mexico*, New York, Doubleday, 1966, p. 24.

17 D. G. Brinton, *Nagualism*, Philadelphia, 1894, p. 56.

18 Alexander von Wuthenau, *Unexpected Faces in Ancient America*, New York, Crown Publishers, 1975, p. 27.

19 Weiner, op. cit., p. 250.

20 Ibid., pp. 258, 259.

21 Gonzalo Aguirre Beltran, "La Ethnohistoria y el Estudio del Negro en Mexico," in Sol Tax (ed.) *Acculturation in the Americas*, New York, Cooper Sq. Pubs., 1967, pp. 161–168. For this reference I am indebted to Ms. Harriet Lehmann, who translated Beltran's article for my personal use.

22 P. Schellas, "Representation of Deities of the Maya Manuscripts," *Papers of the Peabody Museum of American Archaeology and Ethnology*, Harvard University, Vol. 4, No. 1, p. 34.

23 Seler, Codex Borgia, Vol. 1, p. 322.

24 Weiner, op. cit., p. 259.

25 Ibid., p. 230.

26 Ibid., p. 231.

27 Ibid., p. 234.

28 Ibid., pp. 229, 230.

29 Weiner, op. cit., Vol. 2, p. 112.

30 Weiner, op. cit., Vol. 3, pp. 364–365. It should be pointed out in connection with the Arabic words for garments in Mandingo which appear in medieval Mexico that the Mandingo did not change their mode of dress to suit the Arabs. The Mandingo traders simply gave Arabic names to the garments they sold and wore. As Weiner puts it, "They did not adopt the Arabic habiliments [but] those that they wore bore names derived from the Arabic."

31 Weiner, Vol. 3, p. 237.
32 Cyrus Gordon, *Before Columbus*, New York, Crown Publishers, 1971, pp. 92, 93.
33 Weiner, Vol. 3, p. 238.
34 Ibid., p. 369.
35 John Boyd Thacher, *Christopher Columbus: His Life, His Work, His Remains*, New York, G. P. Putnam's Sons, 1903, Vol. 2, p. 694.
36 Albert Idell (ed. and trans.) *The Bernal Diaz Chronicles*, New York, Doubleday, 1957, p. 160.
37 D. T. Niane, *Sundiata: An Epic of Old Mali*, trans. from the Mande by G. D. Pickett, London, Longmans, 1965.
38 Soustelle, op. cit., pp. 2, 3.
39 Bernal, op. cit., p. 87.
40 Weiner, Vol. 2. See comparative plates between pages 176 and 177.
41 Cauvet, op. cit., pp. 132–133.
42 Weiner Vol. 3, p. 365.
43 Weiner, Vol. 2, pp. 249–270; Vol. 3, pp. 230, 239–245, 259. The case for certain West African functions and values of shells as a pre-Columbian influence on Americans is presented by Leo Weiner. This, however, is considerably overstated. While shells found in the burial mounds with other Mandingo artifacts indicate the use of shells as money, this use was very restricted and may have applied to a minor category of exchange. Few native Americans used cowry shells as money until post-Columbian times, when in some cases it was introduced into America through the slave trade. The value-relationship preserved between the "dark" (blue and purple) and the "white" shells and the names given to some of these indicate an imported cultural influence. Among startling identities in the appearance of shells one may mention a variety of "olive" shell found in the interior part of the Congo and in some excavations in Mexico. For reference to the latter comparison I am indebted to an unpublished monograph on shell culture by Dr. Jane Safer of the American Museum of Natural History.

7

BLACK AFRICA AND EGYPT

*What was most characteristic in the predynastic cul-
ture of Egypt is due to intercourse with the interior of
Africa and the immediate influence of that permanent Negro element which had been present in the population of
southern Egypt from the remotest times to our day.*

—RANDALL MC IVER, *Ancient Races of the Thebaid*

*Egypt was the receiver still more than the giver . . . An-
cient Egypt was essentially an African colonization.*

—BASIL DAVIDSON, *The African Past*

If you could stand on the summit of the Great Pyramid of Khufu
at Gizeh, looking south, you would feel your spirit walking down
a street that took you back to the beginnings of man's longest
civilization. As far as you could see on the southern horizon would
lie the conical tents of the gods, pitched upon the earth for more
than sixty miles, pyramid after pyramid, row after row of royal
tombs, skyscrapers of sheer stone, the blocks of which, if laid end
to end, would circle the belly of the world. You could descend
and walk unannounced into this city of the dead, for the doors
of the tombs are standing open.

When Count Volney stood under the shadow of the great Sphinx
in 1783 and looked at these man-made mountains stretching across
the western desert, he was startled and confused. He had walked
across the low flat country, dotted with villages of mud-brick huts,

where stood the tall date palms. The floor of the land was a vivid green, and through the green ran an intricate network of irrigation canals. Brown- and black-skinned men of slender build and dark hair, mostly Negroid, "having a broad and flat nose, very short, a large flattened mouth, . . . thick lips"[1] were seen along the banks of the canals, swaying up and down as they rhythmically lifted irrigation buckets attached to what looked like a well-sweep. These men were native Egyptians, with skins and features like many of the slaves of the French empire. How could things have been turned so upside down? How could history have been so violently reversed?

A strange guilt troubled Count Volney. It was so natural to think of blacks as "hewers of wood and drawers of water." When did this curse begin? "How we are astonished," he later wrote, "when we reflect that to the race of Negroes, at present our slaves, and the objects of our contempt, we owe our arts, sciences . . ."[2]

Fifteen years later an expedition under Napoleon marched into Egypt. The scientists of that expedition were equally astonished and impressed. From what they saw they concluded, as the Greeks had done a thousand years before, that Egyptian civilization owed its inspiration to a black race.[3]

This rediscovery by Europeans of ancient Egypt, and the disclosures of a powerful Negro-African element in the ancestry of a civilization to which Europe owed so much, came as an embarrassment. It came also at a most inopportune time. It threatened to explode a myth of innate black inferiority that was necessary to the peace of the Christian conscience in a Europe that was then prospering from the massive exploitation of black slaves. Africa was being systematically depopulated. Its empires had disintegrated. Its history had been buried. Its movement in step with other world civilizations had been abruptly halted. Only its most backward and inaccessible elements were left virtually untouched to bear false witness in later times to the scale and complexity of its evolution.

The Christian conscience of slave-trading Europe had been assuaged for a while by a myth which drew its inspiration not from the Christian Bible, as some theologians of the day then thought

(for the Bible makes no distinctions between black and white),
but from a very arbitrary interpretation of a biblical story, the
story of Ham, which appeared in the Talmud, a collection of
Jewish oral traditions, in the sixth century A.D. Starting out as an
innocuous little anecdote (Noah curses a son of Ham, making
him and his progeny "a servant of servants" for looking at him
in his nakedness), it grew to become a most pernicious racial
myth. It has affected nearly all histories of Africa and Africans
for the past two hundred years.

The curse of the son of Ham, it was said, was the curse of blackness. The descendants of the son of Ham, according to this interpretation of the story, were the Africans and the Egyptians (who,
at the time the myth began to circulate, had fallen from their pin-
nacle of power). When, however, the Napoleonic expedition uncovered the splendors of ancient Egyptian civilization, a new
version of history was urgently required. The myth of blackness
as a curse had backfired. How could a black and accursed race
have inspired or contributed greatly to the development of a
pre-European civilization?

An ingenious new version was not long in the making. Political
necessity, then as now, is the mother of historical invention. Christian theologians began to suggest that Noah had only cursed
Canaan, one son of Ham, and that therefore the curse lay only on
his progeny, the black race. Another son of Ham, Mizraim, had not
been cursed. From him issued the marvelous Egyptians, the cre-
ators of the greatest of early civilizations.[4] The Christian conscience could sleep peacefully again. Canaan's sons, after all—the
black branch—were only getting what was their terrible destiny
and due. The sons of Mizraim were the Caucasoid curse-free
branch of the Hamites, according to this new version. With the
creation of these two legendary branches—a servile and accursed
Negroid branch and a gifted and blessed Caucasoid branch—the
problem of the Hamitic curse was neatly solved. From then on,
historians and anthropologists would talk of Hamitic culture-
bringers in Africa, meaning whites, fairy grandfathers touching
Kemi (the original word for Egypt, literally "the black lands")
with the magical wand of civilization.

Behind the van of the clergy, to assist and consolidate this version, rose up a scientific establishment that tried to prove that Negro-Africans had nothing whatever to do with the evolution and development of Egyptian civilization. Skeletal material from Egypt was selectively gathered and selectively measured and classified. The American anatomist Samuel Morton—the Shockley of the nineteenth century—using pseudoscientific criteria, flattered and delighted his Negrophobic listeners by demonstrating to their satisfaction that the Egyptians were a Caucasoid race and indigenous to the Nile valley.[5] This finding flatly contradicted the claim of the historian Herodotus that the Egyptians, compared to the Greeks and other European Caucasoids, were for the most part "a black-skinned and wooly-haired" people.[6]

The findings of Morton have been shown to be false. Extensive skeletal surveys of the ancient Egyptians, both before and during the dynasties, show them to be of roughly the same racial composition as the blacks of a modern Caribbean island, with a predominantly Negroid base and traces of Asiatic and Caucasoid admixtures. As Basil Davidson has pointed out in *Africa in History,* "it now seems perfectly clear that the vast majority of predynastic Egyptians were of continental African stock, and even of central-west Saharan origins."[7] These people later mixed with Asians and Caucasians migrating into the north of Egypt. The Nile was the meeting place of races, but the Negro-African element both before and during several of the dynasties was a dominant racial element.

An Oxford professor of anatomy, David Thomson, and an Egyptologist of the same university, Randall McIver, carried out the most extensive surveys of ancient Egyptian skeletal material ever made. They reported in 1905 that from the early predynastic period to the Fifth Dynasty, 24 percent of the males and 19.5 percent of the females were pure Negro. Between the Sixth to the Eighteenth Dynasty, about 20 percent of the males and 15 percent of the females were pure Negro. An even larger percentage were "intermediates" with Negroid physical characteristics.[8]

But the density of the Negro-African racial presence in predynastic and dynastic Egypt is an empty statistic in itself. What should most concern us is the contribution of black Africans to the birth of Egyptian civilization, their participation in the growth and development of that civilization, and the eventual emergence toward the close of the dynasties of a black power—the Nubians —from a land south of the Negroid and mulatto Egyptians, as the source of both spiritual and political authority in the Egyptian world during the significant 800–700 B.C. new world-old world contact period.

Black Africa's influence upon the genesis of Egyptian civilization was profound. What came up to Egypt from south and west of the Nile was seminal. In the early formative centuries the Sahara did not divide the African continent. "Far from being a natural barrier between the peoples of West Africa and North Africa," Basil Davidson has pointed out, "the old Sahara joined these peoples together. All could share in the same ideas and discoveries. Many travellers journeyed through the green Sahara in New Stone Age times. They used horses and carts that have been found along two main trails between North and West Africa . . . new ideas were being taken back and forth by these old travellers . . . we shall make little sense of African history unless we have this picture constantly in mind, this picture of the great regions learning from each other, teaching each other, trading with each other through the centuries."[9]

But in this cultural give-and-take, what did the black African outside of Egypt really give that was so crucial to the foundations of Egyptian civilization?

Recent archaeological studies in the Sahara and the Sudan have shown that much of the art one finds in the tombs of the Pharaohs, many of the bird and animal deities the ancient Egyptians worshiped, the custom and technique of mummification itself, originated among Negro-Africans south and west of the Nile.

It has always been assumed that mummification originated in Egypt. There is evidence to show that it was practiced there as early as the Second Dynasty (circa 3000 B.C.), since J. E. Quibell found at Saqqara several tombs of this date in which the bodies had been elaborately bandaged, the limbs being wrapped separately.[10] From the beginning of the Fourth Dynasty (2900–2750

B.C.) there is the canopic box of Hetepheres (mother of Cheops, the builder of the great pyramid at Gizeh), which still contains packets of what presumably were the viscera preserved in a dilute of nacron, a chemical used in embalming, which is proof that the body had been embalmed, though the mummy was not in the tomb.[11] There is an Egyptian mummy on display in the Museum of the Royal College of Surgeons in London that dates back to the Fifth Dynasty (2750–2475 B.C.).[12]

But going back to centuries earlier than the earliest of these Egyptian mummies is a recent find in the rocky hills of the Fezzan—the body of a Negroid child, mummified, flexed and buried beneath the dirt floor of the family shelter. "The body was carefully preserved (in this case by drying) before burial. The discoverer, Italian archaeologist, F. Mori, claims a date of 3,500 B.C. for his find, and the carbon-14 dates back him up. The spectacular thing about that date is that it makes the Fezzan mummy older than the oldest known Egyptian mummies. There is one thing more. On the wall of the rock shelter in which the child was buried someone had painted a mummy figure bound in many cloths and tied with bands. This is the way the dead were represented in Egypt in later times. And yet Dr. Mori believes the painting may date even further back than the child's burial. Another blow to the Egyptian image, to her reputation as premier undertaker."[13]

The implications of this go beyond mere burial practices. Mummification in dynastic Egypt was part of a complex body of ritual and belief. The concept of the king as divine, as a God in person among men, lay at the root of royal mummification. The particular form of this divine kingship found in Egypt came not from Asia, as was formerly supposed, but from the heart of Africa. "Egyptian ideas of kingship," Bohannon and Curtin have pointed out, "developed in Egypt itself and were developed on an African cultural base. The ideas about the nature of the dead were expressed in the Pyramids (which ideas developed with amazing rapidity once they started) and the forms of the state that emerged are significantly different from similar ideas and practices found in Asia Minor. Divine kingship seems to have been an African invention, for the African form differs radically from the other. Millenia later, it could be found in Uganda, in the Benue Valley, along the Guinea coast and down into Rhodesia."[14]

Prototypes of some of the bird and animal deities of the Egyptians have been traced back to the desert rock art of Negro-Africans in the Tassili mountains. Even the ceremonial costumes of the Pharaohs blossomed out of sartorial styles displayed by some figures on these rocks. Anthropologist Henri Lhote has brought this Saharan art to the world's attention—the beautifully drawn herds and herders, bird-headed goddesses, the hunters dressed in animal heads and tails. "People of Negroid type," claims Lhote, "were painting men and women with a beautiful and sensitive realism before 3000 B.C. and were among the originators of naturalistic human portraiture."[15]

Pottery is now known to have been made by black Africans as early as 7000 B.C. in a fishing-hunting community near Khartoum. The people of this community "fired" pottery and combed it with a catfish spine to give it a basket effect. The oldest ivory figurines found in ancient Egypt were sculpted by the Badari, a Negroid race of the Egyptians.[16] Another form of art found among the Egyptians, which came up from the Sudan and points to a domestication of cattle as early as 4500 B.C. by black Africans, are the rock paintings of cattle with intricately twisted horns. The fanciful shapes of these horns reappear in the temple and tomb paintings of dynastic Egypt.[17]

Discoveries of this nature are of the greatest significance. They give the lie to the Hamitic hypothesis which made claims, still believed by many historians of Africa, that pastoral science (the skills of cattle-rearing) came into Africa through Caucasoid Hamites. Thus C. G. Seligman, the most bigoted and influential British exponent of this racial theory, stated in a book, originally published in 1930 and reprinted without change as late as 1966, that "the incoming Hamites were *pastoral Europeans*—arriving wave after wave—quicker witted than the *dark agricultural Negroes*"[18] (italics added).

The earliest agricultural settlement in the Negro Sudan (that of the Fayum) shows that pastoral and agricultural science existed side by side. British archaeologist A. J. Arkell excavated two sites along the Nile, one near Khartoum, south of Egypt, where the Nile splits, and one in the Fayum area. In the Fayum there was clear evidence that people were growing grain and minding cattle as early as 4500 B.C., while in the Khartoum the blacks were cultivating crops and making pottery.[19] Arkell found something even more interesting, something that connected these two sites to an African source west of the Nile, deep in the Sahara. In both sites were considerable quantities of Amazon stone beads (microline felspar) from the Eghei Mountains, north of Tibetsi (in the Sahara). In the Khartoum site was found dotted wavy-line pottery identical with pottery in the Tibetsi area.[20] What this indicates is that Tibetsi was a dispersal area of cultural influences moving up the Nile from the Sahara, and that when that desert, once a fertile plain, ended its wet phase and began to dry up, black Africans started moving north and east, "following the shrinking tributaries of the Nile until they reached the floodplain,"[21] thereby colonizing Egypt.

Every new archaeological find seems to be pushing the agricultural breakthrough in Africa further and further back in time, and the influence of this breakthrough on the ancient Egyptians should not be underestimated, since the great and early civilizations were built only after mankind had reached the settled agricultural stage. It has always been assumed that Africans were late in the day in this respect, and since the Asian agricultural complex was among the earliest, the agricultural science of Egypt was thought to be largely Asian in origin.

The American anthropologist George Peter Murdock has reclassified the great agricultural complexes in the ancient world— the South West Asian complex (Caucasoid), the South East Asian complex (Mongoloid), the Middle American complex (American Indian) and the Sudanic complex (West African). The Sudanic complex was completely ignored until recently. Russian botanist Vavilov, who listed all plants in the three non-African complexes, never visited Black Africa. Hence, he and others made serious misclassifications, especially with regard to indigenous African crops that had traveled to India and were thought to have origi-

nated in Asia. Murdock, by use of geographical and linguistic distribution of plants and plant names, as well as recent agricultural
finds, has been able to prepare a classification of plants belonging
to the Sudanic complex. He has shown that the Mande people of
West Africa created a center of plant domestication around the
headwaters of the river Niger circa 4500 B.C. He has also shown
that while Egypt gave nothing in the way of plants to Black
Africa, black Africans contributed the bottle gourd, the watermelon, the tamarind fruit and cultivated cotton (*gossypium herbaceum*) to Egypt.[22]

Murdock's claim that crops moved north and east across the
African continent from this center of plant domestication in the
Western Sudan, is borne out by a study of Nubian agriculture.
Nubia, the black state on the southern boundaries of Egypt, in
spite of its long passage under the dynastic Egyptians, has little
in the way of crops that it owes to Egypt. Its basic crops were
"Sudanic" in origin. It seems, whatever the reason, that whereas
West African crops traveled up the Nile and took root in Egypt
and its colonial outposts, Egyptian crops are not to be seen in
sites west and south of the Nile. In one of the fireholes of the
4500 B.C. settlement near Khartoum, excavated by Arkell, the
charred fragment of an oil-palm fruit,[23] an indigenous West African plant, was found located far north and east of its original
home (the agricultural complex of the "nuclear Mande") moving
in an Egyptian direction. No comparable find, indicating the
southward or westward movement of an indigenous Egyptian
plant, exists.

C. Wrigley is critical of specific points in the Murdock thesis
but concludes nonetheless that plant domestication must have
occurred very early in Africa. He argues that the existence of
"wide networks of languages which are only remotely related,"
fine pottery dating back to 5000 B.C. in East Africa and livestock
in the eastern Sudan in 4000 B.C. attest to an equally early emergence of food producers in sub-Saharan Africa.[24] Roland Porteres
presents, as evidence of ancient African agriculture, the fact that
India as early as 1300 B.C. had imported a number of indigenous
African crops.[25] Botanist Edgar Anderson, operating by wholly

different methods and using different evidence, arrives at roughly the same conclusion as Murdock. He agrees that there was a separate African origin of agriculture around the headwaters of the Niger.[26]

The investigations of Delcroix and Vaufrey provide archaeological support for this hypothesis of an early independent center of agricultural domestication in West Africa. Among the numerous archaeological materials that they have studied from west and central Africa, they identify the Toumbien of Guinea and the Para-Toumbien of the neighboring Sudan as the remains of early, simple agriculturalists.[27] Karl Schwerin suggests that the Toumbien culture began somewhere close to 5000 B.C.[28] Radio-carbon dates for these sites have not yet been obtained, but Professor Davies has provided radio-carbon dates for later sites in the Niger area which, while not as early as the Arkell dates in the Sudan, show that the general consensus among these botanists, archaeologists and anthropologists has a basis in fact. For the Tenere Neolithic (a later agricultural phase in the Niger) he gives a date of 5140 plus or minus 170 years.[29]

As I have indicated before, the drying up of the Sahara pushed black Africans northward up from the central Sahara and the Sudan toward the Nile floodplain. This they occupied in fairly dense concentrations in the predynastic period. It is this northern migration of the black African into the basin of the Nile that made the land of Chem (Egypt) "essentially an African colonization."[30]

Thus the blacks in the predynastic period, hugging the banks of the Nile, were responsible for major agricultural innovations along that ancient river. The blacks dominated a land from the twenty-ninth parallel north to the tenth parallel south (see Plate 19) by circa 3400 B.C. This land was the old Ethiopian Empire. In the north, from above the twenty-ninth parallel to the Mediterranean, there was a slice of land, one fourth of Lower Egypt, into which Asians and a sprinkle of Caucasians trickled. These foreigners waged wars with black Africans until the Africans won a decisive victory over them circa 3400 B.C. under the African king Menes. It is from this point that real Egyptian history begins, because it was then that the African king joined the two lands,

Uazit with Nekhebit (Nekheb was the old black capital). It is at this point too that the winged disc motif developed as a political symbol signifying the unification of the two lands.[31] Menes laid the foundations of a city which was to become the capital of the Egyptian kings for three thousand years—Memphis—named after him.*

"During one of the longest reigns in history Menes brought about the kind of stability that not only provided a solid foundation for a first dynasty but also the economic and social conditions necessary for a far more uniform expansion of religion, the arts and crafts and the mathematical sciences. Here too is where Mesopotamia, Palestine and Greece, although not as advanced, may have made cultural contributions to the Africans and received much from them in return."[32]

The unification of the lands led to the mixing of Asians and Africans in the north. The African script, language, the character of the royal dynasties, became a composite of African and Asian elements. In other words, Lower Egypt (the north) became physically and culturally a "mulatto" Egypt. Asians married African princesses, and the integration of the two peoples proceeded apace. Hence, the emergence of Pharaohs with both Negroid and Asian physical characteristics. Some of the royal portraits and sculptures are highly stylized, with the headgear, the false beards, etc., often obscuring the racial detail. It is often necessary to look at other royal representations of the same period to fully appreciate this. But conventional histories have ignored the African beginnings, the African political and administrative structure, the unique African form of the divine-king concept, the African agricultural contribution on the Nile, the African science of mathematics and mummification—all the elements that laid the basis for the first four dynasties. They make no mention of the fact that the Sphinx was a portrait statue of the black Pharaoh Khafre (also called Cephren) nor that the greatest of all the pyramids was built during the reign of the African Knufu (Second Dynasty, 2590–67

---

* Menes built what was known then as "The White Wall," later known as Memphis.

B.C.) nor that the religious cults of Seth and Amon were African.[33]

They by-pass all the Negro-African figures in the dynasties or disguise them with blanket classifications, laying emphasis only on the Asian elements, the men who came in from the north as "tent-dwelling nomads." They credit all the genius of the dynastic period to these infiltrators, inheritors of an African cultural, scientific, and even physical legacy. When the blacks are mentioned at all, they are confined to the Twenty-Fifth Dynasty, which is called "The Ethiopian Dynasty." Even that, as we shall show in our next chapter, has been in dispute until recently, and when it was not contained within a footnote it was classified in such a way as to render it insignificant and unworthy of serious consideration. Labels like "period of decline" are clapped onto these periods. Inscriptions are defaced, Negro-African heads are lopped off, noses are chiseled down, photographs are taken from misleading angles or through misleading filters, nomenclatures meant to confuse are pasted over the archaeological and documentary evidence. One comes upon the scene of history as though a witness to a massive cultural genocide, the perpetrators of which have nevertheless left telltale clues in the graveyard, where a subterranean current, an electric truth, galvanizes still the surviving skeletons and sculptures.

A largely mixed North (Afro-Asian mulattoes) and a largely black South (Negro-African) sums up the racial picture of Egypt, from about 3000 B.C. down to the period just before the birth of Christ. In all her periods of upheaval, when the North was threatened by chaos or the invasion of foreigners, Egypt was rescued and reunited by powerful men from the black South. When it fell into anarchy during the latter years of Pepi II, and was divided into feudal baronies during what is known as the First Intermediate Period (2200–2050 B.C.), a Nubian Southerner, Mentuhotep I, reunited Egypt.[34] When in 1770 B.C. the North was invaded and conquered by the Hyksos, an Asiatic people, the black South remained strong and took into its arms the fleeing mulattoes from the north, transfusing a new stream of Negro-African blood into the mixed pool of the northern Egyptians.[35] When in the Twenty-Fifth dynasty (800–654 B.C.) the Assyrians, the power of Western

Asia, had made vassals of the Northern Egyptian kings, it was the black kings of the South who reunified Egypt under their rule once again and held the Assyrians at bay for nearly a century, ushering in a renaissance, not a decline, of the Egyptian culture and spirit.

It is important to understand that modern Egypt and modern Egyptians are not the direct successors of these ancient peoples. With the fall of Egyptian civilization in the last phase of the pre-Christian era and the massive Arab movement into the North, the sack of Alexandria and the founding of Cairo, Northern Egypt and indeed all Northern Africa changed in its physical and cultural appearance. It is to the last great phase of Egyptian history before this radical change begins that we shall now turn our attention.

NOTES AND REFERENCES

1 For the description of this physical type seen in Egypt in the Napoleonic era, see Baron V. Denon, *Travels in Upper and Lower Egypt*, 1803. For this reference see Herbert J. Foster, "The Ethnicity of the Ancient Egyptians," *Journal of Black Studies*, 5, 2, 1974, p. 177.

2 E. Sanders, "The Hamitic Hypothesis," *Journal of African History*, 10, 4, 1969, p. 525.

3 Foster, loc. cit.

4 Sanders, op. cit., pp. 526–527.

5 Foster, op. cit., p. 190.

6 G. Rawlinson (ed.), *The History of Herodotus*, London, Murray, 1875.

7 Basil Davidson, *Africa in History*, New York, Macmillan, 1969, pp. 21–22.

8 Randall McIver and Arthur Thomson, *Ancient Races of the Thebaid*, London, 1905. For this reference see Foster, op. cit., p. 183.

9 Basil Davidson, *History of West Africa*, New York, Doubleday, 1966, p. 7.

10 J. E. Quibell, *Excavations at Saqqara (1912–1914)*, London, 1914, pp. 11, 19, 28, 32.

11 G. A. Reisner, *Bulletin of the Museum of Fine Arts*, 26, No. 157, Boston, 1928.

12 W. R. Dawson, *Egyptian Mummies*, London, 1921, pp. 74–75. See also A. Lucas, *Ancient Egyptian Materials and Industries*, London, Edward Arnold & Co., 1926.

13 Olivia Vlahos, *African Beginnings*, New York, Viking Press, 1967, p. 44.

14 Paul Bohannon and Philip Curtin, *Africa and Africans* (revised edition), New York, Natural History Press, 1971, p. 87.

15 Basil Davidson, *The Lost Cities of Africa*, New York, Little Brown, 1959, p. 58.

16 Vlahos, op. cit., pp. 41, 42.

17 See the reproduction of "cattle with twisted horns" in a Tassili rock-painting compared with that in an Egyptian temple carving, Vlahos, op. cit., pp. 44–45.

18 C. G. Seligman, *Races of Africa*, New York, Oxford University Press, 1930, p. 96.

19 A. J. Arkell, *A History of the Sudan: From the Earliest Times to 1821*, London, The Athlone Press, 1955, pp. 29–34.

20 Idem.

21 Foster, op. cit., p. 186.

22 G. P. Murdock, *Africa: Its Peoples and Their Culture History*, New York, McGraw Hill, 1959, pp. 64–70.

23 For this reference see Vlahos, p. 57.

24 For the Wrigley reference, see Karl Schwerin, "Winds Across the Atlantic: Possible African Origins for Some Pre-Columbian New World Cultigens," *Mesoamerican Studies*, No. 6, University Museum, Southern Illinois University, 1970, pp. 2, 15.

25 Roland Porteres, *Journal of African History*, 3, 1962, pp. 195–210.

26 Edgar Anderson, "The Evolution of Domestication," in Sol Tax (ed.) *Evolution after Darwin*, Chicago, 1960, Vol. 2, pp. 67–84.

27 R. Delcroix and R. Vaufrey, *L'Anthropologie*, 49, 1940, pp. 265–312.

28 Schwerin, op. cit., p. 15.

29 O. Davies, *West Africa Before the Europeans: Archaeology*

and Prehistory, London, 1967, p. 225. For this reference, see Schwerin, op. cit.

30 Basil Davidson, *The African Past*, New York, Grosset and Dunlap, 1967, p. 43.

31 Donald McKenzie, *Myths of Pre-Columbian America*, London, Gresham Publishing Co., 1924, p. 62. Also see Chapter 5 of this volume.

32 Chancellor Williams, *The Destruction of Black Civilization*, Chicago, Third World Press, 1974, p. 67.

33 Ibid., p. 73.

34 James Henry Breasted, *A History of Egypt*, New York, Charles Scribner's & Sons, 1916, p. 151.

35 John Hope Franklin, *From Slavery to Freedom*, New York, Random House, Vintage Bks., 1969, pp. 7–8.

8

THE BLACK KINGS OF THE TWENTY-FIFTH DYNASTY

As one gathers eggs that have been abandoned in fright
have I gathered the whole earth . . .

—SENNACHERIB, THE ASSYRIAN KING

And then he [Sennacherib] heard say of Tirhakah, king
of Ethiopia, Behold, he is come out to fight against thee . . .

—BOOK II, KINGS, CHAPTER 19, VERSE 9

At the far end of the Dongola Reach, as the Nile bends and swings upward, streaming north toward the Fourth Cataract, it flows through the province of Napata where, in the town of Kurru and of Nuri, lie the ancient graves of kings.

These are the graves of the forgotten kings of Kush, the Black Valhalla through whose ghostly fields may still be heard the distant din of wars, the clash of Nubian and Libyan, of Nubian and Assyrian, over the ailing body of Egypt. Here lay, in their trappings of silver and bronze, the mummified horses of Pi-an-khy, Shabaka, Shabataka and Ta-har-ka (or Tir-ha-kah). Here lay the black princes of the Twenty-Fifth Dynasty who, from circa 751 to 654 B.C., threw their shadow across the length and breadth of the Egyptian empire, from the shores of the Mediterranean to the borders of modern Ethiopia, almost a quarter of the African continent. They were among the last of the great sun kings of the ancient world.

These kings formed the last bastion of Egyptian civilization against the advance of the alien. Black Nubian troops of Kush not only brought Osorkon III, a Libyan king of Upper Egypt, to his knees but crushed the rebellion of the petty kings of Egypt under Tafnak, and seizing power over both Lower and Upper Egypt, rescued it from vassalage to the Assyrians, holding that great power at bay for nearly a century until they were eventually outclassed by the heavier concentration of iron weaponry in the Assyrian forces.

For one brief century they restored Egypt to her former glory, renovated her temples, gave new life and moral authority to the sun god, Amon-Ra,* who had become in that time the chief god among both Nubians and Egyptians.

In the town of Kurru and of Nuri lie the graves of these ancient kings. At the foot of the Pure Mountain, Jebel Barkal, in the Temple of Amon, lay many of their weapons and jewels, statues and stelae. Their graves, though plundered; their mummies, though stolen; their stelae, though partially defaced, give proof nonetheless of their true ancestry and origin. Why then are they not represented as black or, even when so conceded, relegated to a footnote in the conventional histories of the ancient world?

We have seen the attempts to deny black Africa's contribution to the rise of civilization in ancient Egypt. It was difficult for Europeans, during the era of the African's enslavement, when the myth of his fundamental inferiority made his subjugation easier to carry on the Christian conscience, to admit that he once stood on the upper branches in the tree of world civilization. But the seeds black Africa planted, which cross-pollinated with those of the mixed Mediterranean races meeting on the Nile, flowered into that tree under whose branches, and feeding on whose fruit, Greece, Rome and Britain later grew.

As in the beginning, so in the last great phase of the Egyptian world, the black African gained ascendancy. To see him in this light, as a power in the dawn and in the sunset of ancient Egypt, was anathema to the ruling prejudices of imperial scholars. Thus Reisner and Brugsch-Bey, Drioton, Vandier and Moret (to men-

---

* The cult of Amon was a cult of black African origin. It later fused with the worship of Ra, a bird-headed Egyptian sun god. (See Chancellor Williams, *The Destruction of Black Civilization*, pp. 73, 74.)

tion just a few) and even more recently Arkell and Shinnie, seek to by-pass the blackness of these kings.

Dr. Brugsch-Bey, in his book *Egypt Under the Pharaohs*, published nearly a hundred years ago, advanced the theory that the kings of the Black Lands of Nubia and Kush, who rose to power in the eighth and seventh century B.C., were not really black at all, but came from outside to give leadership and guidance to "these imperfectly developed people."[1] He claimed—and later Drioton and Vandier supported the claim—that the royal family of Kush were descended from a certain high priest of Thebes, Hirhor.[2] This Hirhor (also spelled Herihor) had been the founder of the Twenty-First Dynasty. He had seized the Egyptian throne in 945 B.C. and made himself the First Prophet of Amon, but his successors, after 150 years of rule, were eventually overthrown and forced to flee Egypt sometime around 800 B.C.

It was around this time that a great national passion was stirring in Nubia. Nubia, in which was based the kingdom of Kush which was later to expand and embrace the whole Egyptian world, had already begun to feel her native strength, to assert her national independence. Egyptianized though she was in many respects from long colonization, she had gained self-government during the troubled period through which Egypt was passing.[3] Yet these scholars would have us believe that at the crest of this spirit of self-pride and national ambition, the black Nubians— credited at that time with having the finest militia in Africa— without a murmur of protest, with not the slightest show of resistance, allowed the fleeing priests of the house of Hirhor, men who had lost all power and prestige, impotent, defeated refugees, to establish a new domination over them. Brugsch-Bey reveals the racial attitude behind this absurd suggestion when he speaks of Nubia and Ethiopia as places "where the minds of an imperfectly developed people must needs show themselves pliable and submissive to a dominant priest caste."[4]

The only thread of evidence for the theory presented by these historians was the fact that Piankhy, the first important king of the Twenty-Fifth dynasty, had adopted a name which was the same as that used by a son and successor of Hirhor. Piankhy is

Egyptian for "the living one," and considering the number of Egyptian customs, names and religious rituals surviving among their ex-colonials, it was flimsy evidence indeed. Excavations in 1919 by G. A. Reisner, which led to the discovery of the graves of the kings, put an end to this hypothesis.[5] The evidence of the graves made it clear that the kings of Kush could not have been native Egyptians.

But Reisner then advanced a new and equally misleading theory. After a cursory examination of stone arrowheads which he found in several of the graves at Kurru, he decided that some with recessed bases were of Libyan type. With this preconceived notion of a Libyan link he was led into the misreading of a word on the stele of Queen Tabiry (one of Piankhy's queens) as *Te-.mehu*. This word means "Southern Libyans," and he therefore thought she was "great chieftainess of the Temehu." On this slender evidence he concluded that "while the Northern Libyans were entering the Delta or soon after, the southern Libyans, the Temehuw, pushed into the Nile valley."[6] Reisner then began to invent a Libyan chief who settled at Kurru and whose family, according to him, "obtained the domination of Ethiopia." A. J. Arkell in *A History of the Sudan* dismisses this in one sentence, which was all it really needed: the evidence for this, he declares, is "nonexistent."[7] The theory however, gained ground for many years, and in several histories of Egypt, such as Alexandre Moret's *The Nile and Egyptian Civilization*, the kings of Kush are represented as Libyans, although placed in the confusing category "Ethiopian Dynasty."[8]

I say confusing, for the word Ethiopian was used in a very general way in ancient times. Ethiops, literally "burnt face," was a broad catchall word for dark peoples. That was why Peter Martyr referred to the mysterious blacks Balboa came upon in the Isthmus of Darien as Ethiopians. It is also confusing if we think of Ethiopian as an exclusive referent to the people of modern Abyssinia. The Ethiopian Dynasty, a label given by the Egyptian historian Manetho to the "black power" period of Egypt, is really the dynasty founded by the kings of Kush, with its base at Napata in Nubia.

The old notion that the ancestors of the Kushite royal family
were Libyans has been abandoned. Most modern authorities now
agree that they were of native Nubian origin. The way they were
buried is one of several clues to their native roots. The burial practices are not only non-Egyptian but also very different from anything found among the Libyans. In spite of the Egyptian cultural
influence (and the graves of the kings give clear evidence of this)
the manner of the royal burial is distinctive. The black kings are
buried on beds rather than in coffins. "A coffin bench is constructed
with niches cut out near its corners for the legs of the funerary
bed, the frame of which rested on the bench. In one of the queen's
tombs two bronze bed-legs were found still in place." This type
of burial was practiced by the Nubians a thousand years earlier.
"While the furnishing and iconography of the royal tombs in most
respects follow the standard Egyptian practice of the period . . .
they [the Kings of Kush] were reluctant to abandon their ancestral form of burial."[9]

What is even more interesting is that we find close by the royal
burials the graves of people who worked under the black kings—
priests, artists, craftsmen, scribes, some of whom were Egyptian
—buried in the Egyptian fashion, bodies in coffins without beds.
These graves of typically Egyptian style belonged to people of
lower status than the kings. The pits where these bodies lie are
much narrower and very poorly furnished.[10] Another difference
between Egyptian burial and that of the black kings of Kush
should be noted. The mound form of superstructure which occurs
in the royal graves at Kurru had been characteristic of Lower
Nubia since 2000 B.C.[11]

This evidence has convinced Professors Arkell and Shinnie, as
indeed it would convince anyone who has had to examine it, that
the chieftains of Kush were native. But having come step by step
through each archaeological advance to an admission that natives,
not foreigners, provided the power behind the kingdom of Kush,
we find that the question dramatically shifts from what is the
racial origin of the kings of Kush to what is the racial origin of the
natives of Kush. "This," says Arkell, contradicting his earlier
clarity and certainty on other related matters, is "wrapped in

obscurity."[12] His pupil and protégé, P. L. Shinnie, is equally cautious. "The results should be treated with reserve," he declares, when faced with the findings of excavators at Karanog that clearly indicated that the overwhelming majority of skeletons in the Nubian area during this period were Negroid.[13] We are witnessing again the same Negrophobia that afflicted so many European scholars during the heyday of the Hamitic hypothesis. That myth has now been bludgeoned to death, but its mutilated ghost still lingers, particularly within the unconscious racial reflex of British scholars.

When the Nubians were paying tribute and bearing gifts to the Pharaohs, there was no doubt whatever as to their racial identity. Their blackness was not "wrapped in obscurity." There is a representation of Negro-Nubian princes in an Egyptian wall painting in the tomb of Huy at Thebes.[14] This painting has been well circulated. It appears in countless histories of Egypt and owes its popularity to the fact that it flatters the generally accepted notion of the black as colonial or vassal. Little or no use is made of equally "instructive" paintings of ancient Egypt in which the Caucasoid or Asiatic figure is depicted as bound captive and slave. The Nubian princes are seen in the painting sitting in ox-drawn chariots, shaded by parasols. Both they and their attendants are predominantly Negroid. Why then should skeletal surveys, which show the natives of this area to be predominantly Negroid, be "treated with reserve"? Has the Nubian become "faintly negroid" (to use Shinnie's shamefaced phrase)[15] as he leaves the role of vassal behind him and aggressively assumes the double crown of Egypt?

Both Arkell and Shinnie seek to deny the Negro-ness of the Nubian king Taharka. Arkell says that "it is most improbable that Taharka was a negro though he may have had some negroid blood in his veins."[16] Fortunately, we do not have to depend on these gentlemen for proof on the point. We can go to the records of Taharka's enemies themselves, the Assyrians, his contemporaries, who on several occasions both in times of troubled peace and on the brutal field of war met him and his predecessors face to face. They left a vivid portrait of Taharka, who haunted their sleep as they had haunted the sleep of the Egyptians for generations. They met his predecessor, Shabaka, brother of Piankhy, when their ambassadors came to hold peace talks between him and the Assyrian king, Sennacherib. Impressions of Shabaka's clay seal have been found side by side with that of Sennacherib in the royal archives of Kuyunjik at Nineveh. They saw Taharka for the first time when, circa 701 B.C., he appeared as a young man on the battlefield near Jerusalem, coming to the aid of Hezekiah of Judah. Taharka's appearance on the field of battle is mentioned in the Hebrew chronicles of that period.[18]

He was not yet king, but he had been sent out to head the Nubian contingent of the allied Nubian-Egyptian army in preference to his elder but weaker brothers. The Assyrians clashed with him again in the Delta in 673 B.C. when he repulsed the forces of their king Esharhaddon,[19] and at Memphis in 671 B.C. when Esharhaddon drove him south.[20] They faced him finally in 666 B.C. when he regrouped his forces, reoccupied Upper Egypt and forced Esharhaddon's son, Ashur-bani-pal, to march on him once more. Taharka was routed and retreated further south but maintained control of Upper Egypt and Nubia until 663 B.C. when, in the last year of his life, he began to share his throne with a nephew, Tanutamon.[21]

Kings like Taharka would appear in the van of their forces, riding on a swift chariot. He made a spectacular sight. His horses were brilliantly caparisoned. The Nubian kings of Kush made a fetish out of horses: they were buried alongside the royal families even as the earlier Egyptian Pharaohs had buried their favorite *basenji* dogs.[22] To see the black king Taharka galloping across the battlefields of Jerusalem, at Tanis in the Delta, and in the sacred city of Thebes, was never to forget him. The people of Judah saw him and took heart when Hezekiah was wavering in his mind as to whether he should submit to the Assyrian Sennacherib or lean on Egypt for support. The Assyrians have immortalized him. Esharhaddon had a portrait of him carved upon a stele at Sinjirli,[23] which clearly represents him as Negroid. Arkell says that they depicted him thus to show their "oriental contempt,"[24] forgetting that this would have been an anachronistic pathology in that period. J. H. Breasted, in his *History of Egypt*, points out: "He was the son of a Nubian woman and his features, as preserved in contemporary sculptures, show unmistakable negroid characteristics."[25]

An outline of events in the eastern Mediterranean during the reign of these black kings is of great significance in the matter we are examining. It may help to illuminate the state of the time and reveal to us the nature of the pressures as well as capacities within the Nubian-Egyptian world which led to the embarkation of a ship or ships down the Mediterranean toward North Africa circa 800–671 B.C.—a ship or ships carrying Nubian troops in command, one or two Phoenician navigators or merchantmen, and a crew of craftsmen and peasants of both Negroid and mixed Egyptian ancestry, including a few women. The motives for this journey, which never got to the place intended but left indisputable traces at its point of destination, will become obvious as a historical outline of the period unfolds.

Nubia had been moving toward her independence since the tenth century B.C., but it was not until sometime between 800 and 750 B.C. when, taking advantage of the schisms within Egypt, a royal house founded at Napata threw up a king who felt strong enough to extend his power over the south of Egypt (that is, Upper Egypt). This was Kashta.[26] He pushed the Libyan king Osorkon III out of the south, and made himself master of the gold mines and the Nubian militia.

Piankhy (751–716 B.C.), the son of Kashta, pushed farther north into Egypt. Egypt in his reign became a shuttlecock between the Assyrian kings of western Asia and the black kings of Nubia. Lower Egypt (north) was not occupied by Assyrian forces, but its kings paid tribute to the Assyrians and acted as their vassals. Upper Egypt (south) was solidly within the black sphere of power. Middle Egypt, like a kind of no man's land, vacillated between both powers, now playing to the Assyrians, now to the blacks, as power shifted.[27]

The Assyrians were like a great deepening shadow upon the horizon of the Middle East. They were the Huns or Hitlers of that era. They had invaded Iraq, Iran, the Hittite country and Syria.

The Assyrian king Sargon marched into Samaria and transported the Jews in chains from Israel to Iraq.[28] The world was at war. The Asiatics were moving their iron-powered army into the Mediterranean and Africa. But the Assyrians had bitten off more than they could chew. While they had made vassals of many of the native Egyptian kings of the north, they had to be content with merely seeking tribute. They were too tied up holding their ground elsewhere to occupy and consolidate their hold on Lower Egypt (the northern provinces).

Sensing the Assyrian weakness, a local petty king, Tafnak, prince of Sais, a district in the north, rebelled and started to take control of Lower Egypt, forcing allegiance from the other petty kings. But Tafnak did not stop at usurping Assyrian power. He reversed the gains of Piankhy and made the kings who paid the black king tribute "dogs at his feet."[29] It was at this point that the battles, which were to lead to the total conquest of Egypt by the blacks, began. Naval engagements were fought on the Nile, sieges were laid to Egyptian cities, Tafnak was pushed back and back and back, his vassals submitting one by one, until Piankhy, like the great Pharaohs before him, donned the double serpent-crown of Upper and Lower Egypt.[30] In the last great battle of the campaign, at the siege of Memphis, the black king marshaled every kind of watercraft—barges, passenger ships, cargo vessels—using the yardarms as bridges and ladders to scale the walls. Tafnak was forced to retreat to an island within the northernmost reaches of the Nile.[31]

Battles in themselves may be quite meaningless, victories ephemeral and hollow. But something had begun to happen here that gave relative stability, in spite of the fighting that was still to follow, to the black dynasty that was emerging. Piankhy, like his father, established unswerving obedience to his command by both Nubians and native Egyptians through his fanatic devotion to the god Amon-Ra at Thebes. He baptized his vast army in the river before proceeding into battle. In a time of chaos and disorder, when Egypt was indeed "like a bruised reed," the kings of Kush introduced or reinforced the practice of direct divine intervention into the affairs of state, turning Amon-Ra into an oracle so that their orders seemed to come straight from the mouth of God, thereby establishing divine sanction for their dynasty. "The statue [of Amon] was jointed, a priest being especially appointed to work it, and in the sanctuaries hiding places were arranged in the thickness of the wall, from which an officiant skilfully caused the oracular voice of the god to be heard."[32]

The black kings inspired a renaissance of the classical Egyptian spirit. They renovated the temples. They restored royal mummification and pyramid building, which had lapsed for generations,[33] though they built only one kind of pyramid, the truncated step-pyramid. They even restored the concept of "solar blood." Whereas Egyptian Pharaohs had abandoned this custom and had begun marrying Mitannian wives from Hither Asia, the Nubians reinstituted royal incest to preserve the line of the sons of the sun god.[34] Nubia behaved in some ways toward Egypt as America toward Britain, finding herself, two hundred years after independence, the chrysalis of an empire in her own right, powerful and free, yet striving, however awkwardly, sometimes with a naïve idealism, to enshrine and preserve the traditions she has inherited and which, through military might, she alone is equipped to defend and protect, becoming, in effect, a keeper and conscience of her former lord.

Nubia, through Piankhy, and after him Miamum Nut (who fought with Tafnak's son, Bocchoris) and after him Shabaka (who burned Bocchoris alive), and after him Shebitku, who passed over all his brothers for the strongest, Taharka (who had already proven his courage in the van of the allied Nubian-Egyptian forces in Jerusalem)—all these men fought in an unsettled time in a divided world to weld Egypt once more into a unity by virtue of a unifying religious faith. They were all distinguished, in spite of their warlike reigns, by the zeal and piety of men who honestly believe they are agents of a spiritual power. The double-serpent motif dominated the dream life of these kings, and such dreams are described in the stelae of King Nut and King Tanutamon,* a son of Shebitku, Taharka's elder brother, and Qalhata,

---

* Also known and spelled as Tanwetamani.

Taharka's sister.[35] These dreams gave them a single-minded intensity, a sense of mission, of destiny. Thus did their followers fight as fanatically, pursue their enemies as relentlessly, kill with as great a sense of puritan sanctity as did the Christians and Muslims in the later eras of their holy wars. No petty Egyptian king like Tafnak or Bocchoris could arrogate to himself the "divine" titles which these black kings, through their pious dedication to Amon, commanded and assumed. All factions fell, therefore, before the holy march. City after city bowed down in fear and trembling before the messengers of Amon, until from the northernmost head of the Mediterranean down to that southern juncture of the Nile where she splits, branching wide her "white" and "blue" legs, the body of the Egyptian empire submitted to the kings of Kush.

The Assyrians continued to threaten Egypt. They saw the northern provinces fall into the hands of Kush, but even while the battles raged they seemed unable to take advantage of Egypt's internal upheaval and attack her. They too were embroiled on many fronts and dared not overreach themselves, preferring to consolidate their power in Western Asia before risking another naked confrontation with such a powerful adversary.

Many years passed before the inevitable happened. The blacks instituted a policy of "détente" with Assyria. King Shabaka, Piankhy's brother, came to some understanding with the Assyrian king, Sennacherib. Like America and Russia, each decided to observe, or pretend to observe, the other's military and political fief, or sphere of influence. Like the modern great powers they also tried to avert the inevitable clash as long as possible while conspiring secretly to undermine the other through its "satellites" and occasionally fighting "limited wars" not on their own ground but on "satellite" battlefields. Hence, Taharka's appearance on behalf of Hezekiah at Jerusalem. How the battle for the little state of Judah might have ended, had it not been for the mysterious epidemic that broke out among the Assyrians, no one can tell.[36] The Assyrians were not to meet the blacks face to face again on the field of battle for thirty years. Thus their cold war lasted roughly as long as ours has so far.

But Taharka was not idle in those years. He left Upper Egypt (the southern lands) in charge of a black Sudanese high priest, Mentuemhat. Then Taharka came up north to Tanis in the Delta and established his palace in Lower Egypt, where he could be in the swim of things, sensitive to all that was happening in the Mediterranean and western Asia.[37] He became king in 688 B.C., and while playing the policy of détente conspired with the Phoenicians in Tyre and Sidon against the common enemy, the Assyrians. The Phoenicians at that time were vassals of Assyria. They were a defeated but rebellious people, paying tribute to their masters but quietly plotting revenge. So dangerous was the conspiracy they hatched with Taharka that when at last it was discovered by the Assyrians, it unleashed massive and brutal retaliation against both Phoenicia and Egypt. The Phoenician king of Sidon was executed.[38] An insurrection in Tyre, which broke out soon after, was savagely put down.[39] The cold war between Egypt and Assyria came to an end. Esharhaddon, the son of Sennacherib, marched into Egypt and met Taharka's army at Memphis in 671 B.C.[40]

The relationship between the blacks and the Phoenicians, and their common interests in the face of the Assyrians, is an important factor in this period. It may help to explain how a Mediterranean figure with flowing beard and turned-up shoes appears in association with the Negroid figures in ancient Mexico and how certain elements of Phoenician artifacts (such as a model of the Phoenician god Melkart) have been unearthed in America in archaeological contexts related to the African-Egyptian presence.

Egypt had been trading with the Phoenicians for centuries. These people had once been nomads of the desert but had eventually settled on islands in the Mediterranean. They were, however, a people with nomadic urges and soon made of the sea what they had once made of the desert, a field for their restless wanderings. They were extremely poor in metals and so depended for these on their maritime trade, going to Hatus, a Hittite seaport, or to an island later called Cyprus, for copper, to the Iberian peninsula for silver, also to Egypt for the same and Nubian gold dust, and as far as Cornwall in the British Isles, right out into the north Atlantic, for their tin. Although their boats were smaller than those of the Egyptians (seventy feet long was the average), they were extremely maneuverable and equipped with both oar and sail. From their native islands they carried linen cloth and wool, fine jewelry, cedar from which some Egyptian ships were made, perfume and spices; and from their major seaports, Tyre, Sidon and Byblos, things that were rare and treasured in the ancient world—a purple dye, which came to be known as Tyrenean purple and was reserved as the color of royalty in the Mediterranean, exquisite glass from Sidon, papyrus from Byblos, which the Egyptians used to write their very first books. Yet compared to the Egyptians, the Phoenicians were semi-illiterates and have left very few written records. Some scholars have claimed it was not so much a matter of their literacy as a reluctance to put things down, a secretiveness about their markets, searoutes and navigational science. They were always afraid of losing their advantage at sea, for this was their only strength. In spite of their restless energy and enterprise they were a very vulnerable people. They lay within the valley of the giants and became the vassals of many powers (Egyptians, Assyrians, Persians, etc.).[41]

But the Egyptians, Herodotus tells us, even when they made subjects of the Phoenicians, did not stifle their maritime trade. It was as vital to Egypt as it was to them. The more riches they amassed from this trade the more tribute they could pay to Egypt.[42] The practical wisdom of this "laissez-faire" policy toward the Phoenicians appealed to the Assyrians also. And so it was that they gave military protection to the Phoenician caravans on land, while allowing them to move freely at sea,[43] from one end of the Mediterranean to the other, although they were a subject race. A lot of Egyptian trade was carried on in Phoenician ships. The Phoenicians were, although merchants in their own right, often mercenary seamen of the Egyptians. (As late as circa 600 B.C., when Assyrian power had waned and the Phoenicians were once more under the heel of the Egyptians, the Pharaoh Necho II hired them to circle Africa by ship.) In the era of Nubian domination of Egypt, vast supplies of copper and tin were required to provide bronze weaponry for the armies. Phoenicians, as poor in metals as Egypt, made fortunes out of the maritime metal trade.[44]

There was something even more important and urgent about the search for metal supplies in this period. The Bronze Age was coming to an end. The Age of Iron had been ushered in swiftly and terribly by the march of the Assyrians, whose armies owed their superiority to a heavier concentration of iron weaponry. The blacks of Kush had learned of the process of iron-smelting, but Egypt was poor in iron. Taharka is credited in the history of the Sudan with having introduced the ironworks in Nubia at a place called Meroe, but this was after his retreat from Egypt. The sights of the blacks, in this period of their ascendancy, lay in the north, where they could realize their dreams of dominating Egypt; not in the south, their homeland, until their armies were irrevocably pushed back by the Assyrians. The discovery of iron, therefore, in their own heartland, and in considerable quantity, did not come until around 650 B.C., when it was too late to make any real difference in the military struggles.[45]

The techniques of iron-smelting were not the monopoly of the Assyrians. These techniques had been developed among the Hittites[46] before their conquest by the Assyrians, and may have diffused to Egypt and Nubia through Hittite refugees fleeing their bases in the Mediterranean as the great armies of the alien overpowered them. The Hittites fled also to Phoenicia. They became a dispersed people, settling in tiny pockets in Egypt, Phoenicia and elsewhere, intermarrying with, and becoming incorporated into, the culture of their neighbors.[47]

Thus we have a picture of the culture complex of this period and the pressures which made it necessary for Taharka to intrigue with the Phoenicians under the noses of the Assyrians. It is during this period that we find at La Venta in the Gulf of Mexico a complex of figures that were associated in the Nubian-Egyptian-Mediterranean milieu of that period—four massive Negroid stone heads in Egyptian-type helmets and a Mediterranean-type figure standing beside them, carved out on a stele, with a flowing beard, Semitic nose and turned-up shoes (Phoenician merchant captain?).[48] Also, we find overwhelming evidence of African-Egyptian cultural features, some of which had lapsed in Egypt for centuries but enjoyed a revival in the Nubian period, features which had a long and complex evolution in the Mediterranean but seem to have emerged full-born with no archaeological layer of anteced-ents in the American world. We are later to find bits and pieces dispersing from this initial point of contact—a model of the Phoe-nician god Melkart in Rio Balsas,[49] Mexico, identification of Hit-tite glyphs on obsidian discs or "coins" by Mrs. Verrill in the state of Utah.[50] But also, in the most remarkable of combinations and in one single place, a number of reliefs of Negroid "dancers" side by side with reliefs in "Assyrian style" (which style was introduced among the Nubian/Egyptian models of gods at Thebes by Ta-harka's black deputy in the south, Mentu-em-hat)*,[51] a represen-tation of the god Ra in its bird aspect, and a sculpture of the Egyptian sphinx. These were found in a single spot at Monte Albán in the first phase of that civilization, which evolved from the last phase of the Olmec world. What an apparently incongru-ous combination of elements—Negro-Nubian, Egyptian, Assyrian! We can see quite clearly from our outline of history how natural to that period was such a cultural fusion, but it led Egon Kisch, a German journalist, to cry out in rhetorical despair:

"Is there any other spot on earth so completely enwrapped in darkness, so mute in the face of all our questions? . . . What tribe, what race once dwelt at the foot of Monte Albán? Who were the builders, who the architects of these pagan temples? What were the tools of the stonemasons made of? How to explain why sev-eral of the urn figures seem to depict an Egyptian sphinx, another the bird-headed god, Ra, and why the reliefs in the 'Gallery of the Dancers' are partly in Assyrian style, partly a portrayal of Negroid types? How? Why? Whence?"[52]

These elements in combination suggest a crew with Nubian-Egyptian troops in command, a navigator of Phoenician ancestry, probably a Hittite or two, a number of Egyptian assistants, such as attended the black kings at Thebes and Memphis, a number of women, like the black Egyptian woman from the preclassic era of American terra cottas, whose resemblance to the Negroid Queen Tiy Professor von Wuthenau has remarked on.[53] This was a crew

* Also spelled Month-em-ha.

that set out on an important mission and therefore was a fair representative or cultural microcosm of the society and place from which it embarked. Did this ship or ships set out to seek iron ore deposits along the vast iron shield of Africa—or other conventional metals (all of which, because of the war, were sorely needed) —and got lost by force of storm or treacherous current on the North Atlantic? Or was it a flotilla of refugees, fleeing the wrath of the Assyrian Esharhaddon after the discovery of the Nubian-Phoenician conspiracy? The quest for metals is the most likely and logical of all possible explanations. For refugees of Phoenicia had no need to flee beyond the pillars of Hercules. The Assyrians lacked the capacity to pursue them to the western extremity of the Mediterranean. Furthermore, Taharka, facing the first full-scale assault of the Assyrians, would never have committed his badly needed troops to the protection of Phoenicians retreating into the distance of an unknown land. The quest for metals, however, could easily have taken them out into the Atlantic, since it had already taken them there to quarry the tinstone of Cornwall.

This need for metals transcended all other needs. What oil and uranium are to us today, so was iron to the survival of the Egyptian empire in that time. Iron was to change the world. Egypt's inability to redeem her lack of it was the largest single cause of her defeat.[54] Taharka and his successor fought, fell back, regrouped and fought again. But the initiative had been lost. The doom of an iron-poor Egypt was imminent. The Bronze Age was over, and with it Egypt's position of preeminence in the ancient world.

NOTES AND REFERENCES

1 Henry Brugsch-Bey, A History of Egypt Under the Pharaohs, London, John Murray, 1881, Vol. 2, p. 235.

2 Ibid. See also E. Drioton and J. Vandier, L'Egypt, Vol. 2 of Les Peuples de l'Orient, Paris, 1936.

3 A. J. Arkell, History of the Sudan to A.D. 1821, London, The Athlone Press, 1935, p. 113.

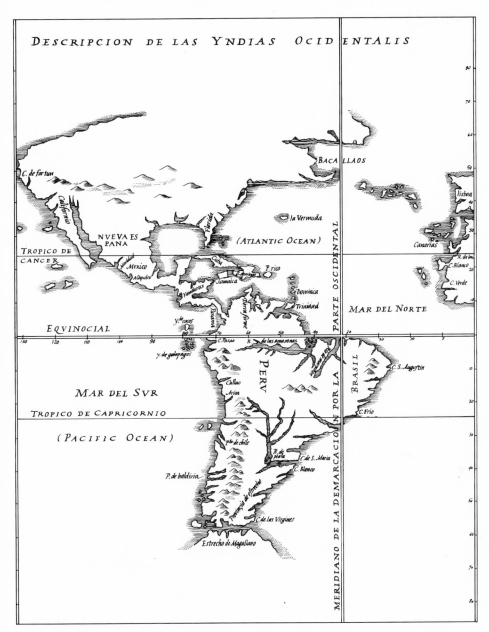

PLATE 1 *The Tordesillas line.* Drawn at the request of King Don Juan of Portugal in June, 1494, before the European "discovery" of South America, on the strength of information gleaned from African mariners in Guinea. The line is 375 leagues west of the Cape Vérde islands (about 1680 miles, using Vespucci's measurement of a league) and was later seen to include roughly 200 miles of Brazil.

PLATE 2   *Negroid heads in pre-Christian Mexico.* (a), (c), (f) from Tlatilco; (b) from Tabasco; (d) from Chiapas; (g) from Guerrero; (h) and (i) from the central plateau of Mexico.

PLATE 3 *African women in pre-Columbian Mexico.* Compare (a) modern Nigerian woman with (b) Negroid Teotihuacán head (Classic period) wearing headkerchief and earrings. (c) Pre-Classic head from Pacific coast of El Salvador. (d) Seated black woman from Vera Cruz (Classic period). Compare (e) Negroid sun-dancer from Vera Cruz (Classic) with (f) Negro-Egyptian head of Queen Tiy, mother of Tutankhamen.

PLATE 4 a   *Negro-Mongoloid mixtures in pre-Columbian Mexico.* Dead man from Vera Cruz. Note hair, goatee beard and mouth. Classic period.

PLATE 4 b   Vera Cruz head, showing a Negroid strain. Classic period.

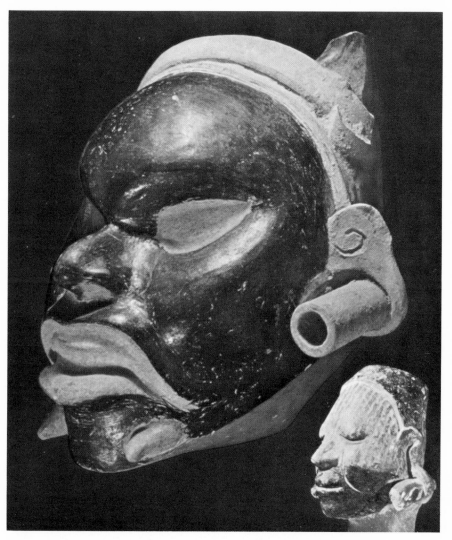

PLATE 5   *Mandingo head in fourteenth-century Mexico.* Made by the Mixtecs, from Oaxaca. Josue Saenz collection, Mexico City.

PLATE 6   Upper row: *Negroid heads with vivid scarification.*(a) Vera Cruz. Classic period. Note headdress. (b) Tattooed head on upper right belongs to collection of pre-Columbian art at Tulane University in New Orleans. Bottom row: (c) *Negroid head.* Worshiped by Aztecs as representation of their god Tezcatlipoca because it had the right ceremonial color. (d) *Negroid mask of Olmec period.*

PLATE 7 *Descendants of black governors of Ecuador.* Zambo chieftains from Esmeraldas (in present-day Ecuador) who visited Quito in 1599. They are shown here in Spanish dress and Indian ornaments but were descendants of a group of 17 shipwrecked Africans who gained political control of an entire province of Ecuador in short order. (see Chapter 2)

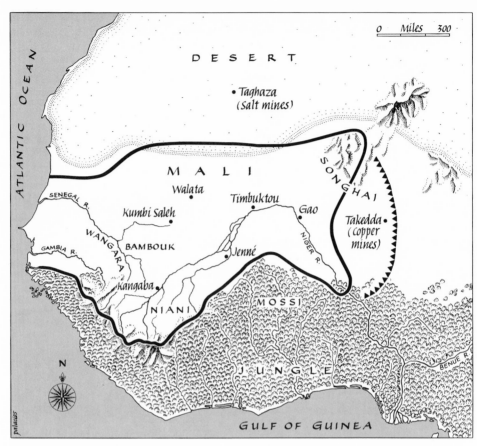

PLATE 8 *Medieval Mali at the time of Abubakari the Second.* It dwarfed the Holy Roman Empire.

PLATE 9 *Abubakari the Second* (Artist's impression).

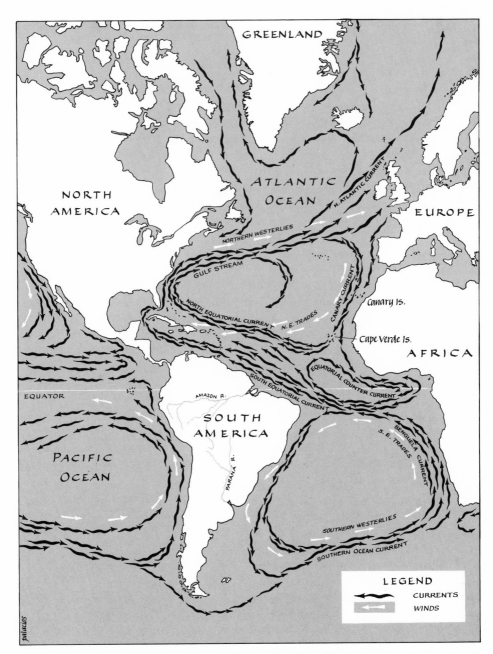

PLATE 10 *World-wide winds and currents, emphasizing Atlantic drift routes from Africa to America.*

PLATE 11 *East African trading ship.* A ship of great antiquity, it sailed the Indian Ocean between Africa and China. Held together not by nails but by palm-fiber lashings, these ships could be as large as 70 tons. The one shown here is from a model in the Fort Jesus museum at Mombasa. The Swahili transshipped an elephant to China in the thirteenth century.

PLATE 13 *African power canoe* (Artist's impression). Type of boat encountered on the Gambia by Portuguese explorer Alvise da Cadamosto in 1455. Similar boat with 48-man crew developed on the Orinoco by South American Indians circa 120 A.D. On this they sailed from Venezuela to Puerto Rico in one day. Average speed was 8 knots an hour in storm-free seasons. This speed was sustainable night and day, since oarsmen worked in shifts, 24 resting, 24 rowing. Note waterproof awning for provisions. (See Desmond V. Nicholson, "Precolumbian Seafaring capabilities in the Lesser Antilles," *Antigua Archaeological Society*, July, 1975.)

PLATE 12 *Heyerdahl's* Ra I, *built by African boatmen.*African boatmen from Lake Chad built this papyrus boat along the pattern of the ancient Egyptians. It left North Africa in 1969 and sailed as far as Barbados. Rudders broke early on the *Ra*, proving that an ancient drift journey in such a boat using Africa-to-America currents was feasible.

a

PLATE 14 (a) *Boat on head of Semitic figure from a stele in Campeche.*
Compare with (b) *Phoenician ships in late dynastic Egyptian period.*

b

a

b

PLATE 15 *Mandingo elements in Mexico.* (a) Cross motif in loop-ended gadwal in Africa. (b) Identical design in Mexico. Cross motif in loop-ended gadwal. (c) Mexican shields with triple crescent. (d) The crescent motif in Arabic-Mandingo blazonry.

c

d

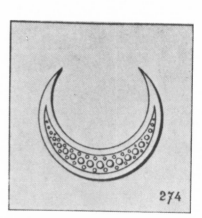

274

279

PLATE 16 *Medieval African smoking pipes, similar in design to American pipes.*

PLATE 17 *Bearded Negroid wanderers in medieval Mexico.* From the Mixtec Codex Dorenberg (fourteenth century). Note beards, lips, noses of these foreigners, who are represented with black skins. While pictorial representations here are not as photographically realistic as some of the terra-cotta portraitures, alien and distinctive features are emphasized.

Abb. 569. Codex Tro 6a.
Der schwarze Gott mit der grossen Nase, Feuer bohrend.

Abb. 570, 571. Codex Tro 19b, 19c.

a

b

PLATE 18 *Black gods in medieval Mexico.* (a) The trader god, Ek-chu-ah. Many Indians of Central and South America and Mexico journey annually even today to what A. Hyatt Verrill of the Museum of the American Indian labels a "shrine or Mecca" in an obscure Guatemalan village. There they worship "the Black Christ," whom they refer to in private as Ek-chu-ah, god of merchants, husbandmen and travelers. (b) The god of jewelers, Naualpilli. Gold pectoral of Negroid god in the National Museum, Mexico City.

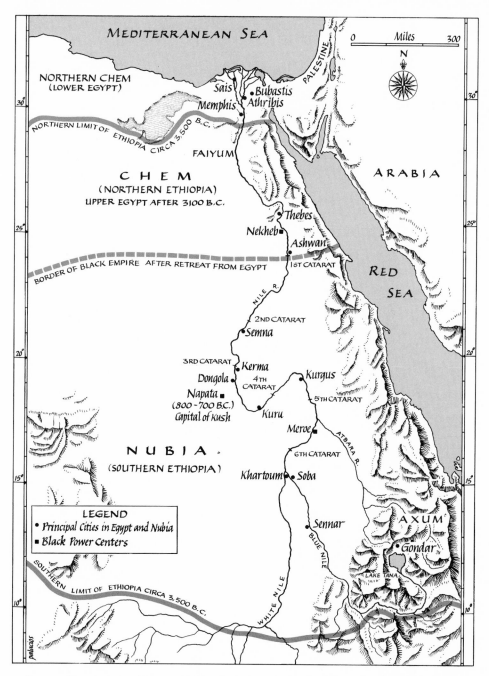

PLATE 19   *Ancient Egypt and Nubia showing principal cities and the black power centers in various periods.*

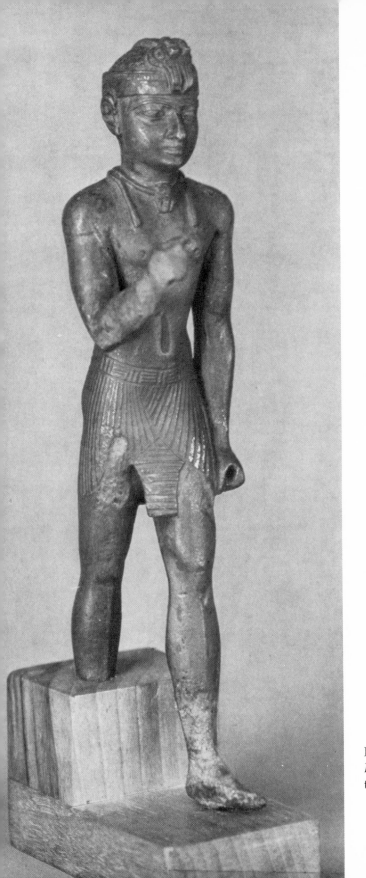

PLATE 20 *The black Pharaoh Taharka.* Twenty-Fifth Dynasty.

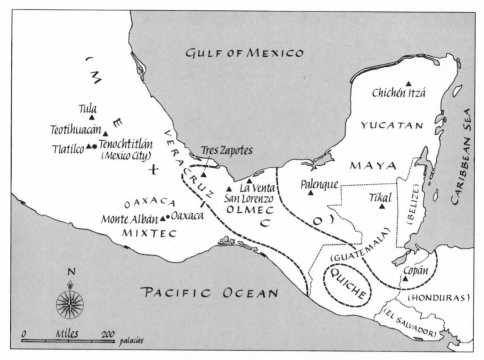

PLATE 21 *Gulf of Mexico indicating the Olmec heartland.* Note centers of La Venta, Tres Zapotes and San Lorenzo, where colossal Negroid heads were found.

PLATE 22 *Phoenician-looking merchant captain.* Found engraved on a stele beside Negroid stone heads at La Venta (800–700 B.C.).

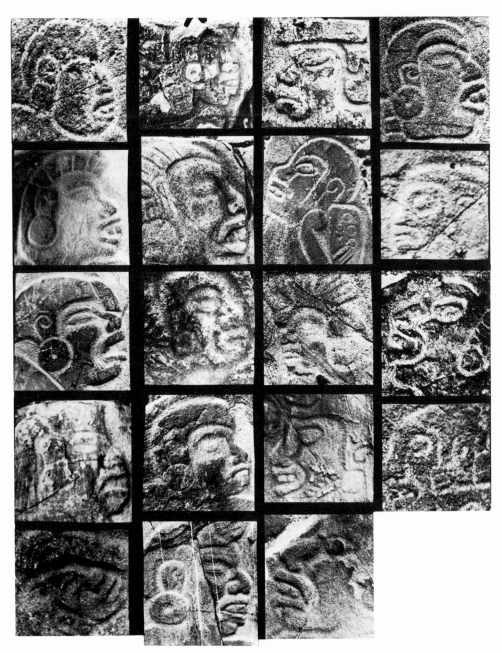

PLATE 23 *Negroid "danzantes" at Monte Albán* These were descendants of the Nubian-Olmec rulers. Some are depicted here slain and castrated in a revolt by natives of Monte Albán, circa 400 B.C.

PLATE 24 *Negroid stone head from Vera Cruz.* Classic period. In American Museum of Natural History, New York.

a

b

PLATE 25 *Negroid magician at Copan, Honduras.* (a) Frontal view. (b) Side view.

PLATE 26 *Negroid boy holding up pre-Columbian altar with trophy heads—Costa Rica.*

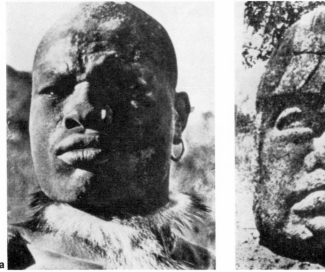

a

b

PLATE 27 Compare (a) *Head of Nuba chief from Africa* with (b) *Olmec Negroid stone head (La Venta 1).*

PLATE 28   *Negroid stone heads in the Olmec heartland.*(a) Tres Zapotes I.
(b) San Lorenzo I. (c) San Lorenzo IV. (d) San Lorenzo VI. (e) Tres Zapotes II. (f) La Venta I.

PLATE 29 *Black warrior dynasts in ancient Mexico.* (a) Olmec Negroid stone head (San Lorenzo V). (b) Olmec Negroid stone head (San Lorenzo IV).

PLATE 30 *Olmec Negroid stone head (Tres Zapotes II).*

PLATE 31 Compare (a) *Head of Nuba chief from Kenya* with (b) *Olmec Negroid stone head (Tres Zapotes F)*.

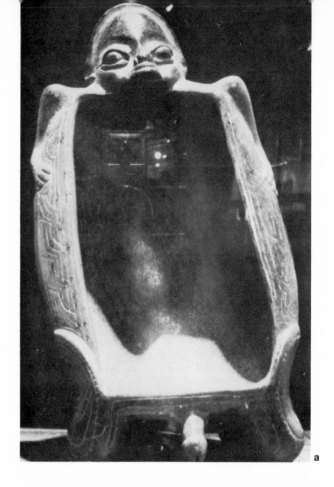

PLATE 32 (a) *Human-headed coffin from Costa Rica* Negroid head with phallus between stylized foot rests. Compare with (b) *Human-headed coffin from Argin, in Nubia.* Both are terra cotta. The phallus in the American model is probably also an influence. See phallic cults in Egypt and America as depicted in Plate 33.

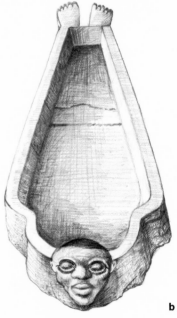

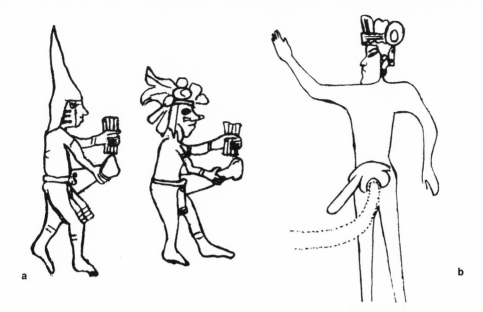

a

b

PLATE 33 *Phallic cults in Egypt and Mexico.*(a) Phallic procession in Mexican Codex Borbonicus holding artificial phalli. (b) Olmec painting of phallic figure from Oxtotitlan with right arm upraised. (c) Egyptian god Min from Medinet Habu holding phallus and raising right hand. (d) Mexican terracotta figure with man holding phallus in the manner of the Egyptian god Min.

c

d

PLATE 34　*Negroid rock mask* At Chalcalzingo, near Morelos, Mexico. Dated 800–700 B.C. by Gillett G. Griffin, curator, Princeton University Museum. Von Wuthenau notes similarity to braceleted arm of Assyrian king Ashurnasirpal II (883–859 B.C.), but this kind of hand seal was also in vogue in the Twenty-Fifth Dynasty, when the Nubian king Shabaka stamped his hand in wet clay beside that of the Assyrian king Sennacherib to sign and seal their truce.

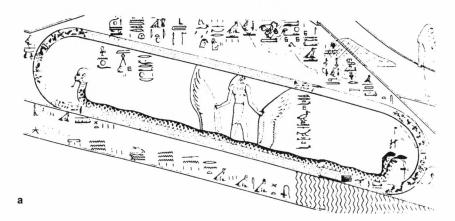

a

b

PLATE 35 *Egyptian gods in Mexico: The God Sokar* (a) Winged god standing on the back of double-ended serpent in Egyptian papyrus painting of the Underworld. Compare with (b) god at Izapa in Mexico. In the Egyptian painting the god stretches out his hands to hold up his wings. In Mexico he does the same. He also stands on the back of the same type of double-ended serpent and wears a foreign beard.

PLATE 36 *Egyptian gods in Mexico: The God Aken* In Egyptian Underworld text "a serpent without eyes, nose or ears, a non-articulated ophidian" (Jairazbhoy) swallows a double-rope. Olmec sculpture in Museum of Jalapa depicts featureless serpent squatting and eating the double-rope.

PLATE 37 *Opening the Mouth Ceremony in Mexico and Egypt.*Compare (a) Egyptian papyrus painting from the *Book of the Dead* depicting the Opening the Mouth Ceremony with (b) wall painting in cave at Juxtlahuaca, with gigantic figure wearing lion skin. He holds two ceremonial objects, similar to the Egyptian, before the kneeling man. Both priests wear skins of beasts whose tails hang between their legs, and both proffer a snake-headed instrument to the kneeling bearded man.

PLATE 38 *Clay dog in Mexican tomb on chariot wheels.*The Mexican never used the wheel for pack transport, since he lacked the horse and other suitable animals. The wheel turns up, however, in a curious association with the dog. Some scholars say they are toys (Eckholm), but they are really funerary offerings. Egyptians mummified dogs. Nubians preserved them only symbolically (funerary tables depicting the dog) but buried horses instead, or sometimes their favorite chariots on wheels, because of their devotion to the military horse. Dog and chariot thus became fused, symbolically in Nubia, but in more concrete terms in Mexico.

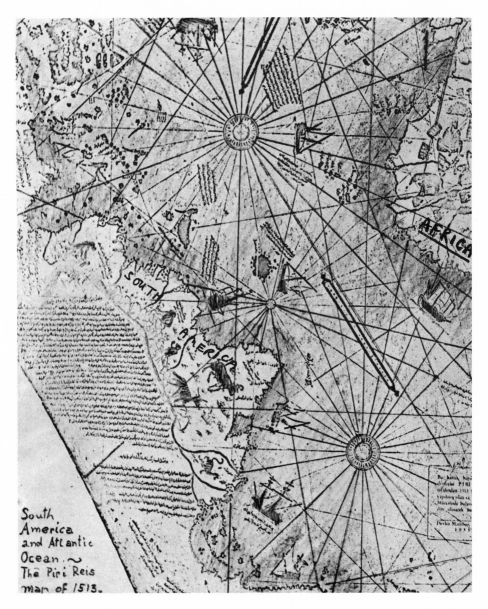

South
America
and Atlantic
Ocean. ∼
The Piri Reis
map of 1513.

PLATE 39 *The Piri Reis map* Drawn in 1513 from earlier maps found in the Library of Alexandria by the Turkish admiral Piri Reis. It depicts fairly accurate latitudinal and longitudinal relationships between the Atlantic coastlines of Africa and South America. Reading of longitude was only achieved by Europeans in the eighteenth century.

PLATE 40 *Negroid heads on pre-Columbian portrait vessels.* (a) Post-classic Negroid head on portrait vessel in Oaxaca with stirrup handle (Mixtec). (b) Negroid head on portrait vessel, also from Oaxaca (Zapotec). (c) A Classic Mochica Negroid portrait vessel from Peru circa A.D. 900 (Arab-African contact period. See Chapter 12).

4 Brugsch-Bey, op. cit., p. 235.

5 G. A. Reisner, "Outline of the Ancient History of the Sudan. IV. The First Kingdom of Ethiopia" in *Sudan Notes and Records*, Vol. 2, 1919, pp. 35–67.

6 Ibid., pp. 41–44.

7 Arkell, op. cit., p. 120.

8 Alexandre Moret, *The Nile and Egyptian Civilization*, New York, Knopf, 1927, p. 336.

9 Arkell, op. cit., p. 120.

10 Idem.

11 Idem.

12 Arkell, op. cit., p. 109.

13 P. L. Shinnie, *Meroe, A Civilization of the Sudan*, New York, Praeger Publishers, 1967. But for a contrasting opinion see C. L. Woolley and D. Randall McIver, *Karanog: The Romano-Nubian Cemetery*, Philadelphia, 1910, p. 4.

14 Plate XXVIII in Davies and Gardiner, *The Tomb of Huy*. See reproduction as Plate 24 of George Steindorff and Keith Seele, *When Egypt Ruled the East*, University of Chicago Press, 1942, 2nd edition, 1957.

15 Shinnie, op. cit., p. 155.

16 Arkell, op. cit., p. 128.

17 J. H. Breasted, *A History of Egypt*, London, Hodder & Stoughton, 1906, p. 553.

18 Bk. II, *Kings*, Chap. 19, verse 9.

19 Breasted, op. cit., p. 555. "His [Esharhaddon's] army was knocking at the frontier fortresses of the eastern Delta in 674 B.C. But Taharka, who was a man of far greater ability than his two predecessors on the throne, must have made a supreme effort to meet the crisis. The outcome of the battle (673 B.C.) was unfavorable for the Assyrian if, as the documents indicate, he did not suffer positive defeat."

20 Ibid., p. 556.

21 Ibid., p. 558.

22 Arkell, op. cit., pp. 123–124.

23 Ibid., p. 128.

24 Ibid.

25 Breasted, p. 554.

26 Arkell, op. cit., p. 121. I have consulted many studies of this
period, Arkell, in spite of his prejudices, provides the most concise outline of the reigns of the kings of Kush. His datings also
are fairly reliable and clear up discrepancies found in the works
of earlier scholars.

27 Brugsch-Bey, p. 237.

28 Arkell, p. 125.

29 Brugsch-Bey, p. 240 (translated from an inscription on a stele
of the Ethiopian king Piankhy).

30 Ibid., p. 246.

31 Ibid., p. 255.

32 Moret, op. cit., p. 338.

33 Moret, op. cit., p. 342. "Whereas no royal tomb is known in
Egypt after the 22nd Dynasty," says Moret, "Napata has
yielded the sepulchres of all the Ethiopian kings." Also Arkell
points to "the political and cultural degeneration in Egypt during the centuries preceding the eighth century B.C. and the
consequent lack [before the Ethiopian dynasty] of written records" (Arkell, A History of the Sudan, p. 114). The blacks left
detailed historical records of their achievements. As Brugsch-
Bey in A History of Egypt under the Pharaohs has pointed out,
kings like Piankhy and Taharka composed "long and memorable descriptions [of their campaigns] preserved on [their]
memorial stones" (p. 238). The cemeteries at Nuri and Kurru
contained the remains of many pyramids and mummies in bead
nets (Arkell, p. 120).

34 Moret, op. cit., p. 316.

35 For dreams of the double-serpent among Nubian kings, see
Arkell, p. 134. For incest among Nubian royalty, see Arkell,
pp. 126, 134.

36 Breasted, op. cit., p. 552. Breasted says Taharka was beaten in
the first round of the battle of Jerusalem, but then the malaria
epidemic broke out, throwing the Assyrian forces into disarray,
thereby saving both the Jews and the allied Nubian-Egyptian
forces.

37 Arkell, p. 127.

38 Arkell, p. 128.

39 Ibid.

40 Ibid.

41 George Rawlinson, *History of Phoenicia*, London, Longmans, 1889. Also, Donald Harden, *The Phoenician*, London, Thames and Hudson, 1962. James Bailey in his chapter on the Phoenicians in *The God Kings and the Titans*, pp. 116–120, makes a number of unsupported claims for the Phoenicians. "They excelled in writing and literature," he declares. This is not the case. It has been shown that while they transmitted the alphabet to the Romans, they did nothing to develop it and were simply culture-carriers in that respect. They took the alphabet from other literate peoples in the Mediterranean. It is true also that the word "book" comes down through the main European languages from Byblos, one of their city-ports, but this has nothing to do with literacy or literature. They were rich in the raw materials for making books, that is all.

42 George Rawlinson (ed.) *The History of Herodotus*, London, Murray, 1875.

43 Ibid.

44 Irwin, *Fair Gods and Stone Faces*, New York, St. Martin's Press, 1963, p. 203.

45 Arkell, op. cit., p. 130.

46 Irwin, op. cit., p. 151.

47 Ibid., p. 147.

48 The finest reproduction of this figure may be found in Thor Heyerdahl, "The Bearded Gods Speak" in Gordon Ashe (ed.) *The Quest for America*, New York, Praeger Publishers, 1971, p. 233 (Illus. 203).

49 George C. Vaillant, "A Bearded Mystery," *Natural History*, Vol. 31 (May–June, 1931), pp. 243–244.

50 Bailey, op. cit., p. 75.

51 Brugsch-Bey, op. cit., p. 278.

52 Quoted by Irwin, op. cit., p. 63.

53 Von Wuthenau, op. cit., p. 149.

54 Arkell, op. cit., p. 130.

9

AFRICAN—EGYPTIAN PRESENCES IN ANCIENT AMERICA

*Is there any other spot on earth so completely enwrapped
in darkness, so mute in the face of all our questions? . . .
How to explain why several of the urn figures seem to depict an Egyptian sphinx, another the bird-headed god, Ra,
and why the reliefs in the "Gallery of the Dancers" are
partly in Assyrian style, partly the portrayal of Negroid
types? How? Why? Whence?*

—EGON ERWIN KISCH, *Entdeckungen in Mexico*

*We can trace the progress of man in Mexico without
noting any definite Old World influence during this period
(1000–650 B.C.) except a strong Negroid substratum connected with the Magicians.*

—FREDERICK A. PETERSON, *Ancient Mexico*

In 1938 Dr. Matthew Stirling led a joint team from the Smithsonian Institution and the National Geographic Society into the
Gulf of Mexico to an obscure spot about a mile outside the village of Tres Zapotes. There, a year earlier, following up a rumor
that some Mexican peasants had come upon a huge stone head
in 1858 but had left it to sink back into its grave, Stirling uncovered what looked like the "helmeted dome" of that head.[1] Spying
out the land within the vicinity of this find, Stirling realized that
it was not buried in isolation but, as certain large mounds indicated, in the company of other huge and probably related objects.

To uncover all these would call for a major digging operation. Stirling therefore returned home to raise money and a team to do the digging. That team, which he brought back with him into the jungles of Vera Cruz in 1939, was to unearth some of the most startling archaeological finds in American history.

Stirling's description of these finds is steeped in his excitement and wonder. When the first head had completely emerged from the dark alluvial soil, he found it, in spite of its great size, to be carved from a single block of basalt and to be a head only, resting upon a prepared foundation of unworked slabs of stone. "Cleared of the surrounding earth, it presented an awe-inspiring spectacle. Despite its great size the workmanship is delicate and sure, and proportions perfect. Unique in character among aboriginal American sculptures, it is remarkable for its realistic treatment. The features are bold and *amazingly negroid* in character."[2] (Italics added.)

This Negroid head was found only ten miles away from the source of the stone from which it was made. The basalt had come from the base of Mount Tuxtla. But what was extraordinary was that the single block of stone from which native Americans had chiseled this portrait was six feet high and eighteen feet in circumference, weighing over ten tons. To bring it from the base of the mountain to the place where it was found called for it to be transported over a thirty-foot-deep gorge. "This problem," remarked Stirling, "would tax the ingenuity of an engineer with the benefit of modern machinery . . . the ancient engineers, however, performed the feat of successfully quarrying a flawless block of basalt and transporting it in perfect condition without the aid of the wheel or domestic animals."[3]

As the diggings at this location continued, a long slab of stone was found—a stele—with dots and crosses, which, when deciphered, yielded a precise date: November 4, 291 B.C.[4] This dating caused an uproar in archaeological circles, and the Herbert Spinden scale for calculating American time inscriptions, which had been used to arrive at this date, was vigorously challenged. Ten years later, carbon datings (which were only introduced as late as 1946 into archaeological studies) were made at a different site—Tikal in Guatemala—and these proved that the Spinden "reading" of American dots and crosses in no way overestimated the antiquity of objects.[5] It was far more accurate, these carbon-14 tests established, than the Goodman-Martinez-Thompson scale which had given much later dates.

The year 291 B.C. was startling enough. It was the earliest date then known for any American cultural find. But greater surprises were in store. Larger heads, earlier dates, more important sites, were revealed as the diggings in Middle America were extended and intensified. They exposed the false, frail ground upon which the historical outlines of pre-Columbian American history had so far been built.

Fourteen years before Stirling's expedition to Tres Zapotes, a team from Tulane University had found a giant stone head pushing out of the ground at La Venta in the Mexican state of Tabasco, about eighteen miles inland from the Gulf of Mexico. The Tulane team, headed by Frans Blom and Oliver La Farge, were only passing through the area and did not have time to dig, but they recorded their find in a photograph.[6] Stirling was struck by something in this photograph: although only the top of the head could be seen, the domelike helmet on this buried figure seemed to match the one he had excavated at Tres Zapotes. Suspecting a link, he headed toward La Venta on his next expedition. What he found there not only confirmed his suspicions but made his work at the former site seem minor in comparison.

When after a relentless search, this head eventually emerged, it was found to be eight feet high, and like the one at Tres Zapotes, vividly Negroid.[7] A native boy, observing the diggings, had seen outcroppings of stone not far from his father's place and led the expedition to that spot. Three more Negroid heads were uncovered. Two of them were so realistic in detail that they even had their teeth carved out, a very unusual thing in American art. Massive, military, menacing they stood, faces of pure basalt stone, dominating the vast ceremonial plaza in which they were found. The lines of cheek and jaw, the fullness of the lips, the broadly fleshed noses, the acutely observed and faithfully reproduced facial contour and particulars bore eloquent witness to a Negro-

African presence. One of the Negroid colossi, eight and a half feet high and twenty-two feet in circumference, wore earplugs *with a cross* carved in each. They all wore headdresses that were foreign and distinctive—domed helmets like those of ancient soldiers. They all faced east, staring into the Atlantic.[8]

Four Negroid heads in all were excavated at La Venta. The largest of the four—nine feet high—had its domed top flattened so that it could function as an altar. A speaking tube was found going in at the ear and out at the mouth; it was used as an oracle, a talking god. It was also, according to Stirling, associated with the first construction phase of the ceremonial court,[9] which went through three phases or alterations. The significance of this and of other objects found on the site could not be assessed until some very hard dating by scientific methods could be obtained. It was not until excavations in 1955 and 1956 by members of a National Geographic–Smithsonian–University of California expedition that the carbon-14 datings began. These were published in 1957.[10] They were astonishing.

At the place where the Negroid figures in association with the Caucasoid figure with the beard were found, the La Venta ceremonial court, nine samples of wood charcoal were taken. Five of these samples related to the original construction of the court. They gave an average reading of 814 B.C., plus or minus 134 years.[11] In other words, the living human figures upon which these heads were modeled, could not have appeared at La Venta later than 680 B.C. and could have entered the Gulf of Mexico anytime between the average 800 B.C. date and the 680 B.C. date, a period which roughly spans the Twenty-Fifth Dynasty of Egypt. Carbon datings cannot be contested, but they must allow for a margin of error about a century either way from the date assessed from samples of organic material. Most Americanists, using other yardsticks to narrow down this margin, agree on 800 B.C. *as the earliest date for the La Venta site.* A study of the known history of the period spanned by these dates, illuminated by other data (for example, aspects of their attire, the relationship of the figures found in juxtaposition, the incidence of foreign cultural elements) may help us to arrive at a more specific dating.

I would put it within the nine years between 688 B.C. (the year of Taharka's assumption of the double-crown of Egypt, his movement north, the beginning of his construction of a new pharaonic palace and gardens at Memphis, the first phase of his diplomatic campaign of alliances and military preparations against the Assyrians) and the year 680 B.C., the latest possible date for the foreigners to be represented in the first phase of the construction of the ceremonial court. Let it be noted, however, that this is simply a selection of the likeliest period and the likeliest set of circumstances. The capacities, the pressures, the potential maritime trading relationship between the black rulers of Egypt and the Phoenician vassals of Assyria existed all through the period 730 B.C. to 656 B.C., from Piankhy's assumption of power over both Upper and Lower Egypt to the sack of Thebes and the final defeat of Taharka and his nephew Tanutamon by the Assyrian king Ashur-bani-pal. The Nubian militia was also a major determinant in Egyptian power politics for centuries preceding the emergence of this black dynasty. Nubia, by her wealth and the power of her army, became a decisive factor in the power politics of Egypt as early as 1085 B.C., even before the actual conquest of Egypt by the black kings of Kush.[12]

That these aliens entered the Gulf of Mexico during the original construction of the ceremonial court (not later than 680 B.C.) is borne out by several factors. One was Stirling's discovery of evidence which indicated that the oracular Negroid stone face, with the altar on the dome of its head, was among the oldest of the figures at the La Venta ceremonial site.[13] Another was the fact that this face and the others were so huge and dominating that they must have affected the shape and size of the ceremonial court itself, presumably built to accommodate and venerate them.

La Venta culture itself—or, rather, the culture of the Olmecs—runs from circa 800 to circa 400 B.C. The original court was renovated and altered three times, and it is from the sampling of the original construction phase and the three renovation phases that the archaeologists who did the tests—Philip Drucker, Robert Heizer and Robert Squier—were able to arrive at the earliest and latest limits of Olmec civilization. During these site construction phases there is no evidence that any significant culture change occurred. In other words, what began to shape Olmec culture at La Venta in the first construction phase dominated it to the last (400–325 B.C.) when the Olmecs abandoned the site. This fact is important in establishing the arrival of foreigners in the first phase (not later than 680 B.C.), for if they arrived afterward, the massive reconstruction work that the sudden and spectacular introduction of the massive stone sculptures would have imposed on the original site, and the changes it would have wrought upon the culture, would have shown up very clearly in the archaeological evidence. "We wish to emphasize," says the joint report of the Drucker-Heizer-Squier team, "that these [later dates] refer to site construction phases only, not cultural stages: we found no evidence of culture change during the time Complex A [the ceremonial site] was in use."[14]

The Olmecs were a people of three faces, that is, a people formed from three main sources or influences. One of these faces was Mongoloid. Elements of this Mongoloid strain may have come into America from Asia even after the famous glacial migrations across the Bering Straits, but they would have blended indistinguishably with the Ice Age Americans. The second face or influence was Negroid. The third suggests a trace of Mediterranean Caucasoids—some with Semitic noses (probably Phoenician)— but this will be shown to be related historically to the second. These faces became one face, to which the broad name "Olmec" was given. I think it is necessary to make it clear—since partisan and ethnocentric scholarship seems to be the order of the day— that the emergence of the Negroid face, which the archaeological and cultural data overwhelmingly confirms, in no way presupposes the lack of a native originality, the absence of other influences, or the automatic eclipse of other faces. Fusion is the marriage—not the fatal collision—of cultures.

La Venta was not alone in its depiction of Negroid faces in stone. Apart from the four found there, two were excavated in Tres Zapotes and five at San Lorenzo in Vera Cruz, one of which, the largest known, is nine feet, four inches high.[15]

Further archaeological evidence of the Negroid presence in an-

cient America is found in stone reliefs associated with an American culture which in its first phase was contemporaneous with
the last phase of Olmec culture and strongly influenced by it. This
was the culture of Monte Albán, located southwest of La Venta.
In what is known as the "Temple of the Danzantes" (dancing figures), a stone-faced platform contemporary with the first occupation of Monte Albán, is found a series of bas-relief figures on
large stone slabs. Over 140 of these figures, most of them Negroid
types and Negroid-Mongoloid mixtures, seem to be "swimming
or dancing in a viscous fluid."[16] Some of them are old, bearded
men. They all have closed eyes, open mouths and are completely
nude.

On closer inspection, we find that this is no ritual dance at all
but men crumpled into grotesque postures by mortal agony. As
Michael Coe has pointed out, "the curiously distorted posture of
the limbs, the open mouth and closed eyes indicate that they are
corpses."[17] Other evidence, such as the mutilation of the sex on
some of the figures, with a depiction of "blood streaming in flow-
ery patterns from the severed part" suggests that they were violently killed. The fact that these "corpses" were given greater
prominence than any other figures at Monte Albán is partly responsible for Michael Coe's assertion that they were "undoubtedly
chiefs and kings slain by the earliest rulers of Monte Albán."[18]

We are therefore left with a picture of a group of Negroid and
Negroid-Mongoloid elements, a second or third generation of the
original visitors to La Venta, migrating southwest to Monte Albán,
only to meet with a violent end. Whatever happened to this migratory group, it did not spell the end to the influence of the Negroid
element in early American cultures. This influence, as marked by
the distribution of the Negroid colossi, radiated outward from
La Venta into Tres Zapotes and San Lorenzo in Vera Cruz. In the
southeastern corner of Vera Cruz, the state where the largest of
the Negroid colossi were found, archaeologists have turned up an
Egyptian bas-relief carving of a Semite on the back of a Totonac
slate mirror.[19] In Monte Albán itself, where the Negroid dancers
or death figures were engraved, carvings closely resembling an

Egyptian sphinx and the Egyptian god Ra, in its bird aspect, appear at the same location.[20] Furthermore, when we move with the wave of Olmec culture sweeping slowly down through that narrow corridor of land that joins the two Americas, linking Mexico in the north with the world of Peru in the south, we come upon the most concrete evidence of an Egyptian presence. This is a find of "patently Egyptian statuettes" buried three meters deep in the eastern beaches of Acajutla in San Salvador.[21] John Sorenson has documented the find, which is now on exhibit in the Museo Nacional "David J. Guzman," San Salvador. A stratum three meters deep brings us clearly within the centuries of the Negro-Egyptian contact with the Olmec world.

What has been made of all this? What theories have been advanced to account for the presence of Negroes in ancient America and for Egyptian and Mediterranean elements in the Olmec heartland? Speculations about an Egyptian influence on pre-Christian America go back almost to the beginnings of Egyptology, long before the discovery and dating of the Negroid heads and Egyptian statuettes in Middle America. These speculations sprang, however, from the pens of romantics, dazzled by sensational legends of the lost city of Atlantis, or facile diffusionists, who saw the world as one vast ecumene and made sweeping claims for all kinds of Old World presences in America, building up their case on the most superficial resemblances, cultural items drawn from all time levels and all possible and impossible places. In their open game of fantasy they jumped at a hundred items belonging to no one cultural milieu or social complex, no particular or definitive period in Old World history. The truth was that until 1955–56, when carbon datings were at last obtained at the La Venta site, these impatient gentlemen were pounding at a closed door. We were only given the keys to this mysterious chamber of history three decades ago.

Constance Irwin was the first writer to make known to the general public some of the implications of these discoveries. Before her book appeared in 1963, only a few archaeologists knew about these heads, and the information was relegated to technical journals. Some scholars, finding it embarrassing to their already settled notions of American history, chose to ignore its existence. Some concentrated on the Caucasoid-type figure (nicknamed Uncle Sam) rejoicing in the belief that they had at last found proof of "a white god of civilization," turning a blind eye on the massive Negroid figures standing beside him. Some picked upon the one smiling Negroid face among the quaternity of heads, nicknaming it "Baby-face" so as to blur the obvious and inescapable distinction between the colossal, realistic representations of the aliens in stone and the smooth, dwarflike Mongoloid figures in clay and jadeite littered beside them. These little figures, in contrast, were stylized in the typical jaguar motif of the Olmecs, with snarling, feline mouths, sexless bodies and infantile faces. Thus has a generation of scholars contrived to silence and side-step these uncomfortable discoveries.

Irwin stepped into the breach with a bold and plausible theory which seemed at first to tie up most of the pieces. She began by looking closely at strange cultural items on these figures. The blacks wore dome-shaped covers on their heads which looked like "football helmets" or "upturned kettles."[22] The large Caucasoid figure (nicknamed Uncle Sam by archaeologists) wore "turned-up shoes." With respect to the latter, Miss Irwin pointed out that there were only three peoples in the ancient world during this time that wore turned-up shoes. These were the Etruscans, the Hittites and the Phoenicians.[23] The Etruscans, she claimed, though she hedged this in with qualifiers, were "the least likely to have found their way to American shores." The Hittites were "land-bound," but apart from that, their empire had disintegrated at the critical period of contact, and they were dispersed in refugee pockets among their neighbors in the Mediterranean with whom they not only intermingled but intermarried. Among their neighbors were the Phoenicians, to whom the Hittite custom of turned-up shoes diffused.[24] The Phoenicians were, by a simple process of elimination, the most logical choice for the identity of the Mediterranean-type figure at La Venta. Moreover, they had a good navy. They were trading along the Mediterranean seeking metal supplies from places far distant from their island complex. To cap it all, a model of the ancient Phoenician god Melkart had turned up in Rio Balsas, Mexico.[25]

Miss Irwin then posed the critical question. What did the Phoenicians have to do with the Negroid figures dominating the La Venta ceremonial site? For the answer, she turned to an Assyrian source which described Phoenician ambassadors and their servants coming to pay tribute to the Assyrian court (circa 849 B.C.) The source describes the headgear of the servants who "*bore* kettles on their heads *like* caps"[26] (italics added). Since one or two people had casually mentioned that the Negroid stone figures at La Venta wore what looked like "upturned kettles," Miss Irwin pounced on the image and suggested that these figures were "a cargo of captured blacks" whom the Phoenicians had turned into their servants, hence the kettle-like caps.[27]

Let us look at her source closely. Nowhere does it mention blacks as servants of the Phoenicians. The Phoenicians in this quotation came to pay tribute to their Assyrian overlords. They were in a state of humble vassalage during the period dated by the quotation (circa 849 B.C.) when the Nubian blacks had gained full independence from Egypt. These blacks in this historical period were servants of no one. The Phoenicians remained in that lowly state all during the time the blacks moved to a position of ascendancy from the ninth to the seventh century B.C. The Phoenicians, in fact, during the whole first phase of La Venta culture, right down to 680 B.C., were either vassals of Assyria or mercenaries and protected traders of a Nubian-controlled Egypt. What is more, the quotation has been ingeniously stretched to convey the impression that the kettles were worn rather than borne. A full unprejudiced reading simply shows us that every available carrying space on these porter-servants was weighted down with tribute. They bore trays of sweetmeats in their hands, boxes laden with blue wool and ingots of gold, silver and lead on their shoulders, and kettles (that is, receptacles of liquid or solid food) on their heads.[28] They *bore* not wore these "kettles," and the word "like" in the phrase "like caps" comes to mean "in the place of," "in the manner of," and *not* "serving the same function as." This style of porterage, in which the head is covered or "capped" by pots or kettles or saucepans of food, is quite common to many cultures. One does not have to be a clever linguist to see how forced and inauthentic the association is.

But there is something else that led to Irwin's assumption that these Negroes were "a cargo of captured blacks." After the Assyrians drove the Nubians out of Egypt, they installed a vassal king, Necho. His successor, Necho II (609–593 B.C.), assumed mastery of Egypt when Assyrian power was on the decline. He hired Phoenician navigators to circle Africa to see if such a thing were possible. They started out from the Red Sea port of Ezion-Geber, proceeded down along the east coast of Africa, rounded the Cape, sailed up along the west coast and entered the Mediterranean through the straits of Gibraltar, returning thus to Egypt.[29] The round-trip took them three years. Evidence for the authenticity of this trip lies in a very strange reading of the sun's position taken when rounding the Cape, a reading which could not have been invented, the validity of which has been crosschecked by later navigators.[30] What Irwin is suggesting is that somewhere around this time "613–580 B.C." (her dates), when the Phoenicians were getting acquainted with Africa, they took some West Africans captive, brought them aboard ship, turned them into their servants (put on the kettle cap) and got themselves blown off-course to America.

There are three objections to this theory. First of all, it is nearly a hundred years later than the latest possible date for the arrival of the Negroid figures at La Venta (680 *not* 580 B.C.). Her downdating is largely influenced by the fact that it was a more favorable period for Phoenician enterprise at sea. I have already pointed to Stirling's evidence that the oracular Negroid figure belongs to the first phase of the construction of the ceremonial site and to the joint report of Drucker, Heizer and Squier indicating that there was no significant change of culture in the succeeding phases. To place the arrival of the outsiders—and their cultural impact—in the second phase, therefore, is irresponsible. Secondly, if the Phoenicians had made servants of the blacks, why were these so-called "captives" and "servants" given such prominence among the native Americans, dwarfing their so-called masters? There were eleven Negroid colossi in all found in the Olmec world. Four of these dominated the La Venta site. Against these massive figures was one major Mediterranean-type Caucasoid.[31] The Mediterranean figure with beard is seven feet in height, carved on a stele which he shares with a headless companion. This is a flat representation or drawing, whereas the Negroid heads are full-bodied realistic sculptures of great size, nearly ten times larger than life. Do people build monuments and altars and oracles to slaves which surpass in significance, size and number those representing their masters? Here is no attempt whatever to perceive the relationship created by the historical realities of the period. All we have, in spite of a revolutionary pre-Columbian find, is a reactionary post-Columbian reflex. Black man found standing beside white man. Relationship? Black man obviously servant or captive or slave. White man obviously master. History in this conception has not changed one whit. 676 B.C. 1976 A.D. Races and people seem frozen in an immemorial stance.

Thirdly, the very "kettle-cap" which was conveniently clamped upon the heads of the black colossi to bring them down to size as "servants," turns out, upon examination, to be the type of battle helmet the Nubians and Egyptians wore in the contact period. This may be demonstrated by a relief from the Temple of Ramses III at Medinet Habu, Thebes, where a naval battle is in progress between the Egyptians (who wear these helmets with earflaps), while the enemy wear crests (the Philistine soldiers) and horned helmets (the Sherden soldiers).[32]

James Bailey recognizes these helmets as military apparel but falls, by virtue of the same automatic racial reflex, into the same trap as Irwin. He conceives of the blacks in ancient America as "mercenary troops" of the Phoenicians. It does not occur to him that the Phoenicians were the mercenaries of the Egyptians and that in the period in question they were in no position to make mercenaries of anyone—least of all the blacks, who, as the then rulers of Egypt, were their protectors against a common enemy, the Assyrians. He talks glibly about the planting of Phoenician colonies along the seaboard of West Africa, circa 425 B.C.[33] Not only is the period too late for our consideration, but the kind of "master-mercenary" relationship he envisions between the Phoenicians and the blacks has no foundation in history. Moreover, a great number of these so-called "colonizers" of West Africa were killed, absorbed or turned into captives and slaves.[34] Even if, to flatter his fantasy, we were to assume that the Phoenicians paid Africans to join their fleet and fight native Americans for their territory, why should these people, crushed and humiliated by black mercenaries, build altars and monuments to them? Out of gratitude for being "civilized"? It's the old colonial fairy story. Its patent absurdity may not strike a man who can refer with insensitive and myopic dogmatism to "Africa that never, outside Egypt, came to anything momentous."[35]

One cannot deny, however, the imagination and scholarship of these two writers. Miss Irwin is sound and cautious on most things. James Bailey, though he trafficks in sensational superficialities, has done some impressive research. He throws a wide net over Bronze Age civilizations and brings up a rich catch of relevant and irrelevant oddities. Both share, however, the same basic weakness: an inability to look through the window of ancient history with eyes untinted by the ethnocentric dyes of their day. They and others have begun to provide a new script for the pre-Columbian drama of America. All the characters in the Old World seem to have been given new lines—all except the Negro.

What was the impact of these aliens (the Negroid and Mediterranean figures) upon Olmec culture? How can we distinguish between what they found on their arrival and what they brought with them? How can a responsible list of loans be drawn up that we may deem a reliable index of cultural contact and influence? Vague coincidences abound. We must be wary. Facile comparisons have led romantic diffusionists to claim an Old World origin for almost everything found on American soil, from the universal legend of the Flood down to the simple bow and arrow.[36] How can we avoid the Scylla of radical "diffusionism" on the one hand and the Charybdis of reactionary "isolationism" on the other?

A fairly safe guideline may be set up to pilot us through this perilous minefield. This guideline counsels us to be time-specific and culture-specific; to cite evidence, where possible, of a long evolution of the habit, artifact, system or technique in the area of the donor and to demonstrate a lack of known antecedents in that of the recipient; to consider levels of "identity in complexity" as against superficial stylistic similarity; to think in terms not of single traits but of complexes or clusters of interlocking parallels.

A number of important items may be seen to survive this critical test.

Let us consider, first of all, the pyramids. They have a very long history in the Mediterranean world. The type found in America— the step-pyramid—may be traced to ancient Babylon and Egypt. It is also known by the name of ziggurat. The ziggurat, step-pyramid or stepped temple is as distinctive a type of religious architecture as a Chinese pagoda or a Mohammedan mosque. It has been found nowhere in the Old World without clear and incontestable proof of diffusion. It goes back three thousand years before Christ. Among the most noted Egyptian step-pyramids are the Pyramid of Djoser at Saqqara (2750 B.C.) and the Pyramid of Medum built for the Pharaoh Sneferu (2700 B.C.).[37] There were no pyramids in America before the "contact period" (800–680 B.C.). The very first American pyramid, or stepped temple, appears at La Venta, the site of the colossal Negroid heads and the stele on which is carved the Mediterranean-type figure with beard and turned-up shoes.[38] Other notable step-pyramids in America are the Pyramid of Cholula, dedicated to Quetzalcoatl (150 B.C.) and the Pyramid of the Sun at Teotihuacán near Mexico City. We should also mention the Cerro Colorado Pyramid in the Chicama Valley in northern Peru, where the influence of the visitors to the Gulf of Mexico later diffused.

It would appear from the above that the major criterion has been met. There is clear evidence of long evolution of a unique architectural configuration in the area from which the aliens are presumed to have come and no evidence of antecedents in the area where they landed. Suddenly in the "contact" period the ziggurat or stepped temple (a particular kind of Babylonian/ Egyptian pyramid) begins to appear in America, and not only is the design identical but, like its presumed prototype, it is sun-star oriented and encircled by a precinct. Not only are the shape and

religious function the same but also the astronomical and spa-
tial relationships.[39] There is, however, one serious objection. The
Egyptians, it would appear, had stopped building pyramids (since
1600 B.C.), particularly this kind of pyramid. In other words, the
American pyramid, if it were influenced by aliens in the "contact"
period, would have had to come from an architect in the migrant
group who was nostalgically returning to classical or early Egyptian architecture. The heyday of the Egyptian step-pyramid was
long over.

Over in Egypt, yes, but not in Nubia. The black kings of Nubia
built the last of the Egyptian-type pyramids above their tombs
(small but elegant copies) and the last of the stepped temples for
sun worship. They also rebuilt and restored a great number of
temples which had fallen into disrepair. Nostalgia for the religious
and architectural past of Egypt was strong in Piankhy and Taharka. Piankhy rebuilt the great temple of Amon, originally built
by Thutmosis III and IV, with additions by Ramses II.[40] Taharka
erected a magnificent colonnade in the great forecourt of the temple at Karnak. One of these columns is still standing today. He
also restored halls of "hypostyle" columns in the great temple of
Amon-Ra at Jebel Barkal.[41] The hypostyle or "forest of columns"
is another architectural feature which we find appearing in America after the "contact" period. Like the Egyptians (and the native
Americans) the Nubians oriented all their religious structures on
earth to cardinal points in the heavens. To assist in his architectural schemes Taharka in 684 B.C. called in "four experts in reckoning the time by star-transits and their astronomical instruments
are mentioned."[42]

Many of these temples have been beaten into the dust by time,
but even as late as 593 B.C. a successor of Taharka (Aspelta) built
the sun temple at Meroe which Herodotus calls The Table of the
Sun. It is the stepped type of temple, and fragments of its ruins
may still be found. A flight of stone steps or Jacob's ladder takes
us up to the platform at the summit, and a colonnade encloses the
sanctuary. Reliefs on the walls of this sun temple have motifs that
occur on similar temples in ancient Egypt and America, like those
showing conquered prisoners supporting the royal foot.[43]

Mummification is another extremely interesting case which merits close examination. Few mummies have been unearthed in ancient Mexico because of the corrosive humidity but we have indisputable proof of Mexican mummification nonetheless. One of the best examples is the mummified figure in the sarcophagus at Palenque. Three features of this Palenque burial indicate an Egyptian influence. The jade mask on the face of the dead, the fact of mummification itself, and the flared base of the sarcophagus. With respect to the latter, it should be noted that Egyptians made sarcophagi with a flared base to enable them to stand it up because their burials were vertical. The Egyptians built their mummy cases of wood, and these cases were often stood on end, the "flared base" feature affording them stability in the standing position.[44] The Mexicans, like the Nubians, buried in a horizontal position, yet at Palenque the flared base is retained although it serves no function.[45] The retention of such a nonfunctional element (especially when, as in this case, considerable time and effort went into chiseling the flared base out of stone) is among the clearest indications of an influence. A borrowed artifact often goes through an initial period of "slavish imitation" before it is restructured to suit local needs. Both horizontal and vertical burials occur in the royal graveyards of Nubia. Egyptian and native Nubian burial customs coexist for a while and then fuse. Arkell has noted that the more Egyptian the burial the poorer are the grave furnishings, indicating that the black kings, whose tombs, though plundered, are obviously much richer, retained around them a nucleus of Egyptian assistants—architects, scribes, priests.[46]

Egyptian mummification techniques (which originated in predynastic Black Africa and were developed and refined in the dynastic period) are most in evidence in Peru. There, in the desert sands, we find very specific and ample evidence of the Egyptian influence. Evidence of mummification, however, is widespread in ancient North America as the practice diffused from the Mexican heartland. "The Indian tribes of Virginia, of North Carolina, the Congarees of South Carolina, the Indians of the Northwest coast of Central America and those of Florida practiced this custom as well as the Incas . . . In Colombia the inhabitants of Darien used

to remove the viscera and fill the body cavity with resin, after-
wards they smoked [that is, fumigated] the body and preserved
it in their houses . . . The Muiscas, the Aleutians, the inhabitants
of Yucatan and Chiapas also embalmed the bodies of their kings,
of their chiefs and of their priests by similar methods."[47]

Dr. Haddon, in 1908, showed that certain refined techniques in
mummification, which were later found in America and also in
East and West Africa and the Canary Islands, "were not adopted
in Egypt until the time of the XXIst dynasty" [1090–945 B.C.].[48]
Some scholars have claimed that the practice of mummification
diffused to America from Asia, but Elliot-Smith has very ably
demonstrated the early spread of this practice to the Far East from
Egypt. As we shall go on to show, the identity of the Egyptian
with the American technical formula in some places rules out an
Asian middle man preceding the Nubian-Egyptian, because it is
not simply the act or practice of mummification which is in question, but the transmission of an "identity in complexity" of the
technical formula.

Mummification as a chemical process had been taken to such a
state of refinement in Egypt that in March, 1963, biologists at
the University of Oklahoma confirmed that the skin cells of the
ancient Egyptian princess Mene were capable of living. The ancient Egyptians, after thousands of years, had come close to the
threshold of the secret of physical immortality. The chemical formula by which this remarkable state of preserving Princess Mene
was achieved had been arrived at through centuries of experimentation. Yet we find in Peru not only the same manner of evis-
ceration through the anus and the same manner of swaddling the
corpse in ritual bandages but, according to Professor L. Ruetter,
who has made an analysis of embalming mixtures in Peru "the
antiseptic substances [used in embalming] are *identical* with those
used in ancient Egypt . . . balsam, menthol, salt, tannin, alkaloids,
saponins and undetermined resins."[49] The ingredients are common
enough. The formula is very complex and elusive.

What is perhaps even more astonishing is that the Egyptians
buried parts of the corpse in four Canopic jars. These were called
Horus jars, since they were dedicated to the Horuses of the four

cardinal points. Certain internal organs were placed in the North jar (small viscera) the South jar (stomach and large intestines) the West jar (liver and gall) and the East jar (heart and lungs). Colors were assigned to these cardinal points. This color configuration associated with the Horus jars reappears in the cardinal color scheme of ancient Mexico. Thus we have a Red North in ancient Egypt and Mexico, a White South, a Dark West (black in Egypt, blue in Mexico) and a Golden East (yellow is the equivalent color for gold in Mexico).[50] This is no simple accident. Chinese and other Asian aboriginal color schemes differ radically in this connection.

Moreover, mummies examined in ancient Peru toward the end of the Olmec phase of civilization show that foreign elements, both Negroid and Caucasoid, seem to have entered the native South American population (400–300 B.C.). Dr. M. Trotter, doing a hair analysis on pieces of scalp from Paracas mummies in Peru, reported in 1943 that "the cross-section form shows so much divergency between the different mummies that they cover *all* divisions of hair form."[51] Dr. Trotter, under cross-questioning by Thor Heyerdahl, indicated that hair color and texture need alter only slightly through post-mortem dehydration and fading. Also, an examination of skeletons in the area, simultaneously conducted by T. D. Stewart, demonstrated the presence of races of greater average height and a different cephalic index (head shape) than the aboriginal Americans. Heyerdahl's questioning of Trotter, and his interview with the mummy specialist W. R. Dawson elicited information that can clearly establish the Mediterranean presence in America through these mummies, but his overwhelming desire to prove the Europoid presence (probably Phoenician) makes him defensively selective in presenting his information, which equally suggests Negroid elements, mulatto curly-haired Egyptians, and a good deal of racial intermixtures.[52]

Dogs were also mummified by the Egyptian Pharaohs. The Nubian kings, on the other hand, were fascinated by horses, and Piankhy (who raged after his victory at Hermopolis because his horses had been badly fed during the siege) started burying horses in the royal graves instead. The full team of four that drew the

royal chariot were buried beside the king and, though the grave-
robbers stripped the chariots of their useful parts, remains of the
rich trappings were found—including plume-carriers, silver head-
bands, beads and amulets.[53] Yet, in spite of this departure from
the Egyptian type of burial, the coexistence of the two cultures
was preserved by a symbolic Nubian homage to the dog. The
Egyptian dog-headed god, Anubis, graces the Nubian funerary
offering tables. These offering tables found in the graves, with
invocations to the gods written in the Nubian script (Meroitic),
show the goddess Nephthys and the dog-headed god Anubis, both
concerned with the cult of the dead, pouring libations.[54] In this
very period the Olmecs begin to sculpt little clay dogs attached
to wheels or to tiny chariots with wheels.[55] In this peculiar blend
of dog and chariot lies virtually their only use of the wheel. The
lack of the horse or other draught animals of comparable size
precluded a more practical use. How they struck upon this ritual
association (dog/wheeled chariot) is an intriguing question. The
full-blown Egyptian practice, however, of mummifying dogs has
been found in Peru. What is even more intriguing is that these
dogs mummified in Peru do not all look like the typical American
spitz and husky types. Some look uncannily like the *basenji*, the
species of Egyptian dog worshiped by the Pharaohs.[56]

The only surviving species of this dog is found today in Africa
(where it is used by the pygmies of the Ituri forest to track and
chase game). It is a very distinctive type, with regal appearance,
stands with feet well apart and ears so taut that they look like
webbed antennae. This dog became a great pet in ancient Egypt
because it has no body odor and it makes no noise. It is known
as the barkless dog.[57] It is upon this animal that the dog-headed
god of Egypt and Nubia was modeled. Columbus reports a species
of barkless dog during his voyages to the Caribbean.[58] The *basenji*
answers to the description in his journals.

Other similarities in burial customs have been noted, such as
twisted rope designs on sarcophagi, golden mummy masks (such
as the Chimu mask of Peru), and a small hole in the top slabs of
death chambers for the release of the soul or the flight of the "bird
of death." Twisted rope designs are first noted in America on

Altar One of the La Venta site, and they later appear on Mexican coffins.[59] The style, according to one investigator (Bailey) is "North Syrian"; the resemblance is rather superficial, although it is not difficult to conceive of a member of the ancient party carrying it over from that area, which neighbored the Egyptian-Phoenician states. With respect to the golden mummy masks, coffins cast in Nubian gold with the detailed features of the mummified kings are not unknown in Egypt (an example is the golden coffin of Tutankhamen, with elaborate facial detail).[60] The golden mummy mask, as such, however, is not common to either Egypt or Nubia (though in the latter case these masks might have disappeared with the plundered mummies, since the golden mummy mask as a ritual practice appears later in the tombs of African chiefs and kings).[61] Irwin has suggested a Phoenician influence for the golden mummy mask in Mexico, and this cannot be ruled out.[62] The Phoenicians, though mercenary seamen in this period in the pay of the Nubian-Egyptian forces, were an element in the mixed party. While they were obviously of a lower order of importance, as the Olmec sculptures suggest, they must have had some influence. Golden mummy masks appear in some of the Phoenician tombs, though mummification was only practiced in Phoenicia occasionally, and in a much cruder form than in Egypt. The holes in death chambers for the flight of the soul or death bird[63] are not on the same level of uniqueness or ritual complexity as other burial customs we have discussed, and could quite easily have been a coincidence.

One other burial practice common to ancient Egypt and Mexico is worth mentioning, if only for the sake of showing how carefully we must apply our test in the study of cultural similarities. This burial ritual involved the placing of a green stone in the mouth of the corpse. Both the Egyptians and the Mexicans saw this green stone as a symbol of the heart and as the prolonger of life. The Egyptians, among whom it took the form of a green scarab, addressed it thus: "My heart, my mother—my heart whereby I came into being." The Mexicans placed the *chalchiutl* (green amulet) between the lips of the deceased, and they also associated it with life-restorative properties. In fact, they called it "the principle of life."[64] The green stone in the mouth of the dead, however, is a very primitive ritual indeed—one may even say primordial. It precedes Egyptian civilization by thousands of years. It was found between the teeth of some of the Cro-Magnon skeletons in the Grimaldi caves near Menton.[65]

The very ancient Chinese also placed green jade amulets in the mouth to preserve the body from decay. Pearls and shells, as mouth amulets of the dead, were substituted for jade: pearls for feudal lords, shells for ordinary officials, jade reserved for stuffing the mouths of dead emperors.[66] Since we find such a custom in vogue even as far back as the Aurignacian stage of Cro-Magnon culture, it might well have traveled from Asia to America in the glacial epoch, when the very first Americans crossed over to this continent on the bridge of ice in their two major migrations, now calculated to be forty thousand and twenty-five thousand years ago.

Some ritual practices that are almost identical in America and Egypt, which we may safely date from the Olmecs onward and which point to an outside influence, are the wearing of false beards by high priests, the ritual use of purple as an exclusively royal and priestly color, incest between royal siblings and a complex of royal paraphernalia, such as the ceremonial umbrella and litter and the bird-serpent motif in coats of arms and royal diadems (for the latter, see Chapter 5). Here we have not one but a cluster of closely linked parallels, some of which are unique to these two areas and some of which, like the wearing of artificial beards, are highly unusual among the beardless American Indians. Heyerdahl has, with a graphic brilliance, indicated the statistical improbability of so many parallels occurring in two culture areas independently—especially when they are known to be joined by a marine conveyor belt.

"A single culture element found to appear at both ends of a natural sea route," wrote Heyerdahl, "may very well be the result of coincidence or independent evolution along parallel lines. To become a reasonable indicator of contact, a whole array of identities or similarities of extraordinary nature must be concentrated in the two areas linked by a land bridge or marine conveyor belt.

... What confronts us ... on both side of the Atlantic are arrays of cultural parallels and when these are dealt with as complexes, we are faced by amazing statistical indications ... When the whole list of Mediterranean-American parallels are considered together as an entity then the probability of diffusion rather than independent development does not increase arithmetically but exponentially; for instance, a cluster of twelve parallels grouped together, say, in Mesopotamia and Mexico does not weigh twelve times heavier in the discussion than a single parallel, but rather, according to the laws of probability, has increased its significance by a truly astronomical amount. Among other things, this means that the Isolationist's technique of negating these parallels one by one by labeling them 'coincidence' is mathematically invalid."[67]

The artificial beard worn by kings and priests is one of the ancient mysteries of Mexico, for the native Mexican (as we know him) has no hair on his chin. The Ainu of Japan are hairy Asiatics, and there is evidence for a pre-Columbian presence of Japanese in America. The Ainu could have been one of the earliest American races emigrating to this continent from Asia. Also, the black stream (the Kouro Siwo) has occasionally cast remnants of Japanese crews onto the American Pacific coast. "White, bearded" figures hunted down in a part of sixteenth-century South America were found to be Japanese,[68] and there is evidence (Jomon pottery) for a late pre-Columbian Japanese influence in Ecuador.[69] All this, however, does not seem to explain the high ritual value placed upon the beard. The Pharaohs (and sometimes the high priests) of Egypt and Nubia wore false beards. These were highly stylized appendages, smooth, long and terminating in a blunt, square tuft. The abstract idea of the beard as a badge of high office may have been influenced by Nubian-Egyptian culture, but the literal image of the beard—textured and tapered, as it is usually represented—was inspired no doubt by quite ordinary human figures, figures most likely from the same party of foreigners. Among these, we may consider the Mediterranean Caucasoid figure at La Venta. In fact, he is the only one who has so far been considered as a likely candidate for the influence of the un-American beard. We should also bear in mind that the smooth-chinned

Negroid figures in stone are not the only type of Negro-African who came in during this period. Von Wuthenau has demonstrated through his terra cottas that there were other ancient Negroid figures in America equipped with beards.

Another practice common to Egypt, Nubia and Mexico is that of royal incest. It is unique to these societies. Royal incest among siblings (brother and sister) is the rarest social institution in the world. In spite of the horror incest arouses in all human societies, secret incestuous relationships may be fairly common. But there are only three societies in the world—Egypt, Nubia and Mexico— where incest was actively encouraged in the royal family, incest between full-blooded brother and sister. The black Nubian king Tanutamon, who succeeded Taharka, was the product of such an incestuous union (see Chapter 8). Egyptian royal incest belongs to an earlier period, and therefore we may say that only two societies in the world at that time (800–700 B.C.) practiced royal incest between siblings—Nubia and Mexico.* The Egyptians, who had practiced it in the belief that they were kings of the sun, and that it would keep solar blood from dilution, had abandoned the practice before the "contact" period. The Egyptian pharaohs started to marry Mitannian wives from Hither Asia and thus "broke with purity of solar blood." Thus we find "solar blood diluted in the veins of the Pharaohs at the end of the Twenty-Third dynasty."[71] The black kings of Kush resurrected this custom,[72] and for the very same reason as it was practiced earlier in Egypt and later in Mexico.

Other practices common to the two culture areas are the use of the umbrella and litter as royal prerogatives. Today these items are so common and have such vulgar functions (the umbrella for weather protection, the litter for the sick or wounded) that it is difficult to conceive of their unique *ritual* use and value as an index of high rank in the Egyptian-Nubian and Mexican worlds. Professor Varron has demonstrated the use of the umbrella as an

---

* The royal family of Hawaii also practiced incest, but this solitary exception among the world's societies belongs to a much later period, and was a result of diffusion.

emblem of dignity and power in ancient times,[73] and a visual comparison of the Mexican royal umbrella with that hovering over the black Nubian princes in the tomb painting of Huy, also of the litters used for transport of royalty in Mexico with those used in Mesopotamia,[74] prototypes of the Egyptian litters, startle by their identity of appearance and function.

The religious value of "murex purple" and its use to distinguish priests and kings and people of high rank from the common herd has its origins in the Mediterranean. First evidence of the extraction of the purple dye from the murex shell occurs in Crete in 1600 B.C., but the religious value attached to it was a consequence of the peculiar behavior of the Nile. In ancient Egypt the riddle of life was read in the Nile which, as it rose in flood, turned green, red, and yellowish and then blue. The fluid of the murex shell, barring a tint or two, behaved in almost the same way, turning from a yellowish cream to green, then blue like the Nile before acquiring its final fixed purple. It thus revealed by its sequence of colors (green, yellowish, blue) the various attributes of the Nile deity. This accounts for the enormous sanctity attached to shell purple, which, according to Besnier, was not only considered a noble and sacred color by the Egyptians but "emblematic of the power of the gods."[75]

The Phoenicians of Tyre and Sidon adopted the industry, and "Tyrian purple" became famous in the Mediterranean, particularly in Egypt, with which the Phoenicians did most of their trade. It thenceforth diffused through the Old World. Purple-yielding shells were searched for far and wide, and in the western Mediterranean. Purple-dye centers were established. The Phoenicians obtained from the British Isles, while shipping for their tin in Cornwall, a dark shade of shell purple called "black purple." Kitchen middens in Cornwall have yielded traces of the ancient industry.[76] Traces of the ancient purple industry have also been found in Mexico, and here the same value and function is attached to it, also the same extraordinary association with the conch-shell trumpet to summon the deity.[77]

Mrs. Zelia Nuttall has published a paper entitled "A Curious Survival in Mexico of the use of the Purpura Shell-fish for Dyeing." She shows in the Nuttall Codex "pictures of no fewer than thirteen *women of rank* in Mexico wearing purple skirts, and five with capes and jackets of the same color. In addition, forty five *chieftains* are figured with short, fringed, rounded purple waist-cloths, and there are also three examples of the use of a close-fitting purple cap."[78] Purple-yielding shells, broken for the dyeing industry, have also been taken from Inca graves in North Chile.[79]

Purple is one of those colors that do not come naturally and easily. As J. Wilfred Jackson points out in *Shells as Evidence of the Migration of Early Cultures*, "the method of its production is a complex and difficult process."[80] Moreover, the ancient purple industry, because of its marine nature, was conducted by Mediterranean mariners and became associated with pearl-fishing and the use of the artificially devised conch-shell trumpet. The earliest use of the conch-shell trumpet, according to Professor Elliot-Smith, was in the Minoan worship in Crete, where the purple industry started. From thence it spread far and wide until it came to play a part in religious services in "the Mediterranean, in India, in Central Asia, in Indonesia and Japan, in Oceania and *America* . . . it was supposed to have the definite ritual object of summoning the deity."[81] In addition to the ritual use of the conch-shell trumpet, identical in the Egyptian and American worlds, Jackson finds an intimate relationship between this (purple industry and conch-shell trumpets) with weaving, as well as mining, working and trafficking in metals (gold, silver, copper). In Mexico and Peru the purple industry was also associated with these pursuits.[82]

The ritual use of purple as an index of rank therefore, and the extraction of purple and the religious use of the artificial conch-shell to summon the deity, and the further association of all this with weaving and metal-working, is one of the most remarkable complexes of interlocking parallels found between Mediterannean and ancient New World civilizations. The Phoenician/Egyptian/ Nubian link and joint influence in the mixed crew of shipwrecks is also most clearly seen in this connection. The Egyptian-Nubian religious link to the Nile which gave the murex-purple shell its sanctity, the Phoenician maritime enterprise which exploited the Cretan discovery of the shell-milk as an indelible dye and the conch-shell trumpet as a summoner of the divine, the use of Tyrian purple among the Pharaohs and high priests of Egypt and Nubia are all seen in the later duplication of this royal and priestly use of purple, with all its complex associations, by the Mexicans and Peruvians.

Since weaving and metal-working were among the pursuits associated with the purple-dye manufacturers, weaving techniques, such as the loom, and metallurgical techniques, such as the refined metal-casting process known as the "lost-wax" technique, were carried from one end of the Mediterranean to the other and so diffused through the Old World. An examination of these two technological achievements in the Old World and the New provides us with further proof of an influence.

Although native Americans in Peru were weaving cloth as early as 2500 B.C., they were not using the loom. Dr. Junius Bird discovered cotton fabrics at Huaca Prieta in Peru carbon-dated 2500 B.C., but 78 percent of the three thousand pieces of cotton cloth examined were *twined* and the rest *netted*—two of the simplest methods of producing fabrics without a loom.[83] When a loom of the horizontal type appeared in Peru it was found to be "identical with a horizontal loom depicted in an Egyptian tomb."[84] When the vertical loom appeared in Peru it was "*identical* with those found in a tomb at Thebes,"[85] the sacred capital of the black kings. Both the New World and Old World looms had the same eleven working parts.[86] To be even more specific, it has been shown that "the vertical-frame loom with two warp beams used by the Incas was the same as that used in Egypt in the New Kingdom [Eighteenth to Twentieth Dynasty, circa 1400–1100 B.C.] . . . the second of the two types of Peruvian looms, the horizontal loom staked out on the ground, as used in the Titicaca Basin, was also the same as that of ancient Egypt."[87] Spindle whorls, also used in weaving, were so *identical* in Egypt, the Mexican capital of Tula and in Peru that "laid side by side, *even an expert can scarcely tell them apart*."[88] (Italics added.)

The metal-casting technique known as the lost-wax or *cire perdue* method is far more complex than the loom and far more unlikely to appear in a place where metals were just luxuries, having a ritual rather than a utilitarian value. Metals in Egypt and Nubia could make all the difference to success and defeat in battle, metal-trafficking was one of the mainstays of Phoenician trade, metal-hunger was the inspiration of many maritime explorations and migrations. But the ancient Americans, as Frederick Dellenbaugh has pointed out, "were unacquainted with the *common use* of metals." They worked metals, all right—silver, gold and copper—but "to a limited extent and in an ornamental way."[89] Ancient American weapons are not of copper and bronze but of flint and obsidian and stone. Metals were mainly used to protect and animate the living and the dead and were offered as gems to the gods. There is no archaeological witness to the stages preceding their sudden leap into highly refined casting techniques developed by people producing metals in vast quantities for a mass utility purpose.

It took centuries of experimentation in the Mediterranean, for example, to reduce tin simply to a subsidiary element or alloy in the production of bronze from its sovereignty as a metal in itself. Yet there is not a single object made entirely of tin by the ancient Americans. The Americans jumped that step mysteriously, and we find them (according to C. W. Mead, a curator of Peruvian archaeology, who has analyzed bronze pieces in ancient Peruvian graves), using only 6 or 7 percent of tin in their bronzes, a technical achievement reached by only the best of the Mediterranean bronze-workers (the ancient European bronzes had an average of tin alloys as high as 10 percent).[90]

As for the lost-wax technique, used in Egypt and Nubia (from where it diffused to the Yoruba and Bini of Nigeria via Meroë, capital of the black kings after their retreat from Egypt) it is a technique that appears nowhere in the Old World without some indication of diffusion from the Mediterranean center. Metal-casting is a highly technical operation, and the lost-wax method is far superior to the common "sand-process." It is considered especially good for reproducing faithfully delicate and intricate detail.

The following brief summary of the technique is presented to give some impression of the complexity of the process which has been found copied by the ancient metal-casters of the New World.

The first step in the lost-wax method of casting is the making of a mold which bears, in reverse, the details of the object to be cast. This is usually dusted with finely ground charcoal and made ready for the wax cast. The inside of the mold is painted with molten wax, which is then reinforced with sheets of warm wax pressed against it. The thickness of the wax must be controlled so that it does not exceed the desired thickness of the final cast in bronze, gold or silver. The mold is then taken off, leaving a hollow wax replica. An opening or vent is made in the object to carry off the melting wax during the baking of the final mold. This final mold is made of a heat-resisting semiliquid compound poured into the wax mold to form the core and built up around the outside to form a jacket. The whole thing is put into a blast furnace (even this has been found to be identical in design in Egypt and America)[91] and baked for a couple of days until the wax has melted away. The mold is then removed from the furnace. Molten gold, bronze or silver is poured into the opening in the mold and fills the space left empty by the melting of the (lost) wax cast. When the metal cools, the jacket is broken away and the job is done.[92]

Many of the Mediterranean-type technical processes, burial customs and royal/priestly rituals that mark Olmec culture in the Mexico of the north are found in the Chavin-Cupisnique culture in the Peru of the south. These are contemporary centers of American civilization (early Chavin levels have been carbon-dated 848 ± 167 B.C.) and the movement of major aspects of culture from the one to the other has been clearly established. They even share the central feline motif.[93]

An Egyptian surgical procedure found in both ancient Mexico and Peruvian civilization is trepanning, or trepannation. It was performed on the skulls of Egyptian-Nubian soldiers, among others, to relieve pressure caused by blows on the skull. Hippocrates recommended it in an essay "On Injuries of the Head."[94] Doctors in ancient Egypt, Mexico and Peru removed plaques of bone from the skull, and in many cases the operation was remarkably successful. Skulls examined in Peru indicate absence of signs of infection and a new growth of normal bone in and about the wound. There are very few cases in which post-operative infection of the skull set in, leading to lethal decay, indicated by a vast cavity. An examination of skulls in Egypt, Mexico and Peru upon which this operation was performed show square and circular holes in the skull. The skullbone was penetrated by scraping, cutting or drilling the bone.[95]

The Egyptians have left us their surgical papyri. The surgical books of the New World lie in the thousands of skulls examined in America, particularly in Peru, where the paleontological evidence is more ample. Skull deformation, deliberately practiced by the Egyptian and ancient American upper class to distinguish them physically from their subjects, is another remarkable trait which seems restricted to these two culture areas.[96]

Another shared feature often noted and calling for serious examination is that of "fitted megalithic masonry." The finest examples are found at Gizeh in Egypt, at Lixus in Morocco (where it diffused), at Saccsahuaman and Cuzco in Peru and across the Pacific from Peru, and on Easter Island. The technique calls for considerable skill, since the massive stone blocks fitted together are not of any regular shape or size (not cut into conventional squares, for example) but display the complex regularity of patterns or designs in a jigsaw puzzle. No cement is used in the building of these massive blocks "so wonderfully exact is the masonry work of which they are composed."[97] The identical methods of quarrying in the New and Old Worlds, which Seton Lloyd's study has demonstrated, may account for this extraordinary building technique. Both the ancient Egyptians and Americans quarried stone by "driving wooden wedges into natural faults in the stone, which cracked when the wedges filled with water."[98] It may be that a whole natural wall of stone or a cliff-face was transported in its entirety from the quarry in its separate bits and pieces. This would account for the irregularly divided blocks being put together again by the masons into a tightly fitting pattern. The pieces or blocks were probably broken off the quarry wall at those points where "natural faults" were exploited to break up the stone. They were then reconstructed as one reconstructs the irregularly shaped but naturally fitting pieces of a jigsaw.

Similar responses to a similar problem may lead to an independent but similar solution. There may have been no other practical method by which massive stone blocks could have been quarried in the Old World, though "fitted megalithic masonry" in itself is unique to an area in the Old World where a certain complex of cultural traits has been found. While the method of quarrying stone, therefore, might have been coincidental, this method of building walls and fortifications certainly was not. The identical technique occurred to no other people outside of this interconnected complex.

Far more arbitrary, however, than a construction technique of this unusual nature is the construction of certain of the world's calendars. Even if astronomical science was as advanced in the Olmec world as it was in Egypt and Nubia before the 800–700 B.C. contact, it could not have led to the whole series of coincidences to be observed in one of the Mexican calendars.

The Abbé Hervas, a Franciscan priest, writing to the historian Clavigero, highlights the remarkable conformity between the ancient Egyptian and Mexican calendars. "The Mexican year," the Abbé Hervas wrote, "began upon the 26th of February, a day celebrated in the era of Nabonassar, which was fixed by the Egyptians 747 years before the Christian era;* for the beginning of their month Toth corresponded with the meridian of the same day. If those periods fixed also on this day as an epoch, because it was celebrated in Egypt, we have here the Mexican calendar agreeing with the Egyptian. But independent of this, it is certain that the Mexican calendar conformed greatly with the Egyptian.

"On this subject Herodotus says that the year was first regulated by the Egyptians, who gave to it twelve months, of thirty days, and added five days to every year, that the circle of the year might revolve regularly: that the principal gods of the Egyptians were twelve in number, and that each month was under the tutelage and protection of one of these gods. The Mexicans also added to every year five days, which they called Nemontemi, or useless;

* This celebration of February 26 begins in Egypt in 747 B.C. The Egyptian calendar, as such, began many centuries earlier. The parallel dating of this day and other remarkable correspondences in America gives us the earliest possible date for the contact, which could not be before 747 B.C.

because during these days they did nothing. Plutarch says that on such days the Egyptians celebrated the festival of the birth of the gods."[99]

The Abbé Hervas goes on to show that the Mexican month was in ancient times like the Egyptian, but for some reason the time reckoning was later altered. "The Mexicans received the lunar month from their ancestors but for certain purposes instituted another." Under the first and older system, dating like the Egyptian from 26th February, 747 B.C., the Mexicans arrived at the same total for the year as did the ancient Egyptians—three hundred and sixty days—"a number," as the Abbé Hervas points out, "which from time immemorial has ruled in geometry and astronomy, and is of the utmost particularity on account of its relation to the circle, which is divided into three hundred and sixty parts or degrees."[100]

The Egyptian influence may be traced not only to those three aspects we have noted, namely, the time the Mexicans began to count the years (February 26, 747 B.C.), the twelve lunar mansions corresponding to the twelve Egyptian gods, the five useless or dateless "festival" days. It may also be seen in the symbols of the Mexican months.

"Respecting the symbols of the Mexican months and year," the Abbé Hervas observed, "they discover ideas entirely conformable with those of the ancient Egyptian. The latter distinguished, as appears from their monuments, each month or part of the zodiac, where the sun stood, with characteristical figures of that which happened in every season of the year.

"Therefore we see the signs of Aries, Taurus and the two young goats (which now are Gemini) used to mark the months of the births of those animals; the signs of Cancer, Leo, and Virgo, with the ear of corn, for those months, in which the sun goes backward like a crab, in which there is greater heat, and in which the harvests are reaped. The sign of the Scorpion (which in the Egyptian sphere occupied the space which at present is occupied by the sign of Libra), and that of Sagittarius, in the months of virulent, or contagious distempers . . . and lastly, the signs of Capricorn, Aquarius and Pisces, in those months in which the sun begins to ascend towards others; in which it rains much, and in which there is abundant fishing. These ideas are similar to those which the Mexicans associated with their clime."[101]

Other symbols, extremely arbitrary symbols, have been found in use by both the ancient Egyptians and the Mexicans. The sun devoured or encircled by a serpent is one of these.

"In the Mexican symbol we see the sun as it were eclipsed by the moon and surrounded with a serpent, which makes four twists and embraces the four periods of thirteen years. This very idea of the serpent with the sun has, from time immemorial, signified the periodical or annual course of the sun. We know that in astronomy, the points where the eclipses happen have, from time immemorial, been called the head and tail of a dragon. The Egyptians agree with the Mexicans for to symbolise the sun they employed a circle, with one or two serpents . . . The symbol of the serpent is a thing totally arbitrary to signify the sun, with which it has no physical relation; wherefore then I ask, have nations [which] have had no reciprocal intercourse . . . agreed in using one same symbol so arbitrary, and chose to express it by the same object?"[102]

This, then, is the case for contact between Egypt and the New World in the 800–700 B.C. period,* a period in which the blacks of Nubia had gained ascendancy over the Egyptian empire and appeared, according to carbon-14 datings, in the Olmec world of Mexico as monumental figures, venerated and revered. These are some of the important influences this alien crew of shipwrecks left upon the face of ancient American culture. Many other claims have been made, but we have confined ourselves to those that can pass a rigorous test and eliminated those such as the Egyptian sandal of coiled rope, the Egyptian throwing stick, the simple fishhook and blowgun, also all so-called similarities in art styles *as such* or symbols without a complex history rooted in particular circumstances originating in the Egyptian/Mediterranean world. A critical but open-minded skepticism is needed in these com-

---

* See *Postscript on Other Finds* for further evidence of an African-Egyptian presence and influence in America.

parative studies if we are to lift the tenor of the debate on pre-Columbian contacts between Africa and the New World from the level of the fanciful and the romantic.

All the features of Egyptian culture noted above were duplicated in the Nubian-Egyptian culture complex of the Twenty-Fifth Dynasty. This phenomenon of separate yet parallel identity emerges with a great clarity when the historical and archaeological data of the period are closely examined. The master-colonial relationship between Egypt and Nubia had ceased. Nubia became the inheritor and custodian of a culture which took as much from black Africa as black Africa was later to take from it. Nubia was so much a part of Egypt that, as Professors Steindorff and Seele have pointed out, "it tenaciously held fast to Egyptian culture in later times when Egypt herself succumbed to foreign influences. When the Greeks came into the valley of the Nile in the seventh century B.C. it was Nubia which was considered the seat of orthodox Egyptian character."[103]

NOTES AND REFERENCES

1 Matthew W. Stirling, "Discovering the New World's Oldest Dated Work of Man," *National Geographic Magazine*, Vol. 76 (August, 1939), pp. 183–218.
2 Idem.
3 Idem.
4 Idem.
5 Robert Wauchope, "A Tentative Sequence of Pre-Classic Ceramics in Middle America," Tulane University, *Middle American Research Institute*, Publication 15, 1950, 238.
6 Constance Irwin, *Fair Gods and Stone Faces*, St. Martin's Press, 1963, p. 139.
7 Stirling, op. cit.
8 Irwin, op. cit., p. 141.
9 Stirling, "Great Stone Faces of the Mexican Jungle," *National Geographic Magazine*, Vol. 78, Sept., 1940, pp. 327–328. "If any extensive gap of time exists between the various monu-

ments on the site," Stirling said, "it appears to me this stone must have been the oldest at La Venta."

10 Philip Drucker, Robert F. Heizer and Robert J. Squier, "Radiocarbon dates from La Venta, Tabasco," *Science*, Vol. 126, July 12, 1957, pp. 72–73.

11 Idem.

12 A. J. Arkell, *A History of the Sudan*, University of London, Athlone Press, 1955, p. 108.

13 See the Stirling quote at Note 9.

14 Drucker, Heizer and Squier, loc. cit.

15 Michael Coe, *Mexico*, New York, Praeger Publishers, 1962, p. 92.

16 Ibid., p. 95.

17 Idem.

18 Idem.

19 This is reproduced in Thor Heyerdahl, "The Bearded Gods Speak" in Gordon Ashe (ed.) *The Quest for America*, New York, Praeger Publishers, 1971, p. 230; also James Bailey, *The God-Kings and the Titans*, New York, St. Martin's Press, 1973, p. 53.

20 Irwin, op. cit. p. 63.

21 John Sorenson, *Dialogue* 4, No. 2, Summer 1969, pp. 80–94.

22 Irwin (on likeness to helmets), p. 141; (on likeness to kettles), p. 122ff.

23 Irwin, pp. 148–154.

24 Idem.

25 See reproductions of this, with claims for Phoenician associations, in Irwin, p. 176; Bailey, op. cit., p. 53; Heyerdahl, op. cit., p. 230; and Alexander von Wuthenau, *The Art of Terracotta Pottery in Pre-Columbian Central and South America*, New York, Crown Publishers, 1969, p. 76. Von Wuthenau identifies this as the Phoenician god, Bes, the others as the god Melkart.

26 Irwin, op. cit., p. 154, quoted from A. T. Olmstead, *History of Palestine and Syria*, New York, Scribner's, 1931, pp. 375–376.

27 Irwin, op. cit., p. 157.

28 Olmstead, op. cit.

29 A concise outline of this journey, with a conjectural chart, may be found in J. V. Luce, "Ancient Explorers" in Gordon Ashe (ed.) *The Quest for America*, pp. 78–79.

30 Idem. They found the sun on their right as they sailed westward around the Cape of Good Hope.

31 For a reproduction of this Mediterranean-type figure on the La Venta stele, see Heyerdahl in Ashe, op. cit., p. 233 (Illus. 203).

32 See naval battle of Ramses III (Medinet Habu) in George Steindorff and Keith Seele, *When Egypt Ruled the East*, Fig. 99, p. 255. A better impression, though of only one section, is to be found in Bailey, op. cit., p. 251.

33 Bailey, op. cit., p. 43.

34 A hint of the fate of some of these explorers may be found in M. D. W. Jeffreys, "How Ancient is West African Maize," *Africa*, Jan., 1963, p. 116, where pale-skinned captives are placed on the auction block for sale. Bailey himself notes in his book *The God-Kings and the Titans*, p. 189, the absorption of the Phoenician into the gene pool of the African.

35 Bailey, op. cit., p. 77.

36 To demonstrate the range and shallowness of claims made by some of the extreme diffusionists, J. H. Rowe in his article "Diffusion and Archaeology," *American Antiquity*, Jan. 1966, lists sixty so-called parallels between the Mediterranean and Ancient America. The list, while mentioning a number of startling identicals (which Rowe could not see as evidence of contact because of his belief that the sea journey from the Old World to the New was impossible), attempts to make mock of the diffusionist case by also including such silly generalities as ducks raised for food, regular discipline in armies, animal excrement used for manure and domestic animals for pack transport.

37 On the question of the possible origin of pyramid-building in Egypt, see Chancellor Williams, *The Destruction of Black Civilization*, Chicago, The Third World Press, 1974. Williams

claims that prototypes for these lay in the early three-chambered brick mastabas the Ethiopians built for burial (pp. 67, 73).

38 Coe, op. cit., p. 87.

39 Peter Tompkins, *Secrets of the Great Pyramid*, New York, Harper and Row, 1971.

40 Arkell, op. cit., p. 124.

41 Ibid., p. 130.

42 Ibid., p. 132.

43 P. L. Shinnie, *Meroe, A Civilization of the Sudan*, New York, Praeger Publishers, 1967, p. 82.

44 Irwin, op. cit., p. 95.

45 Cyrus Gordon, *Before Columbus*, New York, Crown Publishers, 1971, p. 195, Note 33.

46 Arkell, op. cit., pp. 120–121.

47 G. Elliot-Smith, *The Migrations of Early Culture*, London, 1915, and Donald Mackenzie, *Myths of Pre-Columbian America*, London, Gresham Publishing Co., 1924, pp. 104, 105.

48 Idem.

49 L. Ruetter, *Bulletin et Memoires Société d'Anthropologie*, 1915 (6th series, vi), p. 288.

50 Mackenzie, op. cit., pp. 72, 79.

51 Heyerdahl, in Ashe (ed.) *The Quest for America*, p. 206.

52 Ibid., pp. 203–207.

53 Arkell, op. cit., p. 124.

54 Shinnie, op. cit., pp. 113, 114.

55 See Gordon F. Eckholm, "Wheeled Toys in Mexico," *American Antiquity*, II, 1946, pp. 222–228. But also see Bailey, op. cit., p. 142. Bailey reports solid stone wheels excavated at Tiahuanaco "probably for moving the cyclopean blocks of stone used in building."

56 Heyerdahl, op. cit., p. 137.

57 Background material on the *basenji*, which is now becoming as popular among dog breeders in America as it was among the kings of ancient Egypt, may be found in Jack Shafer and Bob Mankey, *How to Raise and Train a Basenji*, New York, Crown Publishers, 1966.

58 Cecil Jane, *The Voyages of Christopher Columbus*, London, 1930, pp. 164, 338.

59 Irwin, op. cit., p. 159; Bailey, op. cit., p. 51.

60 An example is the gold coffin of Tutankhamen (Cairo Museum). See reproduction in Denison Ross, *The Art of Egypt through the Ages*, p. 203.

61 Bailey, op. cit., p. 190, which see for fine reproduction of the golden mummy mask of an Ashanti king.

62 Irwin, op. cit., p. 94.

63 Bailey, op. cit., p. 74.

64 Mackenzie, op. cit., pp. 206, 207.

65 Ibid., p. 206.

66 Ibid., p. 207.

67 Heyerdahl, op. cit., pp. 123, 124.

68 Alphonse de Quatrefages, *The Human Species*, New York, Appleton, 1905, pp. 205, 206.

69 R. Pearson, "Migration from Japan to Ecuador: The Japanese Evidence," *American Anthropology*, 70, 1968, pp. 85–86.

70 Irwin, pp. 136ff.

71 Alexandre Moret, *The Nile and Egyptian Civilization*, New York, Alfred A. Knopf, 1927, p. 316.

72 Arkell, op. cit., p.121.

73 A. Varron, "The Umbrella as an Emblem of Dignity and Power," *Ciba Review*, 9, 1942, p. 42.

74 For a comparison of royal litters in ancient Mexico and the Mediterranean, see S. Miles in G. R. Willey (ed.) *The Archaeology of Southern MesoAmerica*, 3, 1966, pp. 237–273, and A. L. Oppenheim, "The Mesopotamian Temple" in *Biblical Archaeologist*, Vol. 7, 1944, pp. 54–63.

75 Mackenzie, op. cit., p. 307.

76 Ibid., p. 303.

77 Ibid., p. 305.

78 Ibid., p. 303.

79 Ibid., p. 304.

80 Idem.

81 Ibid., p. 305.

82 Ibid., p. 304.

83 Irwin, p. 280.

84 Ibid., p. 298.

85 Idem.

86 Kenneth Macgowan, *Early Man in the New World*, New York, Macmillan, 1950, p. 176.

87 Heyerdahl, op. cit., p. 134.

88 Irwin, op. cit., pp. 297, 298.

89 Mackenzie, op. cit., p. 315.

90 Ibid., p. 314.

91 William Gowland, "The Metals in Antiquity," Huxley Memorial Lecture in *The Journal of the Royal Anthropological Institute*, Vol. XLII, 1912, p. 244.

92 Irwin, p. 298. Also see the description of the process in *The Encyclopaedia Britannica*, New York, William Benton, 1968.

93 There was a cat cult in vogue in Nubia in the Twenty-Fifth Dynasty. Even the names of the Nubian kings, Shabaka and Shabataka, correspond to "the male cat" and "son of the male cat" in the Barabra language of the Nubian Nile valley (see Henry Brugsch-Bey, *A History of Egypt under the Pharaohs*, London, John Murray, 1881, Vol. 2, p. 284). Compare also the cat heads of Colombia and Peru represented by James Bailey, op. cit., p. 77 and those of Nubia in P. L. Shinnie, op. cit., p. 125.

94 Irwin, op. cit., p. 290.

95 William T. Corlett, *Medicine-Man of the American Indian*, Springfield, Illinois, C. C. Thomas, 1935, pp. 38, 39.

96 Irwin, Fig. 89, p. 285.

97 Mackenzie, op. cit., Fig. 31 (facing p. 312).

98 Irwin, p. 296.

99 The Abbé D. Francesco Saveria Clavigero, Charles Cullen (trans.), *The History of Mexico*, Philadelphia, 1804, Vol. 1, pp. 365–366.

100 Idem.

101 Idem.

102 Idem.

103 Steindorff and Seele, op. cit., p. 99.

10

PLANTS AND TRANSPLANTS

The adoption of a new plant is no simple matter. It requires the adoption of a whole complex of knowledge about the plant's ecological requirements, and often also about the human usages of the plant. The presence of even one transferred plant means that a quite effective contact has been made between two peoples.

—G. F. CARTER, "MOVEMENT OF PEOPLE AND IDEAS," IN *Plants and Migrations* EDITED BY J. BARRAU

If someone could only prove that even a few of the basic crop plants of American origin . . . were universally distributed in cultivation in both hemispheres in pre-Columbian times, one might be more lenient in judging the matter.

—E. D. MERRILL, "OBSERVATIONS ON CULTIVATED PLANTS WITH REFERENCE TO CERTAIN AMERICAN PROBLEMS"

I. AFRICAN ANCESTORS OF AMERICAN COTTON

Professor Stephens peered into the pale, subaquean light of the tank. Three weeks had now passed since the cotton seeds were taken out of cold storage and set afloat on the artificial sea water. It was impossible, of course, to simulate all the complex conditions of the ocean in a laboratory tank. The ocean had its own inimitable surfaces—the calm of glass, the turbulence of lava—its own tones of utter darkness and soft subterranean lights, its billion fins in flow, its drift, its detritus. But the important thing in this experiment was the salination and temperature of the water, and he had tried to reproduce this as best he could by adding 35 grams of common table salt to each liter of water and by varying the temperature between 25 and 31 degrees centigrade. He had also changed the water at monthly intervals and not, as in 1964, kept the seeds in a tank under constant aeration, forcing air into the system by means of a small aquarium pump. This aeration had had a curious effect on some of the fibers still attached to the cotton seeds, charging them with air bubbles. He had not counted on that, and he had assured himself it might actually help flotation, enhance, perhaps, the buoyancy of the seeds. The experiment, however, had ended rather disappointingly. He had abandoned it after two months, since by that time there were hardly any seeds afloat.[1]

The new 1965 experiment was more complex. He had introduced a number of things, including tests on the viability of the seeds, their capacity to germinate even after sinking.[2] His eyes moved slowly from one container* to the other, studying closely each seed in the critical samples. There were fifty seeds to each sample. Several botanists had collected them from various parts of the world. Drs. Gaudillot, Kerr, Fosberg, Martorell, Gilham and himself, from the Pacific islands, the Caribbean and the African-Atlantic coast.[3] The direction and speed of currents in the oceans and the points of possible departure and arrival had been carefully studied. The purpose of the experiment was to discover whether the various types of cotton got from one point to the other through simple drift across the surface of the oceans.

In the first experiment he had been primarily concerned with wild forms of cotton found in the South Pacific islands and the Caribbean. A variety of the New World species *Gossypium hirsutum* had been found growing wild on several Caribbean islands from a point on the coast of Venezuela right through the Antillean chain to the Yucatan peninsula and the Florida keys. Their distribution seemed to follow the path of the Gulf Stream current,

---

* The samples were separated in this experiment by plastic containers, and in the previous case by vertical plastic grids placed in the tank.

and he wanted to find out if they could have drifted unaided by man from the coast of South America to their furthest points west and north. The entire journey was more than a thousand miles, but the distances between the islands were quite short. Island-hopping on the warm, fast-moving belt of the Gulf Stream made it a manageable problem. Far more problematic, however, was the movement of the South Pacific cottons which, while of the same New World species *hirsutum*, differed enough from the Caribbean variety of the species to suggest that they started their migration into the Pacific from some other center in the New World, in all likelihood from a Central American base.[4] For them to have made it from there to places like the Marquesas Islands and Hawaii, they would have had to drift along several branches of the Pacific currents, taking, in some cases, more than a year to arrive at their present locations. Could they have floated all that time? And, even if they had, would they have survived intact and potent after so many months of salt-water immersion? It was all very well and good for Professor Watt to have demonstrated in his salt-water tanks that the cotton variety *darwinii*, of the New World species *Gossypium barbadense*, had drifted to the Galá-pagos islands unaided by man from the coast of South America, floating on the Peru current.[5] That was no big drift. It was like the island-hopping of *hirsutum* in the Caribbean. Island-hopping was one thing. Dispersal of seeds over vast tracts of ocean was another.

Stephens frowned. In this new experiment he was involved in an even more critical issue than that of the Pacific cottons. He had introduced two samples of African cottons into the containers. One of these—*anomalum*—although it had remarkably tough seed coats and close affinities with the other variety, had fared very badly. That morning the last floating seed in the sample had sunk.[6] Still, the matter was far from settled. There was another important sample collected from the southern part of Africa, which was doing quite well. On it hung many hopes. For it was a wild variety of *Gossypium herbaceum*, the reputed ancestor of America's cultivated cottons, the grandfather, perhaps, of both species, *hirsutum* and *barbadense*. It lay at the very center of the controversy over the origins of the world's cultivated cottons.

Thirty years before Stephens had started his experiment, Professor Harland analyzed the nature of the distinctions between the species of the world's cultivated cottons. Harland's work led to the acceptance of four species, and four only, to embrace the vast diversity of cultivated cottons.[7] Of these four species, two are known as tetraploids and were formed in the New World, two are known as diploids and originated in the tropical and subtropical areas of the Old World.

But the genetic structure of the two New World tetraploids (*G. hirsutum* and *G. barbadense*) indicates that they are the result of an ancient crossing between an Old World diploid and a wild New World type. Half of the twenty-six chromosomes found in the New World tetraploids are "homologous with the complement of the Old World diploids, and half with the complement of species of the genus growing wild in the New World."[8] These Old World diploids are *G. herbaceum* and *G. arboreum*. *G. herbaceum* is an African diploid cotton, and it is now recognized that *G. arboreum* (common to Pacific Asia) arose through a mutation of a species of *G. herbaceum* from Africa. The African *G. herbaceum* has emerged as the only likely diploid cotton which could have crossed with a wild New World type to form the New World tetraploids.

Where the sample of *herbaceum* had been collected, however (by Dr. Gilham in Southern Rhodesia), it would have taken five months at least, if *unaided by man*, to float across the Atlantic from Africa along the South Atlantic Equatorial Current to South America or the Caribbean. It would have had to drift nearly 3000 nautical miles at the snail's pace of 20 miles a day.[9] It would be of great interest therefore to know whether the seeds could have survived for this length of time.

In the second month, however, the *herbaceum* seeds began to sink. While they might sink below the surface of the water, Stephens argued, reluctant to relinquish hope, they might still remain within the effective belt of the current, probably supported by drifting bits of timber dislodged from coastal forests or vegetation mats. The final test lay not with buoyancy, perhaps, but with viability. Would the seeds remain alive, submerged or not? That was the question. He therefore removed ten seeds from those that had sunk, and air-dried them in a dessicator. These seeds were then acid-delinted. Their seed coats were removed and the seeds were placed on germinating pads. His hunch was right. They were still healthy, fertile seeds. But his excitement over this was short-lived. When he repeated it with some more seeds a little later, he had to admit that the hypothesis that African cotton seeds had drifted unaided across the Atlantic to America could not be supported. The *herbaceum* seeds were all dead.[10]

"Tests of seed buoyancy and seed viability in experimental tanks of saltwater," wrote Stephens in his report on these experiments, "indicate that the upper time limit for seed buoyancy is a little over two months. This is sufficient to effect the transport of seeds over relatively short distances (e.g. throughout the Caribbean islands and from mainland South America to the Galápagos Islands) but totally inadequate for trans-Atlantic or trans-Pacific dispersal."[11]

Stephens' contribution, however, was extremely valuable. He had shown the limited applicability of the Watt experiment. He had forced botanists to look again at this troubling question, "the question . . . concerning the origin of the amphidiploid cottons as a whole, since their putative parents . . . are confined to Africa and America respectively."[12] By what means, then, had the links been made between the two cotton strains? For he had at least dismissed the possibility of unaided oceanic drift.

Some botanists working on problems unrelated to the cotton controversy have considered the possibility of birds' retaining seeds in their digestive tracts over long periods and depositing them on alien shores after transoceanic flights. This hypothesis has been examined by V. W. Proctor, and while it has been found that "seeds of some plant species can remain viable in the intestinal tract of some shorebirds long enough to be transported thousands of miles,"[13] this can offer no explanation in the case of cotton. The cotton boll is not one of the seeds birds feed on. Even

if the boll were swallowed by accident and regurgitated or ex-
creted after an extended flight it would retain neither form nor
potency.

Botanists have tried other ways to account for the meeting of
the Old World and New World cottons. Since tropical parts of
Asia (India/Pakistan) had imported an African type of cotton
(presumably in a wild state), and the domestication of cotton in
Asia was thought to be (until very recently) of much greater antiquity than that in Africa, it was suggested that the Pacific was
the key to the problem. The fragment of a fiber and string was
reported in excavations at Mohenjo-Daro in Sind, Pakistan, by
A. M. Gulati and A. J. Turner in 1928. This fragment is dated
about 3000 B.C., and it indicates a knowledge of cotton weaving.[14]

Now, a movement from Asia across the Pacific to America, not
from outlying islands but from the Indian Ocean, is a far more
problematic proposition than the African-American journey, not
only from the point of view of distance but from the disposition of
world-wide winds and currents. It was a desperate suggestion to
deal with an inexplicable problem. Harland first advanced the
Oceanian-Pacific hypothesis, going so far as to postulate a land
bridge across the Pacific Ocean.[15] No evidence has been found for
any such land bridge, and botanists later suggested that the link
was provided by civilized man, migrating eastward from the Old
World (that is, Asia) and taking his cottons with him.[16] What
lent credence to this theory was not only the "known antiquity" of
Asian cottons but the fact that coastal Peru (which is on the Pacific
side) appeared at one time to be the home of the American
cottons.

The search for ancient New World cotton in Peru was inspired
by this hypothesis of an eastward migration to the Pacific mainland of South America and led to the discovery, in 1948, by Dr.
Junius Bird, of the oldest known cotton textiles* in the New World
in the caves of Huaca Prieta. The Huaca Prieta site in Peru
yielded materials dating back to 2500 B.C.[17] The discovery, however, did not prove that an Old World cotton from the Pacific had

* Handmade, not woven with the help of the loom. See Chapter 9.

fused with a New World species in Peru. An examination of seeds, carpels and lint from the early Huaca Prieta deposits revealed nothing to suggest the presence of an Asian diploid cotton.

Certain evidence seems to point to an eastern South American origin for these Peruvian cottons, although they are distributed west of the continental divide. F. Engel, according to Hutchinson, reported groundnuts (*Arachis*) among the crops of the ancient pre-ceramic cotton-using cultures of the Peruvian coast. These groundnuts "originated east of the Andes, probably in north-western Argentina, suggesting that the cultivators reached the coast from the mountains and *not* from the Pacific. If they came over the mountains, they presumably brought their cotton with them."[18] This takes us back to the Atlantic.

But other alternatives have to be examined. G. L. Stebbins has suggested that the diploid Old World parent of the New World cottons came to this hemisphere by way of China and Alaska across the Antarctic route. Sir Joseph Hutchinson, a world authority on cotton, has shown that this could not be so because cotton is a round-the-year shrub adapted to the arid tropics. According to Hutchinson, "No member of the genus would grow in an ecological situation where temperate woodlands existed and no member of the genus would survive in a climate of winter frosts. It is therefore reasonable to conclude that contact between the Old World and New World Species did not come about by migration round the Pacific, either by a northern or southern route."[19]

Evidence has been presented recently which seemed for a while to rule out the possibility of human transport across the Atlantic from Africa as the origin of the American cottons. Botanists C. E. Smith and R. S. MacNeish claimed in 1964 to have found even earlier evidence for the existence of cultivated cotton in the New World than that found by Bird. Excavations in caves in the Tehuacán Valley area of southeastern Puebla show, they claimed, that "cotton and other plants were cultivated as long as 7000 years ago" (that would be circa 5000 B.C.).

Smith and MacNeish say, "The most remarkable cotton find

is two segments of a cotton boll excavated in Coxcatlan Cave in Zone XVI, and El Riego floor level date between 7200 B.C. and 5000 B.C. Three carbon-14 dates for Zone XVI are all around 5800 B.C."[20]

These claims have been disputed by botanists Karl Schwerin and S. G. Stephens. Schwerin contends that "in spite of MacNeish's claim for an earlier appearance, he has only one specimen from the El Riego floor level (dated between 7200 and 5000 B.C.) and absolutely no evidence of cotton in the intervening Coxcatlan phase (5000–3400 B.C.)." "The best explanation for this apparent anomaly," Schwerin argues, "is that that single specimen was intrusive from a higher level. The most recent discussion of the find (Stephens) reports that this specimen was indeed unearthed in a disturbed level of the Coxcatlan cave. This interpretation is further supported by Stephens' observations that the specimen is nearly identical to modern cultivated upland cotton and very unlike feral or wild cottons . . . it seems more likely that cotton did not appear in Mexico before 3400 B.C. (the next level on which specimens were found)."[21]

Smith and MacNeish have suggested that because of this early find of New World cotton (corrected and dated down by Schwerin and Stephens to read 3400 B.C. at the earliest) botanists should no longer look for an Old World ancestor of the American hybrid cottons but for some native wild American ancestor, genetically similar to the reputed Old World ancestor. These gentlemen, however, despair of ever finding such a native ancestor and try to close the argument by saying that although "the human transport theory is untenable," they must confess that "the parental stocks contributing to the original hybridization may never be found."[22]

Work on the other side of the Atlantic basin, however, in Africa itself, has shown that the agricultural revolution came to West Africa, and particularly to the Mande people, much earlier than was formerly supposed (as early as 5000 B.C.) and that cotton cultivation in Sudanic Africa was of considerable antiquity. (See Chapter 11.) This therefore puts Africa back into the picture. Schwerin's condition—that if Africa is to be considered a poten-

tial area of the Old World from which this introduction may have
been made, it would require a domestication not later than the
fifth millenium B.C.—seems to have been met.

"Agriculture was independently developed (circa 5000 B.C.)
by the Negroes of West Africa," says George Peter Murdock, an
American anthropologist, in his book *Africa: Its Peoples and
Their Culture History.* "This was, moreover, a genuine invention,
not a borrowing from another people. Furthermore, the assem-
blage of cultivated plants ennobled from wild forms in Negro
Africa ranks as one of the four major agricultural complexes
evolved in the entire course of human history . . . The invention
of agriculture in Negro Africa is most probably to be credited to
the Mande peoples around the headwaters of the Niger in the
extreme western part of the Sudan, less than 1000 miles from the
shores of the Atlantic Ocean."[23]

Several botanists still believe that African cotton was introduced into India in a wild form and was domesticated there,
but Murdock, undertaking a tremendous interpretive task based
upon the available literature, claims that "one of the major contributions of the Nuclear Mande people to the welfare of mankind
was the domestication of cotton. Originally ennobled in the Western Sudan, this textile plant was transmitted early to India but did
not reach Egypt *until the sixth century* B.C."[24] (Italics added).

In the last few years several researchers (Wrigley, Porteres,
Anderson, Delcroix and Vaufrey, Schwerin, Davies) have supported the main thrust of Murdock's thesis and have shown that
agriculture, settled village life, and a number of impressive cultural achievements have considerable antiquity in Africa. This has
led to a more favorable reception to the African-Atlantic hypothesis and an abandonment of the Pacific advocacy.

"During the fifties," Schwerin notes, "Thor Heyerdahl alone suggested the probability that cotton reached the Americas by way
of the Atlantic, although he believed it was carried by Near
Eastern sailors. Since that time it has been shown that G. *arboreum*
(common to Pacific Asia) arose through mutation of a species of
G. *herbaceum* from Africa. Furthermore, the African *herbaceum*

itself is more closely related to the New World cottons than is G. *arboreum*. This has led several authorities to suggest that the Old World parent may have come to the Americas across the Atlantic from Africa rather than across the Pacific from Asia. Even Hutchinson, who formerly favored a Pacific crossing, has agreed that the odds (as well as the difficulties) are equally good for a transatlantic introduction."[25]

In fact, Pacific advocates who are so eager to ignore or dismiss the African-Atlantic hypothesis, should bear in mind a number of things that argue strongly against their case but not against the African proposition. The winds and currents in the Pacific do not favor a crossing from Asia to America. The main currents in fact run the opposite way and would be more likely to propel a craft from the Americas to Asia rather than from Asia to the Americas. The prevailing winds (the northeast and southeast trade winds) blow in the same direction as these currents (the north and south Equatorial currents) and make it extremely difficult for a craft without great power to approach the Americas in low latitudes. Furthermore, if the voyage were an accidental drift voyage, it would have been almost impossible for the drifting craft to hold to a steady course right across the Pacific without being blown or pulled off-course to the north or the south and carried back toward Asia, or at least into one of the chains of islands in the Pacific.[26]

It is clear from the above that the Asia to America journey is a veritable nightmare for accidental drift voyagers. The direct, simple, relatively short, almost inescapable West Africa to South America route is so free of these problems that only centuries of blindness to the cultures of the African has made the contemplation of the infinitely more complex drift journey from Asia in a prehistoric time more acceptable and attractive.

Again, it must be noted that cultivated cotton appeared later in Asia than America. As Schwerin points out: "It did not reach China until the seventh century A.D. . . . it was unknown to the original Austronesians at the time of their immigration into the Pacific and Indian oceans . . . furthermore, the cottons of the

Indian subcontinent and of east Asia belong to a species (*G. arboreum*) which, on cytogenic grounds, is unlikely to have been ancestral to the New World cottons."[27]

Finally, while there are many grounds of similarity between African and American agricultural techniques, it has been demonstrated that "the techniques of American agriculture are markedly different from those of Eurasia."[28]

All roads of argument lead back to Africa. A drift voyage by African fisherfolk in the fourth millenium B.C. is the answer. The great antiquity of African agriculture, which began several centuries before that date, the very early "ennobling of cotton," as Murdock puts it, in the ancient Sudanic agricultural complex, and the proven capacity of very small, unsophisticated craft to make it across the Atlantic—all these factors make this suggestion of Schwerin's tenable.

Pre-Columbian contact between Africa and America in the latter half of the fifteenth century has also been proven by another aspect of the cotton evidence. There were Haitian reports of large boats from Guinea trading with them before Columbus. These reports would seem to be supported by evidence that these African-Atlantic traders, on one of their return voyages about the year 1462, brought back a species of New World cotton with them and introduced it into the Cape Verde islands. Europeans first became acquainted with the Cape Verde islands, according to Ribeiro, between the years 1460 and 1462, in which time there were no signs of former habitations. This was approximately thirty years before Columbus sailed to the New World. The botanist S. G. Stephens reports: "Attempts at settlement [of the Cape Verde islands] quickly followed and by 1466 cottons from Guinea had been introduced and had already become semiferal. During the subsequent colonial period, cotton was collected in the wild and also grown under primitive cultivation for export. Today, according to Teixera and Barbosa (1958) it occurs in a wild subspontaneous state in the arid areas of most of the islands. It is a New World cotton (*G. hirsutum* var. *punctatum*). It is clear that if the wild cottons of today are the descendants of the cottons introduced from Guinea between 1462 and 1466, *then a New*

World cotton must have been established in Africa before Colum-bus's first voyage.[29] (Italics added.)

This, then, is the case for cotton. After fifty years of specula-tion, archaeological discovery and botanical debate, Africa has not been dismissed as the source of the ancestor of the New World tetraploids, nor has the African-Atlantic journey and the human transport theory become less tenable.

Several things are clear. First, that an African diploid cotton (*G. herbaceum*) crossed with a wild New World cotton several thousand years ago to form the New World tetraploid cottons (*G. hirsutum* and *G. barbadense*). Second, that seeds of the Afri-can diploid cotton could *not* have drifted by themselves across the ocean but had to come to the New World in the hands of African man. Third, that African man, bearing cottons, made the drift journey to the Americas in the fourth millenium B.C. Finally, that in another series of African-American contacts in the fifteenth century Africans took a tetraploid cotton from the New World (*G. hirsutum var. punctatum*) which was introduced into the Cape Verde islands between 1462 and 1466.

NOTES AND REFERENCES

1 S. G. Stephens, "The Potentiality for Long Range Oceanic Dis-persal of Cotton Seeds," *American Naturalist*, 100, 1966, p. 206.

2 Ibid., p. 207 (Table 4).

3 Ibid., pp. 205–206.

4 Ibid., p. 205.

5 Ibid., p. 199.

6 Ibid., p. 206.

7 For this reference to S. C. Harland, see Sir Joseph Hutchinson, "The History and Relationships of the world's cottons," *En-deavour*, 21, January, 1962, p. 5.

8 Hutchinson, op. cit., p. 5.

9 Stephens, op. cit., p. 205.

10 Ibid., p. 207 (Table 4).

11 Ibid., pp. 208–209.

12 Ibid., p. 208.

13 V. W. Proctor, "Long Distance Dispersal of Seeds by Retention in Digestive Tracts of Birds," *Science*, 160, February,
   1968, pp. 320–322.
14 A. N. Galati and A. J. Turner, *Text and Trans.*, 20, No. I, 1929.
   For this reference, see G. E. Smith and R. S. MacNeish, "Antiquity of American Polyploid Cotton," *Science*, 173, February,
   1964, pp. 675–676.
15 S. C. Harland, *The Genetics of Cotton*, London, Jonathan
   Cape, 1939.
16 J. B. Hutchinson, R. A. Silow and S. G. Stephens, *Evolution of
   Gossypium*, London, Oxford University Press, 1947.
17 J. B. Bird, "South American Radiocarbon Dates," Supplement
   to *American Antiquity*, 17, 1951, pp. 37–49.
18 Hutchinson, op. cit., p.14.
19 Idem.
20 Smith and MacNeish, op. cit., p. 675.
21 Karl Schwerin, *Winds Across the Atlantic: Possible African
   Origins for some Pre-Columbian New World Cultigens*, Meso-
   american Studies, No. 6, 1970.
22 Smith and MacNeish, op. cit., 675.
23 G. P. Murdock, *Africa: Its Peoples and Their Culture History*,
   New York, McGraw-Hill, 1959.
24 Murdock, op. cit., p. 70.
25 Schwerin, op. cit., p. 5.
26 Schwerin, op. cit., p. 10.
27 Schwerin, op. cit., p. 9.
28 Oaks Ames, *Economic Annuals and Human Culture*, Cambridge, 1939. For this reference, see Schwerin, op. cit., p. 9.
29 S. G. Stephens, "Transoceanic Dispersal of New World Cottons," in Riley, Kelley, Pennington and Rands (eds.) *Man
   Across the Sea*, Austin, University of Texas Press, 1971, p. 413.
   On p. 437 of the same volume Herbert Baker comments:
   "Stephens is able to point to features of these cultivated cottons that leave them virtually dependent on human dispersal.
   As a consequence, early occurrences of the linted *G. hirsutum*
   in the Cape Verde islands becomes much more significant and
   worthy of further investigation."

II. PRE-COLUMBIAN BANANAS
IN PERUVIAN GRAVES

As he looked down from the rim of the grave on the top of the mountain, the mourners seemed like a mass of ants writhing their way upward with a heavy burden and morsel.

The slow beat of the drum, sounded at measured intervals, the plaintive flute call, made all the more melancholy the ceaseless wail and lamentation of the women.

Guayanacapa was dead. A king of the Incas had fallen.

The digger leaned on his spade, waiting on the edge of the pit for the body of the great lord. He had dug many graves. Death, the burial of the dead, was mere routine. This time, however, he felt, after hours of labor in the sun, the chill of ice in his bones. He had heard tales of the death of kings. At their passing hundreds of people of all ages were ritually slain. There was no telling who would be called upon today to follow the king on his journey to the afterworld.

Slowly to the pit they came, and he could see the shining skulls of the king's wives, shaved clean out of grief and respect. Some of them had already gone wild, and their wails were no longer in tune with the grieving chorus. They broke from the mass of mourners, uttering shrieks of incredible anguish and terror, hopping, lunging at phantoms, rolling upon the rock and pebbled grass of the ground.

The great mummy pack containing the king was lowered into the pit. A sadness that had nothing to do with grief smote him. There, in the deepest pit he had ever seen dug, they were burying some of the finest treasures in the world. That pack, he knew, contained not only food and drink that the king might not suffer hunger and thirst on his journey but the most marvelous jewels and plumes, the richest, finest cloths. All that was needed to ensure a happy passage were his pets and his companions.

The digger braced himself. The time for filling the pit had come. Some of the king's wives leaped into the bowels of the earth and lay still at the feet of their beloved lord, waiting to be covered. Others were pushed over the side. Some had to be dragged and beaten as they struggled, bludgeoned and kicked as they tried to scramble their way up the steep sides of the pit. He began with the rest of the diggers to hurl the earth full and fast at them, spade after spade, until he could see only the quake and convulsion of living bodies in the ground. Their terrible faces had vanished . . .

These burials in the lofty parts of the mountains had not fully ceased when the Spanish came. It was with Guayanacapa, however, that the ritual slaughter of wives on the death of a king was last recorded. This ancient practice probably passed with his passing, but the burial of the dead with food and drink, jewels and textiles and even arms, continued up to Columbian contact times. It was not the reserve of kings but became widespread among the common people, who kept their dead relatives "happy" by renewing their food and clothes and drink.

There is no graveyard on this continent more steeped in mystery and antiquity than the Necropolis of Ancon in Peru. Here lay the bodies of Inca kings and nobles, their treasures, their retinues and their wives. Some of these ancient graves were opened before the coming of the Spanish and their grave contents renewed. Among these "later" contents (of medieval vintage) which excavators have unearthed, there are items which have never been explained. One of these is the banana. Banana leaves and fruit, the fruit being seedless and belonging therefore to the cultivated species of the banana, were identified by botanists who examined mummy packs in Ancon tombs. No native species of the *musa paradisiaca* (the banana and its sister variety, the plantain) from which this grave fruit could have evolved, can be traced to America. How then did the banana, an Old World plant, arrive in Peru before Columbus?

The botanist E. D. Merrill proposed that the banana was first introduced into the New World by the Portuguese via the Cape Verde islands off Africa.[1] This has since been accepted as the official version, and Thomas de Berlanga, Bishop of Panama, has been credited with the introduction of this plant into the Americas in the year 1516. Both historical and archaeological evidence, however, refute Merrill's theory and those of his followers. This evidence is presented here, evidence which not only points to the pre-Columbian presence of the banana in America but to its introduction from an African-Atlantic source.

Although the *musa paradisiaca* did not originate in Africa and only diffused to Africa by way of the Arabs as late as the thirteenth century, it was definitely in cultivation in West Africa before the Mandingo journey of 1310, and its transference to South America by the Mandingo explorers in the fourteenth century and/or the Songhay traders of the fifteenth (1462–1492)* is the most likely explanation for its pre-Columbian presence in this hemisphere.

Among sixteenth-century chroniclers and historians who claimed the presence of a pre-Columbian banana/plantain in Peru were Father Montesinos, Guaman Poma,[2] Father J. de Acosta, Blas Valera and the half-Inca historian Garcillasso de la Vega.[3] Alphonse de Candolle, in his celebrated botanical classic, *Origin of Cultivated Plants,* dismisses all such claims, particularly the arguments advanced in their favor by the famous explorer Alexander von Humboldt.[4] De Candolle assumed that if these assertions were correct, there would have to be a case for a native banana plant. No such case, he demonstrated forcefully, could be established. Humboldt had argued for a native species on the grounds that there were native American names for the banana. This claim, however, has no validity. Quite apart from any of de Candolle's arguments, we can show that the names he cites are derivations of common Arab-African banana names.

The case for a pre-Columbian banana in South America does not rest, however, on the statements of a few historians or on the arguments of Humboldt. Notwithstanding de Candolle's dismissal of these, extensive excavations by Cessac and Savatier in the Necropolis of Ancon, the sacred cemeteries of Peru, unearthed evidence on behalf of the banana. The botanist A. T. de Rochebrune, reported on the discovery of both banana leaves and fruit

---

* The year 1462 is given as the *latest* possible starting date for African-Caribbean trade contact because of the New World cotton introduced from Guinea into the Cape Verde islands around this time. The African trade with the Caribbean, however, may have started earlier.

in a tomb at Ancon, the fruit being seedless and therefore belonging to the cultivated species of *musa paradisiaca*.[5]

It was the custom of the Peruvian Indians to bury their chiefs in the way the Egyptians buried their Pharaohs. Their wives, attendants, pets, treasures, clothing, food and wine were placed in the graves so as to be close at hand for use in the afterlife. Pedro Ciezza de Leon, who traveled in Peru from 1532 to 1550 and who, according to C. R. Markham, examined every part of the empire of the Incas within a few years of the Conquest, gives an account of how the native Indians buried their dead *caciques* (chiefs).

"When a chief dies," de Leon reported, "they make a very deep sepulchre in the lofty parts of the mountains, and, after much lamentation they put the body in it, wrapped in many rich cloths, with arms on one side and plenty of food on the other, great jars of wine, plumes and gold ornaments. At his feet they bury some of his most beloved and beautiful women alive; holding it for certain that he will come to life, and make use of what they have placed round him."[6]

Ondegardo, another authority on Peru, details the burial ceremonies of the common people. It is easy to see from this why bananas and other kinds of fruit and food were found preserved in the mummy packs. The people believed that "the souls suffer hunger, thirst or other inconveniences" and so "they offer in the sepulchers chicha and food, silver, clothes, wool and other things which may be useful to the deceased."[7]

The sacred cemeteries in Peru date back more than two thousand years. At Ancon, however, numerous mummies have been found at various depths, dating from A.D. 200.[8] The great antiquity of the graves could prove misleading, for the objects within the mummy packs are much more recent, particularly the food and the textiles—thirteenth, fourteenth and fifteenth century. "They are of a relatively modern period," says Gonzalez de la Rosa, "but in any case anterior to when the Spaniards came." *No Spanish objects have been found in these graves.*[9]

The relative recency of the food and textiles is accounted for by the unusual burial practices in Peru. The *huacas* (houses of the dead) were like ancestral shrines. Although in many respects the way the great chiefs of Peru were buried closely parallels the way the Pharaohs of ancient Egypt were buried, the Peruvian burial customs were later "vulgarized." That is, they ceased to be the prerogative of chiefs and were indulged in by almost everyone. In ancient Egypt, there had been a great obsession with the royal dead. Hundreds were slaughtered when a Pharaoh died. Likewise, at the death of Guayanacapa, the last Inca, one thousand persons of all ages were killed.[10] But whatever sacrifices were made at the time of the death of the Pharaohs, however monumental were the tombs built for them, at least they lay in peace for thousands of years before man began invading the privacy of the pyramids. This was not the case in Peru.

In Peru there was an obsession with the bodies of the dead, not only the royal dead but the family dead. The dead were buried and reburied, clothed and reclothed, fed and refed. These people would open the tombs, renew the clothing and the food placed in them and in many instances gather the remains of the dead together and reinter them. This led to the inadvertent or intentional regrouping of ancestors. X-ray pictures taken by A. Baessler of mummy packs in the Royal Museum of Anthropology in Berlin show the remains of several skeletons bundled into one mummy pack.[11] These practices were discontinued under the Spanish.

The Cessac and Savatier excavations which unearthed the bananas in the Peruvian graves also unearthed yams. It is interesting to note that Leo Wiener accepts the yams as African introductions but not the bananas. This is due to a misreading of the stems in African banana names, which led him to conclude that the banana was introduced late into West Africa by the Portuguese. Wiener was not alone in making this linguistic error. M. D. W. Jeffreys has shown how S. W. Koelle (1854), J. W. Christaller (1933) and Roland Porteres (1959) mistook, like Weiner, the *boro* and *poro* stems in West African words as referents for the Portuguese. They regarded, for example, the *poro* in *porobana* (the Vai name for the banana) as proof that the banana was a Portuguese post-Columbian introduction into Africa.[12]

The Arabs introduced the banana into Spain, where it was cultivated in the twelfth century, and it passed into the Arab-African trade not much later. Several West African tribes—the Mano, Kissi, Tshi, Ewe, Ga, Fante and Krepi—all have *boro* and its variants prefixing their names for the banana—*bolo, blofo, borofo, b'lo,* etc. They in no way confirm a European, that is, a Portuguese introduction. These prefixes were used by West Africans as terms for the Arabs long before the coming of the Europeans. As P. K. Reynolds points out: "The Arabs were instrumental in distributing this fruit across equatorial Africa . . . the banana was gradually carried westward by the native tribes and was well established on the Guinea coast when the Portuguese first explored there in 1469."[13]

If the banana, seen in Peru by the early Spaniards and excavated in the pre-Columbian cemeteries of the Incas, did not come from pre-Columbian visitors to America, only one other possibility remains to be examined. That possibility, as Humbodlt contended, is that there was a native variety of the *musa paradisiaca.* What facts support this contention?

Humboldt claimed that there were native words for the banana plant. He points to banana words among two American tribal groups and languages: the name *paruru* in the Tamanaco language, and the name *arata* among the Maypuri Indians. These words seem at first to be far removed from the universal words for the banana and the plantain, the *platena* and *platano* of the Arabs, Africans and Spanish. But when we look at their variants as they pass through a number of American languages, we realize that they are intimately connected with the main source after all, and are not "native" (as Humboldt claims) to these two American tribes and languages. We see *paruru,* for example, very close to *paratunu* (another banana word in another American language), *paratunu* to *paratano, paratano* to *paratana, paratana* to *pratena, pratena* to *platena, platena* to *platano,* the last of these being the source of most of the banana words found throughout Africa and the Arab and Spanish worlds. When we look at the Maypuri word for the banana—*arata*—we see clearly its relationship to *p-arata-no,* which brings us back again to *paratana, pratena, platena, platano.* All these little steps of sound on the staircase of words, which we can climb up and down through the house of American languages, lead us back to the ground words in banana and plantain culture.[14]

A spiral of steps winding its way from the main staircase may be seen in other American words for banana—the small variety—derived from the African *ba-koko*. Thus we have in the American language Galibi, the banana word *baccuccu*; in the Oyapock language, the banana word *baco*; in Oyampi, the word *bacome*; in Tupi, the word *pacoba*; in Apiacas, the word *pacowa*; in Puri, the word *bahoh*; in Coroada, the word *bacoeng*. The African banana word runs right through these American languages.[15]

This word stands for a small African variety of banana, and it is a small African variety that is one of the keys to the question. There seem to have been two main varieties of banana introduced into Africa. The small variety was an offshoot of the Arab transplant in the centuries prior to Columbus and "a larger variety became widespread in the Sudan and the Congo through Spanish and Portuguese influence" in the later period. It is this small variety, popular in pre-Columbian Africa, which da Acosta probably describes when he identifies "a small, white and delicate" banana in Peru during the first decade of the Conquest. Da Acosta testifies that these bananas were grown in Haiti, not Peru, and that they were brought into Peru across the Andes,[16] which fits in with the African-Caribbean contact (Haiti was the first of the islands to report pre-Columbian trade with the Africans) as well as with an African settlement or settlements cultivating this crop along the Atlantic seaboard.

No native variety, as Humboldt claimed, has ever been established. The only other claim of this nature was made by Llano y Zapata, who reported in 1761 that in addition to the bananas introduced into America from the Cape Verde in 1516 and from Guinea in 1605* there was yet another *coyllo* (white) species of banana.[17] As we have shown, this small white banana, as da Acosta describes it, is the African species brought into Peru across the Andes from the direction of the Caribbean. The Peruvians, in

---

* The bananas introduced into America from Guinea in 1605 were first shipped to Panama. From there they made their way to Peru.

fact, have an oral tradition which tells of blacks coming to them from across the Andes.[18]

Asa Gray and J. Hammond Trumbull, in their critique of the first revised volume of Alphonse de Candolle's *Origin of Cultivated Plants*, reopen the issue of the banana: "The Scandinavians, who had carried their expeditions to the northern United States, and the Basques of the Middle Ages, who had extended their whaling voyages perhaps to America, would appear not to have transported a single cultivated species. The Gulf Stream has equally been without effect. Between America and Asia two transplants may have been effected, one by man (*batatas*—the sweet potato), the other either by man or by the sea (the coconut). Perhaps the banana should be ranked with the above in this regard . . ."[19] Like Heyerdahl after them, Gray and Trumbull were suggesting a Pacific origin for the pre-Columbian banana found in America.

This suggestion does not fit any of the known facts. The heaviest concentrations of banana and plantain cultivation, found in places where the Spanish had not yet penetrated, were along the upper reaches of the Amazon River (Atlantic side);[20] bananas were only found in small ritual deposits, but not in cultivation, on the Pacific side; the earliest chronicle which makes reference to a pre-Columbian banana, such as da Acosta's, points to an Atlantic source; all the names of American bananas, post or pre-Columbian, are of Arab-African, not Polynesian or New Guinean origin.

American bananas, we must conclude, both pre- and post-Columbian, disperse from African sources, as the distribution of names for the American varieties of the *musa paradisiaca* clearly shows. The banana, although it did not originate in Africa, was introduced there very early, in Spain as early as the twelfth century, into Africa not much later, at least by the thirteenth, through the Arab caravan trade in the Sudan and through the Asian and Arab maritime trade with East Africa. The research by Reynolds into early banana culture establishes the pre-Columbian cultivation of the banana in West Africa. No extended trip contemplated by the Africans in 1310–1311 or later (in their trade with the Caribbean in the mid-fifteenth century) could have excluded bananas (or plantains, the sister variety of the *musa paradisiaca*). It seems that a small variety of banana was in popular cultivation in West Africa before the coming of the Europeans (Portuguese), who made a larger variety widespread in the Congo and the Sudan. It was a small variety (similar to the West African pre-Columbian banana) that was reported in Haiti and Peru at the time of the contact by Spanish and Portuguese historians.

The explorer Orellana encountered the plantain variety of the species in great abundance all along the upper reaches of the Amazon when he drifted down this river (the longest jungle river in the world) to its mouth in 1540–1541.[21] The plant geographer Carl Sauer has shown how difficult it is for the plantain variety to spread quickly without a very active human crusade on its behalf. Its multiplication is a lot more difficult than that of a seed-bearing plant, which practically spreads itself. "The mature root-stocks [of the plantain]," Sauer points out, "need to be dug up, divided, preferably dried for a while and then replanted. This species is an extraordinarily poor volunteer, and its spread must have been almost entirely by deliberate and rather careful planning."[22]

It is clear from the above that those who still insist on a post-Columbian introduction of the banana by Europeans as the origin of its presence in America not only ignore the eye-witness accounts of the early chroniclers and the archaeological evidence of the Ancon graves, but the intensive cultivation and extraordinary dispersal of the plant and its sister variety on the Atlantic side of the continent and the extremely dependent and slow-spreading nature of the plant itself.

NOTES AND REFERENCES

1 E. D. Merrill, "Observations on Cultivated Plants with Reference to Certain American Problems," *Ceiba* 1, 1950, pp. 161–384.

2 For references to Montesinos and Poma, see Thor Heyerdahl, "Isolationist or Diffusionist," in Gordon Ashe (ed.) *The Quest for America*, New York, Praeger Publishers, 1971, p. 136.

3 (a) J. da Acosta, *Historia natural y moral de las Indias*, Madrid, 1894, 1, p. 377.
(b) Garcilasso de la Vega, *Historia general del Peru*, Cordova, 1617.
For refs. 2(a) and 2(b) see Leo Weiner, *Africa and the Discovery of America*, Vol. 2, pp. 73–74.

4 Alphonse de Candolle, *Origin of Cultivated Plants*, New York, 1885.

5 Leo Weiner, op. cit., p. 73. Rochebrune's list of plants is published in the botanical encyclopedia *Botanisches Centralblatt*, London, Cassell, 1880, 3, p. 1633.

6 C. R. Markham, *The Travels of Pedro de Cieza de Leon*, London, The Hakluyt Society, 1864, p. 65.

7 Ondegardo, *Coleccion de libros y documentos referentes a la historia del Peru*, Lima, Peru, 1916, 3, p. 194, and Weiner op. cit., p. 69.

8 Weiner, op. cit., p. 58.

9 Ibid., p. 60.

10 Ondegardo, op. cit., p. 118, and Weiner, op. cit., p. 69.

11 Arthur Baessler, *Perunische Mumiem, Untersuchungen mit X-Strahlen*, Berlin, 1906, and Weiner, op. cit., p. 71.

12 M. D. W. Jeffreys, "How Ancient is West African Maize?" *Africa*, January, 1963, pp. 115–131.

13 P. K. Reynolds, "Earliest Evidence of Banana Culture," Supplement to the *Journal of the American Oriental Society*, December, 1951.

14 Weiner, op. cit., p. 130.

15 Idem.

16 Weiner, op. cit., p. 74.

17 Weiner, op. cit., p. 73.

18 Harold Lawrence, "African Explorers in the New World," *Crisis*, June–July, 1962, p. 7.

19 Asa Gray and J. Hammond Trumbull, "Origin of Cultivated Plants," *American Journal of Science*, 3, No. 25, 1883, pp. 241–255 and 3, No. 26, 1884, pp. 128–138, 370–379.

20 Thor Heyerdahl, op. cit., p. 136. Heyerdahl not only cites the

1540–41 discovery of intensive cultivation of plantains along the Amazon River by Orellana but points out that sixteenth-century chronicles described it as cultivated from Jalisco in Mexico to the southern coast of Brazil.

21 Idem.

22 Carl O. Sauer, "Cultivated Plants of South and Central America," in J. Steward (ed.) *Handbook of South American Indians*, Vol. 6, pp. 487–548. *Bureau of American Ethnology*, Bull. 143, Washington, 1950.

III. OTHER CROPS

It was the season of spring tides, and the great sea vaulted and tumbled on the land with a terrible force. Even far inland, where he lived in his little cave, he could hear the tremor of distant waters in the veins of the earth on which he slept. Vast mountains must have been pounded to a powder over the ages under the shock, he thought, whole forests made to rock and shudder in their roots until they fell. For there came drifting now the detritus of battered coastlines—the skeletons of trees, large floating mats of grass and vegetation, carcasses of animals in a mantle of poisonous fumes, partly picked by the fish, birds fallen exhausted from the clouds, flowers and wild fruit.

He was drawn to the domed-shaped object bobbing up and down on the current not far from his feet. It looked at first like the head of a bald man with a solitary tuft of hair done up in a curious knot in the middle of his skull. He guided it in with a stick and picked it up. It was larger and lighter than a human head and the mysterious knot in the center of the skull was a stem.

After the day's hunt he took it back with him to his cave. He tried to break it open with a stone to see if it was indeed a fruit and if the flesh within was good and sweet. The stone only made slight indentations in the brittle shell, which was as protective and tough as the hide of an animal. In a rage he threw it down and stamped on it. It broke into two halves. It was quite hollow

inside. A film of flesh, which may have once been soft, still clung
to the inner rim of the shell. It seemed infested with seeds. The
man spat. It was certainly not good for meat. But perhaps . . . perhaps . . . The thought was to return to him much later, more complete. But this time he simply threw the gourd down on the trash
heap . . .

The bottle gourd picked up on the beach by this aboriginal
American is an ancient plant. It is among man's first cultivated
plants. It served many functions before man began making pots
from clay. It could be used as a float, a container, a scoop and a
dipper, and was probably used for all these purposes by prehistoric fishermen. Gourds occur very early in both the Old and New
Worlds, but in spite of the differences in the shape of the seeds
from the two hemispheres, the varieties are known to branch from
a single species. This species originated in tropical Africa and,
according to the botanists I. H. Burkill and Oaks Ames, was originally *domesticated* there.[1] Thomas Whitaker, the leading authority on the cultivated cucurbits, also leans toward that view.[2]

The early branching off from the African *Lagenaria* has produced New World seeds of the bottle gourd that are "small, narrow and without wings," while seeds of the African gourd are
usually "broad and corky." There are, however, New World seeds
of the gourd found in early archaeological sites, from Peru to Baja
California, Mexico, that are "broad," just as there are African
types that resemble "the slender, hard and wingless seeds" of the
New World.[3]

Most botanists hold that the bottle gourd was introduced into
the Americas by natural drift across the ocean. Karl Schwerin suggests that in some prehistoric time (beginning about nine thousands years ago) bottle gourds got caught in the pull of currents
from the African coast and drifted to America across the Atlantic.[4]
Experiments have shown that such a drift voyage could in fact
occur. Thomas Whitaker and G. F. Carter showed that gourds are
capable of floating in sea water for at least seven months, long
enough to reach South America from Africa, without appreciable

loss of seed viability. Salt water does not harm these seeds, just the opposite. Direct immersion of *Lagenaria* seeds for up to four-teen weeks actually seems to have a stimulating effect.[5]

As we have seen, this kind of occurrence would have been im-possible for the African cotton seeds. The botanist S. G. Stephens demonstrated this in laboratory tests.[6] Only man could have trans-ported African cotton seeds across the Atlantic.

Man, it would appear, was not really necessary for the diffusion of the bottle gourd. There is, nonetheless, one problem in connec-tion with the gourd that has caused several authorities, including Whitaker, to add the cautionary note that "introduction by hu-man transportation remains a distinct possibility."[7] The bottle gourd is not a littoral plant. That is, it does not grow along the shoreline of the Atlantic, where it would have landed after its long slow drift. If it is true that African gourds simply got lost and drifted westward until they hit the American mainland, why did they never appear in cultivation along the waterline or littoral, but only far inland? This has led to the speculation that an ancient American may have picked up the gourd on the seashore, taken it inland with him to his settlement, and breaking it open, inadver-tently dispersed the seeds, which then took root in the New World.[8] This seems a plausible explanation. Bottle gourds appear so early in America that it would be rash to claim unequivocally a direct introduction by African man. In fact, as Whitaker at one point suggests, the diffusion of the gourd from one continent to another may even have preceded its domestication by man. On the northern borders of Mesoamerica, the gourd is reported at Tamau-lipas in Mexico from strata radiocarbon-dated at 7000–5500 B.C. It occurs much later in South America. The earliest firm date in South America is 3000 B.C. at Huaca Prieta on the northern coast of Peru.[9]

Other crops, of definite African origin, which have turned up in pre-Columbian strata in the New World, include a species of jack bean (*canavalia sp.*)—the result of an ancient crossing be-tween African and American beans—and a West African yam (*dioscorea cayennensis*). Some scholars have argued for an introduction of both the bottle gourd and the jack bean from Asia. This is hardly worth consideration. First of all, they are both found earliest in America on the Atlantic side. Secondly, bottle gourds and beans appear in much later archaeological contexts in Asia than they do in America.[10] Thirdly, the Asiatic jack bean (*canavalia gladiata*) is quite distinct from the New World species.[11]

The member of the bean family we are considering, the jack bean (*canavalia sp.*) grew from an early marriage between African and New World beans. Red seeds from Africa (*canavalia virosa*) hybridized around 4000 B.C. with white seeds (*canavalia plagiosperma*). These "mottled" seeds, when carried into the Amazon lowland, a habitat like that of the ancestral red seeds of Africa (*c. virosa*), gave rise through repeated backcrossing to brown seeds (*c. piperi*).[12] *Beans, unlike gourds, could not have survived a transatlantic drift.* The red seeds can float for a short time, but they are not impermeable to water, and so swell up and sink. Other canavalia beans are neither buoyant nor impervious to the effects of water. And so the explanations put forward for the pre-Columbian transfers from Africa to America of the jack bean include: 1) a sealed gourd with the seeds packed inside; 2) storm-driven fishermen bringing the beans; and 3) an abandoned watercraft with the beans on board. The sealed-gourd explanation is highly improbable (why should Africans seal a gourd packed with jack beans and set it adrift?), and with respect to the abandoned watercraft, one has to imagine that the Americans who found the craft knew the usefulness of the beans and the technique of their cultivation. That men came in on the watercraft, surviving the long drift journey, is not to be dismissed as improbable, in view of what is now known of the seaworthiness of small craft, the currents traversing the floor of the Atlantic, and the capacity for storm-driven fishermen to survive much longer accidental ocean voyages, utilizing their equipment, which turns the ocean into a mobile food-store. These men, moreover, would know both the usefulness of the plants and the technique of propagating them.

The journeys of these prehistoric fisherfolk, as Schwerin has pointed out, are matched in improbability only by other explanations. "Because fishing cultures are uncommon in West Africa they have been neglected ethnographically. Yet fishermen have probably been important as specialists for a long time, catching and drying great quantities of fish which could be traded long distances inland . . . Indigenous peoples of West Africa were no strangers to travel on the open sea prior to European contact . . . and fishing *in the open sea* has continued among scattered West African groups down to the present . . ."[13]

Very early drift voyages *without man* are postulated for the diffusion to America of the African bottle gourd, and *with man* for a species of *canavalia* bean. Yams, however, were a much more recent introduction, and their pre-Columbian presence in the Americas may be seen as further evidence of the medieval African contact with America. The Spanish naturalist G. F. de Oveido makes it clear that yams were not native to America. "*Nname* (pronounced "nyam") is a foreign fruit," writes Oveido, "and not native to these Indies, having been brought to this Hispaniola (Haiti) and to other parts of the Indies. It came with the Negroes and it has taken well and is profitable and good sustenance for the Negroes . . . these *nnames* look like *ajes* (the sweet potato) but they are not and generally are larger than *ajes*. They cut them in pieces and plant them a hand's distance from the ground and they grow."[14]

Yams were another of the cultigens found preserved in the mummy packs of the Incas in Peru. One of the problems that has arisen in discussions of the yam is the confusion over its name. Wiener says, "*Aje* is the original name of the yam and not of the sweet potato but throughout the world the two were confused and the same name often served for both."[15]

After reviewing many of the early chronicles on this point, Schwerin is convinced that "the *ajes* reported by Oveido, Las Casas and others represent a species of yam (*Dioscorea*)."[16] He holds that a species of yam that may have been introduced into America in a pre-Columbian time is *Dioscorea cayennensis*, which is widespread in tropical America, and which most authorities consider had its original home in West Africa.[17]

NOTES AND REFERENCES

1 Karl Schwerin, *Winds Across the Atlantic: Possible African Origins for Some Pre-Columbian New World Cultigens* (Meso-american Studies, No. 6, 1970), p. 4.

2 Idem.

3 Idem.

4 Schwerin, op. cit., p. 22.

5 T. W. Whitaker and G. F. Carter, "Oceanic Drift of Gourds: Experimental Observations," *American Journal of Botany*, 41, 1954, pp. 697–700, and "Note on the Longevity of Seed of Lagenaria Siceraria after Floating in Water," *Torrey Botany Club Bull*. 88, 1961, pp. 104–106.

6 S. G. Stephens, "The Potentiality for Long Range Oceanic Dispersal of Cotton Seeds," *The American Naturalist*, 100, 1966, p. 209.

7 T. W. Whitaker, "Endemism and Pre-Columbian Migration of the Bottle Gourd," in Riley et al. (eds.) *Man Across the Sea*, Austin, University of Texas Press, 1971, p. 327.

8 Ibid., p. 324.

9 Ibid., p. 327.

10 Schwerin, op. cit., p. 9.

11 Idem.

12 Ibid., p. 22.

13 Ibid., p. 19.

14 Oveido in Weiner, *Africa and the Discovery of America*, Philadelphia, Innes and Sons, 1922, Vol. 1, pp. 203–204.

15 Ibid., p. 204.

16 Schwerin, op. cit., p. 23.

17 Idem.

SMOKING, TOBACCO AND PIPES IN AFRICA AND AMERICA

The black people have practiced the same manner and use of the tobacco as ye Indians have . . .

—N. MONARDES, *Joyfull Newes Out of the New-Found Worlde*

The people of Africa have surpassed every other people in inventing various contrivances for smoking, rising from the very simplest apparatus to the most elaborate. . .

—G. SCHWEINFURTH, *The Heart of Africa*

There is a decidedly classical character about them [Ashantee pipes] as if started from Roman lamps and Pompeian ideas . . .

—R. T. PRITCHETT, *Smokiana*

I. SMOKE CURES, SMOKE WORDS AND THE ORIGIN OF SMOKING

Jean Nicot, French ambassador to Portugal, stood on the balcony of his house, looking out on the garden. He was struck by the luxuriance of the new plant which the Keeper of the Royal Prisons in Portugal had sent him. It had come in recently from Florida, a place somewhere in the new dominions of Spain. He had heard of a plant like this among the Moors used for curing the *Noli me tangere*, but he had dismissed this as irrelevant. All he wanted of the plant was for it to adorn his garden. It was almost as tall as a man, full of leaves, large and long-bearded. He felt, indeed, as if he had acquired from some secret garden a rare and exotic flower of the new-found world.

Later that day a friend of Nicot's page boy, walking and talking in the garden, felt a sharp itching on his cheek by the side of his nose. It was an ugly little growth, halfway between a purulent boil and a cold wart, vexing him continually, and because he had nothing on hand he impulsively tore a leaf from Master Nicot's prize plant and rubbed the spot. A slimy, sticky substance came out of the leaf, but it cooled and tightened the skin like an astringent. To his astonishment the itching stopped for all that day and the next.

The page boy told Nicot of this. He called the young man in, and for a week and a half every day he squeezed the viscous juice of the leaf onto his face. The growth completely vanished. But this was only the beginning. In the kitchen of the embassy a week later, one of the cooks nearly severed his thumb with a great chopping knife. The steward of the house dressed the wound quickly, using the leaves of this plant as a bandage. The thumb was good within a month. News like this travels with the wind. People flocked to the embassy as to the miracle waters of Lourdes—there was the page boy's father, who had a chronic ulcer in his leg, and a woman whose face was so completely disfigured by the ringworm that it looked as if she wore a visor of boils. The juice of this extraordinary plant was applied. Within two weeks, the ulcers, the ringworms, dried up; the sufferers were pronounced healed.

It began to be known as the Ambassador's herb. Nicot called in doctors to confirm the cures. He wrote to King Francis the Second and prescribed it for all nobles in the French court. The Lord of Iarnac, Governor of Rogel, a close personal friend, was so impressed by the reports that he had the juice of the plant distilled and drunk at the Queen's table, claiming that it cured short breath . . .

What has become the king of vices, the sovereign lord of tooth and lung decay, of dentine tartars and pulmonary cancers, was once, from Greco-Roman to medieval times, a sovereign remedy, killer of all aches and worms that attacked tooth or lung, liver or skin, bladder or brain. Thus tobacco began about two thousand years ago as one of the great curers of all ills and evolved into what it is today, one of the great killers of all times.

Smoking in ancient times, however, was no pleasant after-dinner custom. Like the modern enema, the smoke was sometimes funneled into the body through the anus, and smoking through other apertures, like the mouth and nose, was like taking an emergency draught of oxygen in rarefied atmospheres.

Various viscous substances were burned in a vessel, and the fumes, rising in a hot thrust, would pass up through a funnel into a distilling cup or glass. The fumes distilled and condensed in that cup were used to fumigate (smoke) the patient. They were led out of the distilling cup by way of another tube into some opening (mouth, nose or anus) to heat, soothe and clean the affected parts. In that funneling tube (or *embocus*, as the alchemists called it) lay the beginnings of our pipe stem: in that receiving cup of distilled vapors (the *ambix* or *mastarion*) lay the beginnings of our pipe bowl.

The alchemists looked upon their distilling apparatus in a very novel way, as a union of male and female. They saw the *mastarion* as a uterus (and nipple-like appendages studded this container), the funnel or *embocus* as a penis, the hot power of the fumes charging up the *embocus* as "the male sperm which is transformed into the new chemical combination . . . deposited in the glass vessel at the end of the tube of the mastarion."[1]

This distilling apparatus or smoking machine reappears in the most ancient pipes found so far. These are taken from Roman graves and are described by B. Reber in *Les Pipes Antiques de la Suisse*. A glance at the pipes shows they are *mastaria* turned upside down, and the large pipe bowl seems to feature a knob or nipple like the *mastarion* of the alchemists. The pipe stems come out of the bowl at such an angle as would suggest they were intended to be set into a distilling glass. It is hard to escape the conclusion, particularly when one looks at the survival of the nipple or knob and the lids on some of the bowls, no longer utilitarian, that these pipes are, as Leo Wiener claims, "a direct development of the distilling apparatus of the alchemists."[2]

The substances used for medicinal smoking in these early times did not include tobacco. Henbane and alcyonium, a substance close to what is now in use in the manufacture of pipe heads (meerschaum), were the favorites in smoke medicine. In the Salerno school of medicine, henbane was as popular a pain reliever as aspirin is today. The *Catolica Magistri Salerni*, a medical textbook, says, "Henbane seed wrapped in a little wax may be put on hot coal and the smoke should be drawn into the tooth and the worms will soon be killed."[3] There is also a poem on the toothache, which appears in the textbooks of the Salerno school. This is a free translation of the Latin verse:

> To treat bad teeth that ache and rot
> Put grains of leek into a pot
> Mix well and burn with henbane root
> Then heat with smoke the ailing tooth.[4]

Smoke was also recommended for troubles of the chest, especially coughing. According to one medical treatise, also of the Salerno school, "the smoke of colt's foot [a plant] taken through an embocus into the mouth would cure a cough."[5] The ancient Greeks also used the inhalation of smoke through a reed for medical purposes, and they knew of this remedy for coughs.

Thus, Pliny wrote of colt's foot, "The smoke of this plant in a dry state, inhaled by the aid of a reed and swallowed, is curative of chronic cough; it is necessary, however, at each inhalation of the smoke to take a draught of raisin wine."[6] Through Pliny and other Greek writers like Dioscorides, a clear picture emerges of the early smoking apparatus and the many cures attributed to smoke inhalation or fumigation, but the best description of an ancient pipe evolving from this process is given by a Roman, Marcellus Empiricus. Speaking of the colt's foot for an old cough, he tells how "it is gathered in the old moon, dried on Thursday" and then "put in a new vessel with burning coals . . . the top closed carefully with clay and a reed inserted and through it the humor or hot smoke is drawn into the mouth, until it penetrates all the arteries and the stomach."[7]

Many substances were smoked, and many cures were effected. These substances, although as various as the ailments they were concocted to cure, had to be fatty and viscous so as to emit a smoke that was not only strong but of a consistent intensity and duration. Powders in themselves, it was found, did not yield (in the words of medieval surgeon Ambrose Parey) "so strong and so long a fume," but when a viscous substance was mixed and burned with powders "it doth yield them a body and firm consistence." Parey describes smoking cures for obstructions of the brain, ulcers of the lungs, chronic coughs, pains in the ears, pains of the sides, pains of the womb, and even *luis venerea* (venereal disease), which called for a thorough smoking out of the whole body through all of its openings.[8]

The smoking cures of Greco-Roman medicine were passed on to the Arabs, and so was the smoking apparatus. The Arabs, however, although using some of the substances made popular by the Greek and Roman doctors, developed their own smoke-medicine chest. This included the viscous and gluey leaf and juice of a plant which came to be known as the *tubbaq*. This word was chosen because it is derived from the Syrian word for viscum and glue, *dubbaq*.

It is in an Arabic medical treatise that one first becomes aware of *tubbaq*, "a species of tree growing upon the mountains of Mekkah, having long, slender, green leaves, which slip between the fingers when squeezed, applied as a dressing to a fracture, which, remaining upon it, they consolidate; it is beneficial as an antidote against poisons, taken internally or applied as a dressing, and as a remedy for the mange or scab, and the itch, and fevers of long continuance, and colic, and jaundice, and obstructions of the liver . . ." The Arab physician Ibn-al-Baitar, also adds in his description of the Arab species of tobacco plant that "it attains the size of a man . . . lives in groups . . . one never finds one alone."[9] The word *tubbaq*, as used by the Arabs, was not restricted to this

plant, but was extended to apply to a number of viscous substances used in medicinal smoking.

The Arabs alerted Africans to the value of tobacco as a smoke
medicine. Yet they were not responsible for introducing the plant
itself into Africa. The Africans already had tobacco. An indigenous
species was growing wild and plentiful there. As this plant, however, was initially associated with Arab smoke medicine, even
though it was later used by the African medicine men and
magicians for other purposes, it became known by the Arab smoke
word *tubbaq*, and this name was disseminated over a great part of
the Sudan. Thus we have the roots *taba, tawa, tama* in the Mande
languages.

A pre-Columbian poem on smoking in Africa documents the
early use of tobacco. "At Kubacca," Captain Binger wrote, "tobacco serves also for money. By a singular homophony with the
Eureopean name the inhabitants of the Darfur call it in their
language *taba*. Moreover, this is the usual name in the Sudan. In
Fezzan and at Tripoli in Barbary it is called *tabgha*. I have read
a kasidah or poem, composed by a Bakride or descendant of the
Khalif Abu Bakr, to prove that smoking is no sin. These verses, I
think, date back to the ninth century of the hegirah."[10]

That would be circa 1450. It would imply, however, a much
earlier invention of tobacco smoking in the Western Sudan before
it spread to the north and seduced Muslims. One of the verses of
the poem quoted by Binger is a defense of the new-found habit of
smoking against possible Islamic injunctions.

A later reference by O. Houdas shows that Africans introduced
oral smoking of tobacco for pleasure and relaxation among the
Arabs of North Africa: "As the result of the arrival of an elephant
from the Sudan in the city of El Mansur, the use of the dire plant
called tobacco was introduced into the Magreb since the Negroes
who had brought the elephant also had brought tobacco which
they smoked, claiming that the use of it offered great advantages.
The habit of smoking which they brought with them became general in the Draa, later at Morocco and at last in the whole
Magreb."[11]

An important distinction should be pointed out here. Tobacco, as such, was not new to the Arab world. A species of the tobacco plant had been used by the Arabs in early medieval smoke medicine. The medical uses of this plant and other viscous-like substances grouped under the general name of *tubbaq* had diffused to the Africans. But the Africans not only introduced their own brand of *tubbaq* along with other aromatic herbs they imported, (as did the Arabs, for that matter, along with what they inherited from the Greco-Roman medicine chest), they also introduced a range of new functions. They used tobacco for all sorts of things—money, magic and meditation. Among Africans, smoking the *tubbaq* did not remain a painful fumigation of the insides in times of illness. Rather, from their emphasis on oral smoking and their refinements on the pipe, smoking became a source of great meditative and tranquilizing pleasure. It was this latter function that spread to the Arab world as an innovation and an influence. The Arabs had also smoked for the pleasure that the burning and inhalation of hallucinatory or narcotic substances brings, but they knew this function only in relation to hemp and opium. Tobacco was simply medicine to them, smoked or raw.

It is remarkable that the word *tubbaq,* which was used in pre-Columbian Africa, should be found at the time of the Spanish contact already in use among the American Indians for the "smoking reed" and "the act of smoking." *Tubbaq,* as the name for the plant, did not originate in America, as later scholars have assumed, for the plant (at the time of Columbus' arrival) was not called *tubbaq* by the natives. The Mexican word *picietl* was among the several native American words for the plant (although Wiener claims the word has an un-Mexican formation, the initial morpheme *pic* being found in no other Mexican word, and the *yetl* being a possible corruption of *yuli,* which in several South American languages is an approximation of the Mande word for smoke, *duli*). Wiener also makes a case for an Arabic derivation of the American "smoke word" *petun* from *betume* (the letters b and p are interchangeables) from *bitumen,* the main viscous substance in the Greco-Roman smoke-medicine chest replaced by the general Arabic term for smoking substances, *tubbaq.*

On the strength of his philological computations, Wiener insists that the plant itself was an importation into America by the Africans. The evidence, however, seems to suggest that the functions, not the plant itself, diffused to the New World from Africa. The applications of tobacco within the African and New World medieval cultures are so remarkably similar as to establish the case for a pre-Columbian diffusion of medicinal and ritual uses of tobacco, but the methods of cultivation are so different as to suggest independent origins of the tobacco plant. The Africans, for example, are reported as "pounding it while it is fresh, as soon as it is picked, without curing or drying it, pressing the leaves and making them into bricks which they then dry slowly in the shade,"[12] while the Americans are found in most cases doing the opposite, drying the tobacco first and then crushing the leaves.

What was new, what was African, was the habit of smoking the tobacco orally and the instrument developed for such smoking (which is not as natural as it is assumed today). In one Caribbean island, where the habit had probably not yet fully diffused, some Americans were first seen by Columbus smoking with a Y-shaped reed through the nostrils.[13] Hence, when oral smoking and the instrument for oral smoking (the pipe) was introduced into some parts of the Americas by the Africans, the Americans borrowed the Arab-African name (*tubbaq*) and used it to name the act of smoking and the pipe but *not* the plant itself, for which presumably they already had a native name.

Observations by the naturalist G. F. de Oveido support this:

"The Indians of this island use, among other of their vices, one which is very bad and that is smoking which they call *tabaco*, in order to lose consciousness....

This instrument with which they take the smoke the Indians call *tabaco* and not the herb."[14]

On their arrival, not only did the Spanish find this word *tabaco* used both for smoking and for the instrument used for smoking, but also encountered another smoke word which is found in the Mande language group and in a wide range of American languages. The Malinke words meaning to smoke are *dyamba* and *dyemba*. These can account for South American smoke words such as the Guipinavi, *dema*; Tariana, *iema*; Maypures, *jema*; Guahiba, *sema*; Caberi, *scema*; Baniva, *djeema*; and so on. The Mandingo word *duli* (to smoke) which also occurs in the same form in Toma and Bambara, and in its variant forms *nduli* and *luli* in Mende, can be found among the American languages Carib, Arawak, Chavantes, Baniva, Acroamirin and Goajira. *Taba* and *iouli* both stand for tobacco in the Carib and Arawak languages spoken in the Guianas. Weiner has tracked down the deterioration of the *duli* words in geographical sequence. In Haiti, the word is *iouli*. As one moves from the Mandingo central base in Darien to the northern shore of South America, one finds the Arawak *yuli, yeuri, yaari*; further to the west in the Goajira language, *yulli, yuri, yure*; in the interior this further deteriorates into *eeli, eri, wari* and *oali*.[15]

The "discovery" of tobacco in America did not make much difference to Europe for a long time. Specimens of the plant were brought back "to adornate gardens with the fairnesse thereof and to give a pleasant sight."[16] The curative powers known to African and American medicine men did not come to the serious attention of the Europeans until about 1570, when Liebaut made Jean Nicot's observations on tobacco famous. The Spanish were uneasy about the habit of smoking that was so prevalent among the African slaves. On the one hand, they encouraged tobacco cultivation on the plantations because tobacco was good for trade with the Indians, who valued it much. On the other hand, the Spanish saw smoking as the opium of the people, with possibly injurious effects on the quality of the labor force.

Wide as the use of tobacco became among the Indians (as medicine, particularly in the form of powders, juices, leaf poultices; and as food, in the form of tiny balls for chewing), the burning of the tobacco for oral puffing and inhalation (true smoking) was a habit only of the American Indian elite. Indulged in by nearly all Africans, men and women, it was largely restricted to Indian chiefs, wealthy Indians with many wives, or the Indian priests and medicine men. The common people would usually smoke on ceremonial occasions, at a celebration or festival. Thus, we learn of some Indian tribes in the far north of the American continent (now Canada) who smoked heavily at a *tabagie*. *Tabagie* is a word for festival or banquet that closely resembles the

Wolof words *tabasquio, tabaskie* (the December feast), the Mandingo *tabaski,* and the Peul and Berber *tabaske* (feast of the sacrifices).[17]

In 1560, the French ambassador to Portugal, Jean Nicot, became
aware of the use of tobacco among the black Moors as a cure
for the *Noli me tangere* (cancerous ulcers) and fistulas. He wrote
to the Cardinal of Lorraine in April of that year:

"I have acquired an herb of India [America in these years was
still being called *India* and the Americans, *Indians,* the distinction
being made between Oriental India and Occidental India] an herb
of marvellous and approved property against the *Noli me tangere*
and fistulas, declared incurable by the physicians but by this herb
of prompt and certain cure among the Moors. As soon as it has
produced its seed, I will send it to your gardener, at Marmoustier,
and the plant itself in a barrel with the instructions for trans-
planting and caring for it."[18]

As we have noted, Nicot was given this herb by the Keeper of
the Prisons in Portugal. At about the same time, a specimen of
one of the African species (later to be labeled *Nicotiana rustica*)
was sent from Italy to Matthioli in Austria, who falsely identified
it with henbane. Nicot, partly on the scant information about the
tobacco plant that was recorded from Africa and America, and his
own experiments on the relatives of the page boy and the cook in
his embassy, "discovered" tobacco (at least as far as Europe was
concerned).

After Liebaut published his *L'agriculture et maison rustique*
in 1570, highlighting the creative wonders of the tobacco plant,
the experiments of Nicot, and the manner of cultivating tobacco
(which was soon followed by a book on tobacco and sassafras by
Monardes), tobacco became the rage of the time. Nicot was immortalized. Hence, the botanical labels *nicotiana tabacum, nicotiana rustica,* and the crucial element in tobacco, *nicotine.*

Today, when twenty-five million Americans have succeeded in
abandoning the tobacco-smoking habit to save themselves from
possible cancer, the thought of tobacco as one of the great curative
herbs comes as something of a shock. What is a life taker in one

preparation is a life giver in another. From the works of Liebaut
and Monardes the stories of a miracle unfold. The juice of the
tobacco leaf "glewth together and soldereth the fresh wounds and
healeth them: the filthy wounds and sores it doth cleanse and reduce to a perfect health."[19] The Indians chew tobacco for food
"when drought and hunger attack them . . . they can chew it for
days and eat nothing else. The bear does the same thing in hiber-
nation. Without meat or drink he just lies and chews his paw. The
circulating saliva retains body heat."[20] Sir John Hawkins also, in
1564, observed this capacity of tobacco takers to withstand hunger
and thirst. However, in the experience he describes, smoking
rather than chewing achieved this. "The Floridians when they
travell, have a kind of herbe dried, who with a cane and an earth-
ern cup in the end, with fire and the dried herbs put together, doe
sucke thorow the cane the smoke thereof, which smoke satisfieth
their hunger, and therwith they live foure or five dayes without
meat or drinke . . ."[21]

In its various preparations—powder, juice, dried or fresh or
burning leaf—tobacco was used to heal skin diseases (ringworm,
acne, warts, sores), to relieve pains of the head, pains of the chest
(congestion by phlegm), pains of the stomach caused by wind or
gas, labor pains, constipation and vomiting, pains of the limbs from
cold (arthritic pains) toothaches, chilblains, swellings, kidney
stones and short breath. It could cure carbuncles, cankerous ulcers,
shooting pains, fevers, the mange and the itch, cold affections of
the liver, the worms, dropsy, the most stubborn of old corruptions
and the freshest wounds of war. Tobacco juice was a powerful
antidote to the stings of scorpions and the deadly effects of
poisoned arrows.

Tobacco was also used as a tranquilizer in Africa and America.
"The black people," wrote Monardes, "have practised the same
manner and use of the tobacco as ye Indians have, for when they
see themselves weary, they take it at the nose and mouth, and it
happeneth unto them, as unto our Indians, lying as though they
were dead three or four houres, and after they remain lightened,
without wearinesse, for to labour againe: and they do this with

great pleasure, that although they bee not weary yet they are verie desirous to doe it."[22]

The use of smoking as a tranquilizer was secondary to its use for magic and sacred ritual. The first place in the magician's pharmacopia is occupied by the aromatic plants for burning. There is no important ceremony and no invocation of the spirits without specific instructions as to what aromatic plant is to be burned. From this use of the *tubbaq* in Africa there arose the habit of oral smoking (that is, smoking as it is known today).

Some of the ritual and divinatory uses among the American Indians are identical with those among the Africans. "One of the marvelles of this hearbe, and that which bringeth most admiration, is, the manner howe the Priests of the Indians did use it, which was in this manner: when there was amongst the Indians any manner of businesses, of great importance, in which the chiefe Gentlemen called Caciques or any of the principall people of the Country had necessities to consult with their Priests in any business of importance, then they went and propounded their matter to their chiefe Priest, foorthwith in their presence, he tooke certeyne leaves of the Tabaco and cast them into ye fire, and did receive the smoke of them at his mouth, and at his nose with a Cane, and in taking of it, he fell down upon the ground, as a Dead man, and remayning so according to the quantity of the smoke that he had taken when the hearbe had done his worke he did revive and awake and gave them their aunsweares according to the visions which he sawe . . ."[23]

Schweinfurth in his book *The Heart of Africa,* has commented upon the remarkable correspondences between tobacco cultures in the Old and New Worlds. "Of all the plants that are cultivated by these wild people none exhibits a more curious conformity amongst people far remote."[24] Assuming the Africans knew nothing about tobacco in pre-Columbian times, he cannot understand how Africa took to tobacco so quickly and how its culture was so deeply affected by it. "It must be a matter of surprise," says he, "that even Africa, notorious as it has ever been for excluding every sort of novelty in the way of cultivation, should have allowed the Virginian tobacco to penetrate to its very centre."[25]

Not suspecting the linguistic derivation of the word from Arabic, he wonders how it is that "there is not a tribe from the Niger to the Nile" which has any other word but *tubbaq* to denote the plant. (Apart from *tubbaq* to denote both *nicotiana tabacum* (Virginia or American tobacco) and *nicotiana rustica,* there are a number of African words for the *nicotiana rustica.* The *nicotiana tabacum* is always and only known as *tubbaq.* Schweinfurth points to one exception, the Niam-Niam tribe, which calls the American brand of tobacco *gundeh* to distinguish it from their native *tubbaq* (*nicotiana rustica*). On the question of the native home of the *nicotiana rustica,* which grows wild and plentiful in Africa, Schweinfurth is cautious. "Quite an open question I think it is, whether the *Nicotiana rustica* is of American origin. Several of the African tribes had their own names for it. Here amongst the Bongo, to distinguish it from the American brand they call it 'masheer.' Schweinfurth further points out that African *nicotiana rustica* is "distinguished by the extreme strength and by the intense narcotic qualities it possesses."[26]

After pondering the question of the original home of the *nicotiana rustica* species, which he leaves open, Schweinfurth concludes: "At all events the people of Africa have far surpassed every other people in inventing various contrivances for smoking, rising from the very simplest apparatus to the most elaborate." He conjectures that the Africans, although they must have had their own tobacco "favored the foreign growth (nicotiana tabacum) because smoking either of the common tobacco (nicotiana rustica) or some other aromatic weed, had in some way already been a practice amongst them."[27]

Schweinfurth correctly assumes, like the botanist de Candolle, that the wide distribution of *tabba* words in Africa indicates that they proceed from some common source. His mistake in placing the original source of the word in America is based on the accepted theory that it was first used there, but Weiner's investigation of the medical method of fumigation makes it certain, without any dispute, that the *tubbaq* of the Arabs spread throughout Africa without any American influence. There are a number of other linguistic clues to this, which have not yet been mentioned, such as the African *cassot* or pipe (from the Arabic *qasa-bah*) and *buckoor* in the Niger valley (from the Arabic *bahur*), which is "incense smoked with tobacco for cold."[28]

II. ORAL SMOKING AND THE PIPE

There were hundreds of people strolling up and down the streets of Tlatelulco. It was market day and the murmur of the vast crowd was so great that after a while he could hear nothing but a humming, as though he were walking under the lake. There were women cooking on their stoves in the open air—stews and spiced maize porridge, sweetmeats made of honey, maize cakes and those savory *tamales* whose steamed maize crusts were stuffed with beans and meat and pimentos. He was tempted to stop and regale himself, but he wanted to get to the far end of the marketplace, where they sold those quaint little smoking tubes they called *tabaco*.

They were such exquisite things, though the best of them, such as those the priests and *caciques* used, were not commonly on sale. Behind the stall stood a black-skinned trader from the Hot Lands. He was selling mostly cotton mantles and *quetzalli* feathers, but on one side, spread out on an animal hide, lay the smoking tubes. He had thought the purchase would be quick, but he was startled by the variety of the merchandise. Some were so tiny that they were lost between the fingers, some so long that one could sit by the *tabaco* in the cool and place the bowl of burning *picietl* at one's feet. Some seemed showered in fine gold, and it was difficult to tell how this effect and sparkle was achieved. Others were blackened and polished with coal or painted in the white bright powder of chalk. Flowers, fishes and eagles adorned many of them, and the bowls were sometimes the vivid heads of these foreign blacks or the forms of tropical animals.

He chose a cylindrical tube. The interior was stuffed with aromatic herbs and charged with something he knew burned long and slow. He could hardly wait to light it. He drew the smoke in deep and would not let go of the vapors until he felt giddy.

Then at one point there was a rich, pure flame without smoke. In this flame he saw a hidden painting uncoil like a snake aroused. It came and vanished in an instant. It was the body of a woman who danced into life and death as the fire started and stilled her . . .[29]

Our pipe smoker is taken from the early fifteenth-century marketplace of Tlatelulco. "Oral Smoking" in America, and the instrument specifically designed for this, were introduced about a century before then, but it has always been assumed that the habit and the pipe (both called *tabaco* in a great part of the New World) were of great antiquity in America. A reexamination of the evidence shows that this was not the case. Evidence of smoking pipes in America does not go back beyond a century and a half, at most, before Columbus. Some receptacles, in the bowls of which certain substances were burnt, were misclassified as smoking pipes, but the orifices are too large for "oral" smoking, almost as large as the mouths of chimneys.

An ancient Mexican painting of a man "blowing out air" from a trumpetlike object has been falsely identified as evidence for a very early pipe. Other so-called "ancient" pipes have been misdated through carelessness. A pipe with wooden stem is featured in W. K. Moorehead's *The Stone Age in North America*, but this is no Stone Age pipe.[30] It comes from the basketmaker caves in Arizona. Pipes found in these caves are described in considerable detail by S. J. Guernsey and A. V. Kidder in their studies *Basketmaker Caves of Northeastern Arizona* and *Archaeological Explorations in Northeast Arizona*.[31] A stone pipe and part of a clay pipe were found in a plundered grave in Arizona, but according to Weiner "plundered graves cannot form the starting point for any chronology or the ascertainment of culture to which the objects belong, since these pipes may have gotten much later into the open graves."[32]

As for clay pipes, these could not belong to a culture as early as that of the so-called "basketmakers" because the ancient basketmakers did not yet know how to work in clay. "No specimens of true pottery," say Guernsey and Kidder, "either vessel or sherd have yet been found by us under circumstances indicating that it was a basketmaker's product . . . Clay jars found in the cave were undoubtedly cached at a comparatively late date . . .[33] A broken pipe made of clay was excavated at Casa Grande, and another was found on the ground. The former object has a slight enlargement of the perforation at one end. Although much of the stem is missing, there is no doubt that this pipe belongs to the type called the straight-tube variety which is considered to be the prehistoric form in the Southwest."[34]

Specimens of this "straight-tube variety" are to be found in the Moundbuilder culture. The Moundbuilder culture extends from Florida to the country of the Hurons, and within its wide arc are found three types of pipes having a common origin. According to J. D. McGuire, there is the "monitor" type, which is found in the whole Atlantic region down to South Carolina and as far west as Missouri, the "straight-based" or southern mound type, which extends from Florida to North Carolina and Tennessee, and the misnamed "curved-based" mound type found in the regions of the Great Lakes and as far east as Virginia.[35] Whatever the difference in these pipes, they all have a flat base, contends Leo Wiener, and they are nearly all ornamented by animal motifs.

Artifacts in these mounds were thought to be of great antiquity, dating back about two thousand years. They are now known to have been much more recent. Squier and Davis, reporting on pipes found in the mounds, date them as late *pre-Columbian*, therefore, not earlier than the fourteenth century. A few are of contact period manufacture (that is, after Columbus) the latter dating based on the European substances used in the manufacture of these later pipes. Why these mounds were built is still a mystery. Similar mounds were used for the protection of Mandingo trading posts. Wiener, on the strength of the similarity observed between this type of African defense structure and American moundbuilding, argues a direct African influence and claims the mounds are African-type stockades. His comparative plates are revealing.[36]

The influence of Africa on medieval American pipes is best demonstrated by the animal motifs found on the pipes. Most of the sculptured monitor pipes found in the mounds represent animals. Among these are seven pipes that represent the manati or sea cow. "The sculptures of this animal" say Squier and Davis "are in the same style and of like material with the others found in the mounds. One of them is of red porphyry, filled with small white and light blue granules . . . another pipe, delicately carved from compact limestone, represents a toucan, a tropical bird and one not known to exist anywhere within the limits of the U.S. . . . a pottery fragment either from a vessel or pipe, taken from a mound in Butler County, Ohio, is an unmistakable representation of the Brazilian toucan."[37]

This would seem merely to prove that there was traffic going on between the northern and southern halves of the continent, because the toucan and the manati may be found in tropical latitudes farther south. But there is more to it than that. Some of these pipes, as reported by J. D. McGuire, have excellent designs of African totem animals.[38] The elephant totem is one of these, as are the manatis, frogs, serpents, alligators and birds. Some anthropologists claim the elephant motif is an Asian influence. There is a good case for this. The others, however, though also found in tropical latitudes in South America, feature prominently as totems among the Mandingo, and their selection from a range of tropical fauna for pipe design is no accident.

Captain Binger gives the following *tenne* (totem, fetish) for some of the Mandingo. The Mande proper have the manati as their good and bad genius, the Samankhe have the elephant, the Samokho, the snake; the Bambara, the crocodile. These totem animals on the pipes were first represented on Mandingo amulets worn on the arm (known as *cibe*), only later do they appear on the monitor pipes. These totemic amulets or fetishes (called by the Americans *cibe* and *colecibe*) are mentioned by the Franciscan priest Ramon Pane as in use among the American Indians, who wore them around the neck or on the arm. They were made of a stone resembling marble. The extraordinary flat base of the bowl of the monitor pipe and its totemic representations can be seen as a consequence of its evolution from the Mandingo amulet or *cibe*.[39]

R. T. Pritchett in his book *Smokiana* remarks on the amazing
similarity between the Guinea pipes and those of the North American or "Red" Indians. Of the two Ashantee pipes (see Plate 16)
one of them has for ornamentation a bird looking back at the
bowl. Pritchett comments on their beauty, antiquity, and possible
source of inspiration in the Greco-Roman world. "The light-
colored red clay of the Ashantee pipes is very striking and the
form of the bowls still more so. There is a decidedly classical character about them, as if started from Roman lamps and Pompeian
ideas." Another plate features a long Dahomey calumet pipe with
hair-tuft adornment. "The hanging tufts," Pritchett comments,
"are of Red Indian character."[40]

The human form is also frequently represented on the pipes,
either the head alone or a man crouching with head turned back.
Of the first types, E. G. Squier reproduces one, of which the
workmanship "is unsurpassed by any specimen of ancient American art which has fallen under the notice of the editors, not ex-
cepting the best production of Mexico and Peru."[41] One of the
finest crouching figures is that on the bowl of a long pipe, with
a large orifice. It is now in the Museum of the Historical Society
of New York, but its history is unknown. The front and side views
are given in L. Choris' *Voyage Pittoresque autour du monde.*[42]
The thick Negroid lips and broad, generous nose of this figure
are well defined. Besides, the compound bracelets—five on the
wrists, six on the upper part of the arm, and four on the calf of
the leg—are of a type found only in Africa. The headgear consists
of whirl figures on the right and left, and the tuft in the middle.
The whole seems to be a kind of hood the flaps of which come
over the neck. It is to be noted that the majority of the pre-Columbian heads on pipes have just such a tuft in the middle. Even
where the bowl obliterates this tuft, we still find the two knots at
the side.

This African topknot, represented in an exceedingly large number of figurines found on pre-Columbian American pipes and
pottery, is not the only African feature. Equally interesting are
the striations or markings on the faces of the figures. Captain

Binger has given elaborate tattooing tables for a large number of African tribes, and some of the Mande striations are identical with the American.[43]

Negroid heads and masks in pre-Columbian American art have already been dealt with in Chapter 2. A number of other finds should be noted here. Terra-cotta masks that Désiré Charnay, a French anthropologist, picked up on the site of the Pyramid of the Sun at Teotihuacan, Mexico, included several that are unmistakably Negroid. One of these has woolen hair and two side knots, another has a head adornment with three excrescences, yet another has a knot with a rosette design, all familiar characteristics of West African coiffure.

In summary, the smoke medicines of the Arabs classified under the general name *tubbaq* were passed on to the African medicine men. These smoke medicines had been passed on to the Arabs earlier by Greco-Roman medicine, except that for the bitumen, henbane and other viscous plants that the Greeks and Romans used, the Arabs substituted their own herbs, particularly the *tubbaq* (as described by Ibn-al-Baitar). The Africans likewise used their own native *tubbaq* as a smoke medicine. Jean Nicot specifically refers to tobacco cures among the Moors before American tobacco began to be imported into Africa.

From the medicinal use of *tubbaq* among the Arabs, and the medical and magical use of it among the Africans, there arose the habit of oral smoking. This led to the development and refinement (if not the innovation) of pipes among the Africans. This habit of "oral" smoking, several medicinal and magical functions of the *tubbaq*, smoking words and smoking pipes, some with animal motifs and Mandingo totems, were transferred from the Africans to the Americans in pre-Columbian times.

NOTES AND REFERENCES

1 Leo Weiner, *Africa and the Discovery of America*, Philadelphia, Innes & Sons, 1922, Vol. 2, p. 91.
2 B. Reber's plates of ancient pipes published in *Les Pipes An-*

tiques de la Suisse, and reproduced by Weiner on p. 93 of Vol. 2 of his trilogy, strongly support this contention. The nipple-like protuberances on the pipe bowl clearly show that these are survivals of ancient mastaria. In fact, were the plates inverted, they would appear identical with the mastaria of the alchemists.

3 Weiner, op. cit., p. 87.

4 For this poem, see S. de Renzi, *Collectio Salernitana*, Napoli, 1852, Vol. 1, p. 509. A literal prose translation of the Latin reads: "This is the way to treat the teeth: Collect the grains of leek and burn them with henbane, and catch the smoke through an embotus into the tooth." See also Weiner, op. cit., p. 88.

5 Weiner, Vol. 2, p. 95. Quoted from Giacosa, *Magistri Salernitani*, Torino, 1901, p. 205.

6 Pliny, *Historia Naturalis*, Vol. 26, p. 30. J. Bostock and H. T. Riley (trans.), *The Natural History of Pliny*, London, 1855. See also Weiner, Vol. 2, p. 95.

7 Weiner, Vol. 2, p. 96.

8 Thomas Johnson, *The Workes of that famous Chirugion Ambrose Parey*, London, 1634, p. 1072. See also Weiner, op. cit., p. 97.

9 L. Leclerc, *"Traits des simples par Ibn El-Beïthar,"* Notices et extraits des extraits des manuscrits de la Bibliothèque Nationale, Vol. 25, No. 1581. See also Weiner, op. cit., pp. 123–125.

10 G. Binger, *Du Niger au Golfe de Guinée*, Paris, 1892, Vol. 2, p. 364. See also Weiner, op. cit., p. 127.

11 O. Houdas, *Histoire de la dynastie saadienne au Maroc 1511–1670*, Paris, 1884, p. 264. See also Weiner, op. cit., p. 127.

12 J. B. Labat, *Nouvelle relation de l'Afrique occidentale*, Paris, 1728. See Weiner, op. cit., p. 130.

13 Even this, Weiner argues (Vol. 1, p. 107), has its prototype in the "errhine" used by the Greeks and Romans (and later the Arabs) for the inhalation of medicinal powders. He feels, however, that Columbus did not actually see people smoking

them but rather inhaling powders through the nose by means of these reeds. Both A. Ernst and L. Weiner contend that smoking with a forked reed is a physical impossibility. See Ernst, "On the Etymology of the word Tobacco," *The American Anthropologist*, Vol. 2, 1889, p. 134.

14 G. F. de Oveido, *La historia general de las Indias*, Madrid, 1535, Book 5, Chapter 2. See also Weiner, Vol. 1, p. 115.

15 Weiner, Vol. 2, pp. 154–155.

16 N. Monardes, *Joyfull Newes out of the New-found Worlde*, London, 1596. See also Weiner, op. cit., p. 159.

17 Weiner, op. cit., p. 179.

18 E. Flagairolle, *Jean Nicot, Ambassadeur de France en Portugal au XVIe siècle*, Paris, 1897, p. 50. See also Weiner, op. cit., p. 151.

19 Monardes, op. cit., pp. 33b–41b.

20 Idem.

21 R. Hakluyt, *The Principal Navigations, Voyages, Traffiques and Discoveries of the English nation*, New York, 1904, Vol. 10, p. 57.

22 Monardes, op. cit.

23 Idem.

24 G. Schweinfurth, *The Heart of Africa*, New York, 1874, Vol. 1, p. 254.

25 Idem.

26 Idem.

27 Idem.

28 Weiner, op. cit., p. 132.

29 This dramatization of the sale of smoking tubes and pipes in the Mexican marketplace is based on facts gathered from D. Jourdanet and R. Siméon, *Histoire générale des choses de la Nouvelle-Espagne par le R. P. Fray Bernardino de Sahagun*, Paris, 1880, p. 630. See also Weiner, op. cit., Vol. 1, pp. 148, 149.

30 W. K. Moorehead, *The Stone Age in North America*, Boston, 1910, Vol. 2. See also Weiner, Vol. 2, p. 198.

31 S. J. Guernsey and A. V. Kidder, "Basketmaker Caves of North-

eastern Arizona, Report on the Explorations 1916–1917" in *Papers of the Peabody Museum on American Archaeology and Ethnology*, Cambridge, Harvard University, 1921, Vol. 8, No. 2, p. 98.

32 Weiner, op. cit., p. 199.

33 Guernsey and Kidder, op. cit., p. 98.

34 *Twenty Eighth Annual Report of the Bureau of American Ethnology to the Secretary of the Smithsonian Institution (1906–1907)*, Washington, 1912, p. 135.

35 C. Thomas, *The Cherokees in Pre-Columbian Times*, New York, 1890. See Plate 1 (the curved base mound type), Plate 3 (the southern mound type) and Plate 4 (the monitor pipe).

36 Comparative plates of the Peul African stockade from F. Moore's *Travels into the Inland Parts of Africa* (London, 1738) with Le Moyne's drawing of a Florida stockade made in 1564 and reproduced in De Bry's *De Commodis et Insularum Ritibus Virginia* (Frankfurt, 1590) are reproduced side by side in Weiner, op. cit., Vol. 2, between pp. 176 and 177.

37 E. G. Squier and E. H. Davis, "Ancient Monuments of the Mississippi Valley" in *Smithsonian Contributions to Knowledge*, Vol. 1, Washington, 1848, p. 260.

38 J. D. McGuire, "Pipes and Smoking Customs of the American Aborigines" in *Annual Report of the Board of Regents of the Smithsonian Institution for 1897*, p. 523.

39 Weiner, op. cit., Vol. 1, p. 178. Weiner shows that Ramon Pane's *cibe* and *colecibe* (American terms for stone amulets worn on the neck and arm) and *guanini* (for an amulet worn in the ear) are both Mandingo words, and that the *cibe* refers to the amulets worn on the· arm. "But a stone amulet," Weiner argues, "must be curved and flat to adapt itself to the arm. When the Negroes and Arawaks came to Florida, they naturally brought with them the new amulet par excellence, the tobacco pipe, hence the necessity of making it in the form of a *cibe*, with the bowl of the pipe in the middle of the base."

40 R. T. Pritchett, *Smokiana*, London, 1890, p. 33. See also Weiner, op. cit., p. 176.

41 Squier and Davis, op. cit.

42 L. Choris, *Voyage Pittoresque autour du monde*, Paris, 1822. See Table 10.

43 Binger, op. cit.

44 D. Charnay, *Ancient Cities of the New World*, (trans.) J. Gonino and H. Conant, London, 1837, p. 132.

12

THE MYSTERY
OF MU-LAN-P'I

*Far beyond the Western Sea of the Arabs' countries
[Atlantic Ocean] lies the lands of Mu-lan-p'i. The ships
which sail there are the biggest of all. One ship carries a
thousand men; on board are weaving looms and market
places. If it does not encounter favorable winds it does not
get back to port for years.*

—*Chau-ju-kua: His Work on the Chinese and Arab Trade
in the Twelfth and Thirteenth Centuries*, FRIEDRICH
HIRTH AND W. W. ROCKHILL

At Sea, circa A.D. 900

The wind dropped to a calm, and the sea became quite still. We
lay like swans asleep on a lake of blue glass. The *rubban* [cap-
tain] gave orders to let down all six of our stone *angar* [anchors],
and as we did so I saw the large, white *shirāʿ* [sails] of our companion ship, large as a cloud, shrivel slowly down to the foot of
the *daqal* [mast]. Thus we lay, staring into the emptiness of the
sea and the sky for three days.

On the fourth day our *angar* were hoisted aboard. Half a hundred men went down into two *qārib* [lifeboats], and ropes were
attached to the stern of the ship, which stretched taut over the
water as the men rowed and rowed. They were like ants dragging
a mountain. We made one knot an hour. But it stirred us back to
life, and we had only done it to kindle a spark from the smoke of
our souls. This, above all, we who sailed in the great ships feared

most—the calms—even more than the fury and violence of *al-khabb* [the typhoon]. Our ships were as large as ten houses, and we felt we were in a fortress, the walls of which were impregnable against the battering rams and catapults of the waves. It was the waiting that filled our hearts with terror, the windless silence, the siege of space. We feared we would suffocate on the dry decks, drowned by the ocean of space itself, like fishes beached on the waterless sands, drowned in pure air.

Allah be praised, the mercy of God on those who magnify him, for a gentle and favorable wind began to blow at last over the vast pool. Our great sails were unfurled, and once again we moved across the ocean like clouds. There were about eight hundred men on board the two ships, and we magnified Allah and congratulated each other and wept from the intensity of our own happiness. Toward evening birds came circling above us. They alighted on the look-out posts at the top of the *daqal*. But even as we rejoiced at the winds of the day and heard the song of the land in the shrieking banter of the birds, a shaft of lightning shone from the direction of the east. Thunder followed, and a rainstorm, and all the horizons were completely darkened. A powerful gale caught us and started to shake, and beat upon, our ship with a thousand hands.

A great darkness fell upon us, a darkness so deep that for the rest of the night and far into the morning of the next day we could not see our companion ship, the flashing of the waves, nor the still, far lamps of our heavenly pilots, the stars . . .

Thus would an Arab-African sailor, if he had kept a log, have written of some of his adventures on the high seas. It would be unlikely, however, that such a log would have survived the whole-sale burning of Moorish documents and libraries in the squares of Granada by Cardinal Ximenes in the late fifteenth century.[1] Fortunately, in spite of all the burning of ancient and medieval manuscripts, Arab shipping in both the Mediterranean sea and Indian Ocean is well documented. There are surviving narratives in Arabic, describing voyages in ancient and medieval times.[2] There are paintings, wrecks or later copies of some of these ships, as well as *rahmāni* (books of nautical instructions), *dafātir* (sailing directories), and *ṣuwar* (expertly drafted sailing charts).[3] There are historical records of splendid Arab naval victories, like the one against the Byzantine fleet (500 ships strong) in A.D. 655.[4] We have already drawn attention to the Arab influence on European shipping via the Mediterranean, the invention by the Arabs of the lateen sail which Columbus and Vespucci used on their caravels. We should also make mention of the refinement and later transmission of the magnetic needle as a mariner's compass from China to the Mediterranean by the Arabs in the age of the Crusades.[5] Their influence on European as well as on African shipping was considerable. The *mtepe* is an East African version of an ancient Arab ship, just as the main nautical instruments used by Columbus were European versions of early Arab inventions and transmissions.

The Arab ship dramatized above, with six stone anchors, rowing boats large enough to tow the ship in a calm, crews of four hundred, sails as large as clouds, plied the Indian Ocean in the tenth century.[6] Such ships were ten times larger than any ship Columbus sailed to the Americas.[7] It was in the tenth century that Arab ships were reported to have visited Atlantic islands. We find this report in the works of the Nubian geographer Idrisi (*The Third Climate*, 1151 A.D.). The Atlantic islands referred to, however, were just the Canary Islands. There the Arabs, who had set out from Lisbon, found to their surprise that speakers of Arabic had already preceded them. They came upon "an Arab interpreter to the king of the Canary islands."[8]

There is evidence also that they had visited and charted all the islands in the North Atlantic—not just the Canaries but the Cape Verde Islands and the Azores. A *Geography of the World*, published in Europe in 1350 A.D. by a Franciscan friar, lists all of these islands, and they are all given Arabic names.[9] This merely proves, however, that Arabs were navigating in the Atlantic. The one remarkable piece of cartographic evidence confirming pre-Columbian contact with America lies in the map of the famous Turkish admiral Piri Reis. The Piri Reis map was discovered in 1929 in

the old imperial palace of Istanbul. It was painted by Piri Reis
on parchment in the year 1513 from maps partially destroyed in
the library at Alexandria.[10] Parts of the reconstruction are probably not as old as the sack of Alexandria itself. Who is to say that
Piri Reis did not add to the ancient materials? The question in-
evitably arises: Could he not have inserted the South American
continent since, at the time of the reconstruction of the map, South
America had already been visited by Vespucci (June, 1499) and
Cabral (April, 1500)?

There is something unexplainable, however, about this map.
Europeans did not rediscover the technique of determining longitude until the mid-eighteenth century.[11] Maps drawn more than
two hundred years after Columbus do not show South America
in its proper relationship to Africa. Yet this map, redrawn in the
Arab world in 1513, features the accurately charted east coastline
of South America in its right longitudinal relationship with the
Atlantic coast of the Old World (Africa).[12] Also, it has Cairo,
capital of the Arab world, as the center and base for its global
computations.[13] The astronomical and navigational knowledge
demonstrated in the Piri Reis map is so astonishing that no map
until those of the twentieth century surpasses it in terms of the
precision of its latitudinal and longitudinal coordinates in the representation of coastlines of Africa and South America. Clearly it
was drawn by a people who saw South America before Columbus,
a people, moreover, who knew how to plot latitude and longitude. Only the Chinese and the Arabs mastered this knowledge
long before the era of Columbus.[14]

A recent find in South America seems to suggest an Arab presence there as early as the eighth century A.D. "Off the coast of
Venezuela was discovered a hoard of Mediterranean coins with
so many duplicates that it cannot well be a numismatist's collection but rather a supply of cash. Nearly all the coins are Roman,
from the reign of Augustus to the fourth century A.D.; two of the
coins, however, are Arabic of the eighth century A.D. It is the
latter which gives us the *terminus a quo* (i.e., time after which)
of the collection as a whole (which cannot be earlier than the

latest coins in the collection). Roman coins continued in use as currency into medieval times. A Moorish ship seems to have crossed the Atlantic around A.D. 800."[15]

Because Roman and Arab coins were not only in use by Romans and Arabs, this evidence cannot stand alone. It is supportive but not conclusive. The evidence we shall present to establish contact is historical (Sung dynasty documents), agricultural (the pre-Columbian transmission to Africa and Asia of American *zea mays*) and linguistic (Arabic words in Africa, Asia and Europe for the maize plant, as well as seventy-seven clan names and place names shared by the Berbers of North Africa and a group of American Indian tribes).

We shall see, however, from our examination of this evidence that the Arabs returned home rather than settling in America, and hence, like the Vikings, left a very negligible influence upon aboriginal Americans. We shall discover also such a strong Negroid element among the Arab-African mariners, an element numerically if not politically dominant, that as a consequence, there are no skeletal remains or traces of cultural influence in America that can be distinguished from the earlier or later African-Negro presence with but one signal exception. This exception is in the area of family and tribal names. And here we shall see the very strong possibility that the shared nomenclatures of the North African Berbers and a number of American aboriginal tribes were as much the result of journeys by Americans to Africa as the reverse. Of these journeys by Americans to the Old World there are four documented instances,[16] and the American aborigines, unlike the Arabs, lacked the capacity to return home, thereby leaving a marked influence *through settlement*, which influence extends beyond a linguistic to a physical and architectural presence in some Berber villages.

Let us first look at the case for an Arab journey to America and back. A Chinese professor, Hui-Lin Li, presented a paper to the American Oriental Society in 1961.[17] In this paper Professor Li highlighted two geographical works of the Sung dynasty—the *Ling-wai-tai-ta* (1178) by Chou Ch'ü fei and *Chu-fan-chih* (1225) by Chao Ju-kua. These are documents on the Chinese and Arab trade in the twelfth and thirteenth centuries. Both works claim that Arab ships headed west of "Ta-shin" (the extremity of the Mohammedan world, which would be the Atlantic coastline of Africa), and traveling on a great sea "sailing due west for full one hundred days" discovered a new country.

The Chinese knew the Arabs as "Ta-shih"[18] and extended that term to embrace the dominion over which they had political or spiritual influence. Ta-shih came to stand for the Arab Muslims as well as the Arab-Mohammedan world. The ocean west of that world would be the Atlantic. One hundred days' sailing by a large slow ship across the Atlantic from an Arab port "sailing due west" could only bring one to America. It should be noted that the journey takes almost twice as long as that by an African small boat, but allowance should be made for the calms. Thus Lindemann and Bombard made it to America in African-type boats in just a little more time than it took Amerigo Vespucci in his caravel.[19] The boats that sailed for a hundred days west of Ta-shih, according to the Chinese, carried several hundred men to a boat. This is no exaggeration. Buzurg has recorded that large Arab ships of this period could carry on an average four hundred men.[20]

Both the Sung geographers derived their information from Arab merchants who visited the trading ports of Southern China "translating foreign products into Chinese equivalents and transcribing foreign place names into Chinese sounds."[21] They describe the ships that made the journey and the things they found there, particularly plants not familiar to the Arabs or Chinese. The new country indicated in the Sung documents was known as Mu-lan-pʿi, which may be translated as "land reached by great ships." These ships sailed both the "Southern" and "Western" seas. Hui-Lin-Li, on the strength of all the references in the Sung documents, identifies the "Southern sea" as the Indian Ocean and the "Western sea" as the Atlantic Ocean. A sea so vast that there was nothing to be seen for a hundred days of continuous sailing, and which was entered on from a seaport west of Ta-shih, the westernmost part of the Moslem world, (a seaport just off North Africa), could only be the Atlantic.

The following passage from Chou Chʿü-fei, translated by Friedrich Hirth and W. W. Rockhill, gives a detailed account of these large ships. The bracketed insertions are mine, but are based upon Professor Li's interpretations.

"The ships which sail the Southern Sea [Indian Ocean] and south of it are like houses. When their sails are spread they are like great clouds in the sky. Their rudders are several tens of feet long.* A single ship carries several hundred men. It has stored on board a year's supply of grain . . . The big ship with its heavy cargo has naught to fear of the great waves, but in shallow water it comes to grief.

"Far beyond the Western Sea of the Arabs' countries [Atlantic Ocean] lies the land of Mu-lan-p'i. Its ships [that is, the ships which sail there] are the biggest of all. One ship carries a thousand men; on board are weaving looms and market places. If it does not encounter favourable winds it does not get back to port for years. No ship but a very big one could make such voyages. At the present time the term Mu-lan-chou is used [in China] to designate the largest kind of ship."[22]

Hirth and Rockhill, the first translators of the Sung dynasty documents, thought that (to judge from the reports) the crops of the new country were so exaggerated in size and abnormal appearance that they either gave them incongruous locations or dismissed them as fantasies. An assiduous reinspection of the weights, appearance and storage properties of some of the plants seen in the land reached by these ships, has helped Professor Li to identify some of them as New World products. Of those mentioned by the first geographer, Chou (1178), there are three which are distinctive: a large grain, a large gourd, and a strange sheep.

"A cereal grain three inches long,". Hui-Lin-Li comments, "is indeed something unusual, and this one has the property of surviving long storage . . . This strange cereal cannot be wheat, rice, barley or even rye or oats, all of which are not only of smaller size, but were familiar enough to both the Chinese and the Arabs at that time not to have aroused special interest. Judging from its

---

* The rudder was a large oar. That is why it was of such extraordinary length. See G. F. Hourani, *Arab Seafaring in the Indian Ocean*, Princeton University Press, 1951, p. 98.

large size and distinctive storage properties, the grain described is apparently maize or Indian corn, *zea mays*, an American plant . . . Its grains are much larger than any of the cereals of the Old World; and because of its very low protein content, it can be stored for a long time, a characteristic which would certainly have impressed Old World observers."[23]

Chou also describes a gigantic gourd, which was "big enough to feed twenty or thirty persons." This Professor Li identifies as the pumpkin (*cucurbita pepo*), a plant of American origin. These gourds attain a great size, some varieties occasionally weighing as much as 240 pounds.[24] There are large gourds of Old World origin, Professor Li points out, such as the watermelon and the wax gourd, but these would not have been singled out for special mention because they were long known to both the Arabs and the Chinese.

In addition to the strange cereal and gourd cited by Chou Ch'ü-fei (1178), the later geographer, Chao Ju-kua (1225), gives four other unusual plant products: a "pomegranate" weighing five *catties*,* a "peach" weighing two *catties*, a "citron" weighing over twenty *catties* and a "lettuce" weighing as much as over ten *catties*.

There are a number of plants, unknown to the Old World at the time of Chao Ju-kua, with which these four items might be identified. Fruits of American origin, long cultivated in the northern part of South America—the avocado, the cherimoya, the sweetsop, the soursop, the guava, the papaya and the pineapple—grow to a substantial size. Some, like the pineapple, may weigh as much as six pounds. This makes the unusual weights assigned by Chao Ju-kua to his several strange fruits come within reasonable bounds. Professor Li, on the strength of the weights and descriptions, tentatively identifies the "pomegranate" as the several species of *annona* (that is, the sweetsop, soursop and cherimoya); the "peach" as the avocado or papaya; the "citron" as the pineapple.[25]

With respect to the "lettuce," Hui-Lin-Li comments: "The let-

---

* The *cattie* is an Asian weight, approximately 1⅓ lbs.

tuce cited by Chao could be the South American tobacco plant. Chinese lettuce is an open leafy plant, more resembling the tobacco plant in general appearance than the lettuce plant of the Western world. It is used by the Chinese as a salad and both the fleshy stem and the green leaves are eaten either pickled or raw. Tobacco is now known to most people in the form of the aged and processed leaves, used for smoking, chewing or snuff taking, but it should be noted that the cured leaves can also be used immediately for chewing, a practice which very likely was in more general usage among the American Indians in former times. The comparison of the tobacco plant to the lettuce plant is, therefore, not too far-fetched."[26]

In addition to the plant products, both Chou and Chao spoke of sheep of unusual height with large tails. Professor Li identifies these as the llama and alpaca, which are not really sheep, but which, in some respects, so closely resemble the sheep of the Old World that they have been mistaken as such even by travelers in post-Columbian times. They are, according to Professor Li, two domesticated breeds in South America of the wild guanaco, "one being bred as a beast of burden and the other for its wool . . . They are members of the camel family although they lack humps. They closely resemble a sheep, except for the long erect neck, which makes them look much taller than sheep. Both the *llama* and *alpaca* also have large tails."[27] The unusual height and the large tail are features particularly emphasized by Chou Ch'ü-fei.

The strange cereal cited by the Sung geographers as "three inches long" and "with the property of surviving long storage" was in all likelihood *zea mays* (or "American corn," as it is more popularly known). Maize or "American corn" has been firmly established as an indigenous American plant, but there is equally firm evidence that it traveled to the Old World in pre-Columbian times.

Professor M. D. W. Jeffreys, formerly attached to Witwatersrand University, has pursued the matter of pre-Columbian maize in the Old World for the last twenty years. He cites a number of archaeological and botanical finds and unravels a remarkable tapestry of linguistic threads running across Africa and Asia and

Europe that form too consistent a web of clues to be summarily
brushed aside.

He dismisses, first of all, the popular assumption that the
Portuguese and the Dutch introduced maize into Africa after
their acquaintance with America. There seemed at first to be clear
confirmation of this assumption in the names for maize distributed
along the Guinea coast. These maize names—which are linked to
vernacular stems used by Africans to refer to "Europeans,
strangers, white men"—were thought to indicate that Europeans
(the Portuguese and Dutch) had introduced maize into Africa
in the early sixteenth century after the discovery of America. Jeffreys has shown that the terms were in use long before the arrival
of the Europeans and that they were used to refer to Arabs as well
as Berbers; and Arab-Berber, Arab-Negroid light-skinned mixtures.

The Portuguese raid for slaves on the Guinea coast in 1444, for
example, records that when African captives in the mid-fifteenth
century were exposed for sale in Lagos, Portugal . . . "it was truly
a thing astonishing to behold; for among them were some well-
nigh white . . . others were black as Ethiopians."[28] It would be
absurd to assume, argues Jeffreys, that these people "well-nigh
white" had no name among the black Africans until the latter
encountered the Portuguese. The word *Turawa*, for example (*Tur*
means Arab; *awa* means people), mentioned by Ibn Battuta as
early as the mid-fourteenth century in the record of his visit to
Mali, is also in many West African languages (Nupe, Kapa, Ebe,
Hausa, Kambali, Nguro and Moni, to cite just a few) the general
term for white man.

Other popular stems and their variants found in maize names
(such as *buro, boro, poro, puru, pura, poto, putu,* and so on) were
thought to be exclusive referents to Europeans (that is, the
Portuguese). Porteres' interpretation of the term *puto,* Koelle's of
poro, and Wiener's of *aburo,* are all part of the same mistake. Jeffreys shows that the similarity between the sound *put* in African
vernaculars and the sound *port* in Portuguese is purely coincidental. The Arabs, for example, have clearly been established as
the distributors of the plantain and banana in West Africa. The
Vai, a West African tribe, call the banana *poro-bana,* which is the

banana of the *poro* (the stem *poro* standing in this case for the Arab—as in later times it came to stand for the Portuguese and other Europeans). The case is amply demonstrated with both the plantain and banana names, using the following tribes as test cases—The Mano, Kissi, Tshi, Ewe, Ga, Fante, Krepi, Ashante and Kassena. Further, the pre-Columbian Arab trade in spices and the aromatic seed Aframomum led to a number of African names for these spices and aromatics in which these stems reappear, linking their origin to the Arabs. For example, among the Yoruba and Ibo of Nigeria and the Aku of Sierra Leone, stems which are terms for Arabs, *polo, buro, opolo, aburo*, may be found in the names for a number of Arab trade items. It would be strange indeed if so many peoples trading in plantains, bananas, spices, peppers, and perfumes had to wait for the Portuguese to arrive before inventing names for these.

No African maize name (which is usually a compound of the name for the local sorghum and the name of the people from whom maize was obtained) connects the European unequivocally with the introduction of maize. Even the Mpongwe, whose word for maize is associated with a phrase meaning "people of the sun," cannot be shown to have got maize from the Europeans, as Professor Porteres has claimed. The phrase "people of the sun" is widespread in Africa and is pre-European; it was used to refer to those Egyptian Pharaohs who were light-skinned.[29]

Not only have these claims (like those of Willet and Porteres) that there is a linguistic link between the Portuguese and maize in West Africa been exposed by Jeffreys as untenable, but historical documents of the Portuguese and the Dutch themselves show that the equally insistent claim that "maize first arrived in Africa across the Atlantic having been brought from the Guianas and Brazil by Portuguese and Dutch vessels to the Guynee coast"[30] has no foundation. The discovery of Brazil by the Portuguese explorer Alvares Cabral in 1500 makes no mention of maize, and Cabral did not sail to Guinea from Brazil but went direct to Calicut in India, where he stayed for a while to found a trading station. Even the possibility of his taking maize to India must be ruled out, because there maize is known by the same name as in

East Africa—"the sorghum of Mecca." Another Portuguese expedition visited Brazil in 1501, but *not* the Guinea coast. As for the Dutch, their visits to America were later still, and 1595 was the year of their first expedition to West Africa.

But what of the Spanish. Surely Columbus could have brought maize grains to Spain. Brazil, after all, was not the exclusive home of *zea mays,* and the Portuguese and the Dutch were not the only potentially maize-carrying Europeans to set foot on West African soil in the late fifteenth and early sixteenth centuries. Willet contends, "In 1493 Columbus probably introduced maize from Haiti into Spain. Certainly *mahitz* or *maritchi* arrived in Spain from Cuba in 1520, although its cultivation appears to have been attempted in Seville in 1500."[31]

On the first point, Jeffreys shows that Columbus did not, at that date [1493], introduce maize into Spain. He quotes P. Weatherwax, who notes that "it [maize] is generally supposed [to be] among the New World curiosities taken back by Columbus on his return from the first voyage and purely imaginary pictures of the Admiral being received by Ferdinand and Isabella sometimes show ears of corn. . . . We have searched the old chronicles with some care on this point and have failed to find any explicit support for this quite plausible inference." Jeffreys also points to this lack of evidence for a post-Columbian introduction of maize highlighted by the Italian Bertagnolli, who, writing in 1881, states, "It is generally accepted that maize was imported from America by the Spaniards . . . But this opinion is not substantiated by any definite documents."[32]

Even if the Spanish had brought maize to Guinea in 1496, it could not account for what the evidence suggests—that as early as 1500 maize was already a staple crop and regular food on the Guinea coast. By 1502, it was being exported to Sãn Thomé. The first reference to this exportation of maize from the Guinea coast was made by the Portuguese Valentim Fernandez, who in 1506 said that maize (Fernandez used the term *zaburro,* which will be discussed later) was exported from the Guinea coast to Sãn Thomé and grown there for the first time in 1502. Fernandez, describing the Wolof, whose country lay between the Senegal and

Gambia rivers, also remarked, "They eat rice of which they have little, of maize they have much."[33] The Mandingoes (the largest group in this area) were also noted in this reference as cultivators of *milho zaburro*. Some critics of Jeffreys have suggested that maize could be confused with African sorghum, and that Fernandez's use of *zaburro* for maize is not conclusive. The distinction between sorghum and maize, however, was known—or rather, sorghum was too well known to be confused with maize. It had been cultivated in the Iberian peninsula for some centuries before 1502 and acquired its own names there. Names for sorghum are mentioned by the Arab writer D'Ibn-Al-Awan in his treatise on agriculture in the Iberian peninsula, *Kitab-al-Felaha*, published in 1158 in Seville. In Spain sorghum was and still is known as *melica, saggina, mazorca* and *mazaroca,* and in Portuguese as *sorgo* or *mexiora.* Why, asks Jeffreys, should Fernandez use *zaburro* for sorghum, which has its own separate constellation of names. The term *zaburro* was further qualified by Fernandez (*milho zaburro he grāde*) to indicate the extraordinarily large maize grain that an anonymous Portuguese pilot to Guinea (according to Serge Savoglot) described in 1520 as being of the size of chickpeas. "Much of the early maize of West Africa," Jeffreys notes, "was flint maize, whose grains are generally large" and "the only cereal in the high rainfall areas of the West African coasts which produces a grain comparable in size with chickpeas is maize."[34] There is also another and more serious argument against the possible confusion of sorghum with maize. Jeffreys contends that "Cultivated sorghum is not able to grow in the rainforest regions where maize flourishes. The sorghum grains in the humid climate are rapidly attacked by mildew."[35]

The Portuguese pilot paid five visits to Sān Thomé, describing the maize there in considerable detail. He also commented that it was everywhere. While it is true that the pilot's visits and references postdate Fernandez by about fifteen years, there could not possibly have been a shift from heavy sorghum cultivation to ubiquitous maize cultivation in the intervening period. Dr. H. Lains e Silva said of the pilot's evidence that the *zaburro* he describes "certainly does not refer to sorghum but to *zea mays,* whose grains can roughly be compared with those of *Lathyrus cicera* which is indigenous in the South of Europe and therefore known to the author."[36] An earlier Portuguese reference, suggesting the pre-Columbian cultivation of maize in Guinea, comes from a record of the ordinances of the Portuguese king Manoel (1495–1521), who allowed for the purchase of maize from Guinea by those ships which were sent to embark slaves at Sãn Thomé.[37] An even earlier dating is given by Santa Rose de Viterbo, who, in his supplement to the *Elucidario* (written in 1798 on the authority of earlier writers), states that "maize was brought into Portugal in the reign of King John (1481–95) after the discovery of Guynee."[38]

A considerable number of references are quoted by Jeffreys to demonstrate the widespread cultivation of maize along the Guinea coast in the sixteenth century. These other references, however, while they certainly establish the ubiquity of maize and its use as a staple food in West Africa, are too late, I feel, to be of value in this argument. What is more relevant and persuasive is his contention that the Portuguese terms for maize are African terms, and that on finding maize in the Americas the Portuguese neither invented new names for it nor did they adopt the local American Indian name. Rather, they referred to maize as *milho de Guynee* or *zaburro*.

Jules César Scaliger, as early as 1557, stated that the word *zabur* for a cereal was of African origin. He remarked, "Milium is called by the Ethiopians *zabur*, by the Arabs, *dora*."[39] Jeffreys, in an article on *zaburro*, shows that the evidence points to the origin of the word among the Akan (a Twi-speaking people), who he claims acquired maize from the Arabs while in the Djenne-Timbuktu region (circa 1300) and acquired the name at the same time. Because the Twi, Fante and Asante do not have the *z* sound in their languages, *zaburro* would appear in these languages as *aburro*. Over a wide area, *Za* and its variants mean sorghum, and *buro, buru* are variants of the term for Arab. Thus *za-buro* or *a-buro* means sorghum of the Arab. Even in East Africa, among the Siangazija, the term for maize is *mrama buru*, which means "the sorghum of the *buru*," where the word *buru* would never be taken to mean anyone but an Arab.

The possible alternative origin of this word *zaburro*—from *ceburro,* meaning cattle fodder—has also been considered by Jeffreys. That possibility does not upset his case. The early use of maize for fodder may have easily led to the phonetic and semantic fusion of these verbal twins—*zaburro, ceburro.* Leo Wiener quotes Soares de Souza as saying in 1587 that "in all of Brazil there is a native plant which the Indians call *ubatim* (maize) which is Guinea millet and which in Portugal is called *zaburro.* The Portuguese (in Brazil) plant this millet with which to feed the horses, cattle, chickens, goats, sheep, and pigs . . ."[40] In Italy, notes Jeffreys, quoting Bertagnolli, "Maize at first was grown as a food for cattle."

Jeffreys has followed the trail of maize across vast areas of Africa—west, east and south, finally to Asia and Asia Minor (the empire of the Turks and Saracens) and from Asia Minor to Europe. The evidence he unearths is not simply based on linguistics (that is, names for maize) but also on archaeological finds, such as the Goodwin finds at Ile Ife, the Summers and Wild finds in the Inyanga ruins of Monomotapa (now Rhodesia), and the Vishnu-Mittre and Gupta finds in India—all pre-Columbian.

A. J. Goodwin in 1953 reported that pots decorated by rolling a maize cob over wet clay were found at Ile Ife (Yoruba territory in Nigeria). Goodwin noted, "As vast numbers of specimens were collected from a pavement of potsherds that provided a clear dating line for certain sites, it became important to note whether or not the maize cob decoration occurred. It did, and it is abundantly clear that this particular paving is subsequent to the introduction of maize."[41]

This pavement was laid while Ile Ife was the ritual capital of the Yoruba kings. No more precise dating is given, although there is no question that the pavement is pre-Columbian. Jeffreys attempts to date it, and the maize-cob potsherds found on its surface by reference to Yoruba traditions. These traditions, according to R. F. Burton, state that maize was introduced among the Yoruba by yellow-skinned foreigners who crossed the Niger from the northeast.[42] This would rule out Europeans as "bringers" of maize to Africa since, apart from the fact that they do *not* fit the physical description, they came much later and from the west.[43]

Maize, according to Yoruba traditions (recorded by Babalola), arrived in Yorubaland while Ile Ife was still the capital.[44] Talbot writes that between A.D. 600 and A.D. 1000 a wave of immigrants from the east invaded Yorubaland and made Ile Ife their capital, but later this capital was moved to Old Oyo.[45] Jeffreys says, "If now one takes the latest date for their invasion as say A.D. 1000 and that Old Oyo was founded around A.D. 1100, then it would appear that somewhere about this time maize appeared among the Yoruba."[46]

Jeffreys has done another important test to confirm the Yoruba oral traditions that maize reached them from the northeast. As one progresses inland from the coast, he notes, the tribal names for maize indicate the route by which it migrated. "Thus the name for maize in Tribe A is the sorghum of Tribe X where X is found ultimately to be the name of a tribe east or north of the receiving Tribe A." Two or three examples may make this clearer. The Hegi receiving their maize from the Kanuri call it the sorghum of the Kanuri to distinguish it from their local brand of sorghum— African sorghum; the Jukun receiving it from the Pabir call it the sorghum of the Pabir; and the Yakutare receiving it from the Kwona call it the sorghum of the Kwona, and so on.[47]

The evidence Jeffreys presents for pre-Columbian maize in East Africa is equally impressive. The Arabs were trading on the East African seacoast from Sofala to Arabia long before the Portuguese had rounded the Cape of Good Hope. The Arabs penetrated far inland, for when the Portuguese first visited Zimbabwe—then the capital of Monomotapa (the present Rhodesia)—they found Arabs already established there. Jeffreys shows that, starting from Sofala and proceeding north along the coast until Madras in India is reached, all the names for maize among the coastal tribes of East Africa are connected with the Arabs.

V. d'Almeida, the first viceroy of India, noted on his arrival at Kilwa on the East African coast in 1505 that that city "had plenty of *milho* like that of Guynee."[48] The Portuguese had for centuries known what sorghum was like, but here at Kilwa was a grain like that found on the coast of Guinea. (Again, it must be pointed out that two hundred inches of rain fall on the coasts of Guinea, and so no cultivated sorghum will grow, but maize grows and produces two crops a year.) Hence it follows that the remark by d'Almeida—"*milho* (grain) like that of Guynee"—can only point to maize. In 1505, then, maize was a staple crop in places as far apart as Kilwa (East Africa) and the Guinea coast (West Africa).

Chinese sources establish an even earlier date for maize in East Africa. Duyvendak mentions that the Chinese between 1405 and 1422 sent six expeditions by sea to East Africa. These Chinese navigators sent back reports of things seen there, among which were an unknown cereal "with extraordinary large ears," a vegetarian tiger (which has been identified as the African zebra), and "sweet dew."[49] With respect to the first item, it should be noted that the Chinese were well acquainted with the Old World cereals —rice, wheat, barley, and sorghum—none of which carries "extraordinary large ears." Therefore, one is forced to the conclusion that the cereal referred to was maize. The size of maize would strike the Chinese who, according to the botanist Alphonse de Candolle, have annually, since 2200 B.C., ceremonially sown five kinds of seeds—wheat, rice, sorghum, *setaria italica,* and soy—none of which, it must be repeated, carries extraordinarily large ears. How and when maize got to China is another intriguing side to the story.

The first European to reach Mozambique around the Cape, Vasco da Gama, recorded maize there in March 1498. In an account of the capture of two boats in the Mozambique channel, da Gama wrote, "In the one we took we found 17 men, besides gold, silver and an abundance of maize (milho) and other provisions." (The word *milho* Jeffreys claims, on the strength of all the documents he has examined, was the standard Portuguese official name for maize and was used for maize in the early records of the Portuguese administration.)

Recordings of maize in Southern Africa by Europeans are all post-fifteenth century, but they are well before the movement of the Europeans as settlers into that area. They found maize already growing there when they arrived. Reports in the sixteenth century attest to the pre-European presence of maize in Southern Africa. Accounts of a shipwreck on the South African coast in 1554, and of a murdered priest at Zimbabwe (now Rhodesia) in 1561, both tell of a cereal in terms that leave little doubt as to its identity as maize. A survivor of the wreck of the *Esperanca* in 1554, Manoel Perestrello, not only uses the term *milho zaburro* for the grain offered by the Africans at the mouth of the Pescaria River, but the priest who was murdered, Father Gonzalo de Silviera, was noted in a Portuguese account for his daily consumption of "roasted grain cooked with herbs," a detail that distinguishes maize from African sorghum. This is so because Indian corn (maize) in Southern Africa, unlike kaffir corn (African sorghum), is "roasted on the heads in the embers and eaten parched in hot ashes" or "cooked with herbs and served as a vegetable relish," which is still the practice among the Bantu today.[50]

Further evidence of pre-Columbian maize in Southern Africa has been found in the Inyanga ruins of Monomotapa. The Inyanga site was abandoned in the fifteenth century, according to R. Summers. H. Wild, in his botanical report on these ruins, states: "Portions of a maize cob (zea mays L.) were found on the surface of a grinding place on Site IV, although no actual seeds were discovered."[51]

How did maize reach Southern Africa *before* the Dutch or the Portuguese? As a consequence of the movement, says Jeffreys, of two Bantu tribes, the Nguni and the Bavenda, from East Africa into Central Southern Africa. Jeffreys traced the names for maize among these migrating Bantu tribes, and he found that South African Bantu tribes either have stems of the Nguni words for maize and maize loaf or "call maize by a name similar to that by which they knew the Nguni," while the maize words of the Bavenda tribe form a linguistic island, (that is, are words used for maize only by the Bavenda). This clearly suggests that "the Nguni arrived with maize before the Bavenda came, and in disseminating this crop disseminated the maize names linked with them."[52]

Arab trade in the Indian Ocean closely linked the East African coastal territories with the world of India and China. The pre-

Columbian appearance of maize in India, therefore, can be explained in the same way. Chinese documents of the Ming dynasty (the *Pun Ts'ao Kang-Mu*, the *Nung Chêng Ts'uan Shu* and the *Ke Chih King-yüan*) also point to a pre-Columbian introduction from territory west of China, the latter document specifically pinpointing Kan-su, where there was a large settlement of Arabs.

In 1928 the Russian botanist N. N. Kuleshov published the results of his investigations into maize in Asia. These results point to a feature in Asiatic maize, which, if it is a mutation of the American plant, would call for "an earlier cultivation of maize in Asia than the time of the first landing by the Portuguese on the shores of Asia in 1516 . . . The facts, which were established by us (Kuleshov and Vavilov) return us anew to this supposition and this time with a great deal of conviction."[53]

Maize names in India all suggest an Arab introduction. "In the whole of Southern India," says Sri P. Krishna Rao, in a personal letter to Professor Jeffreys, "maize is known as Mekka sorghum, the word *sorghum* being rendered into the respective local Indian languages. The names all strongly point to the fact that maize has come from Mecca." (Mecca here refers not to a specific place but to the symbolic heartland of the Arab-Mohammedan world.)

The Vishnu-Mittre and Gupta finds are the strongest evidence supporting the pre-Columbian presence of maize in Asia. Vishnu-Mittre, describing carbonized food grains and their impressions on potsherds from Kaundinyapur, an archaeological site in Madhya Pradesh, north India, wrote that "the evidence of maize in India is not in any case later than 1435 A.D. . . . and tends to establish its pre-Columbian age."[54] From both Asia and Asia Minor (which circa 1320 was the empire of the Muslim Turks and Saracens) maize spread to Europe, and hence it is referred to in European countries as Turkish wheat, Saracen wheat, wheat of Asia or Arabian wheat. "Turk" was once the generic name for the Arab in the Mediterranean. Thus, we have *grano turco*, *grano Saraceno*, *frumentum Saracenium*, *frumentum Asiaticum* (Italy), Turkish corn, Tartarian wheat (Great Britain), *Turks tarwe* (Holland), *Turkish hvede* (Sweden), *Turetzki chelb* (Russia), *frumentum*

Asiaticum (Germany), *blé de Turquie* (France), *Tshurkiya* (Morocco) and *Arabosite* (Greece).[55]

The pre-Columbian appearance of maize in Asia is well known. Botanists who knew nothing of the African pre-Columbian evidence unearthed by Jeffreys were claiming an Asian origin for the grain. In fact, no one ever suggested that maize was originally brought to Europe from America in the first thirty years of the discussion of the plant.[56] Europe, as Jeffreys has shown, has almost all of its names for maize associated with Asia (i.e., that part of Asia within the pre-Columbian Mohammedan world). Asia, on the other hand, has no names for maize associated with America or Europe.[57] Even in Spain an early name for maize was *trigo de Turquia,* not the American word "maize" (from the Arawak *mahiz*), and in Portugal (as mentioned earlier) it was referred to as Guynee wheat.

To return to the central question, How did maize get to Africa, to Asia, to Asia Minor, and to Europe in pre-Columbian times? Who orignally brought it from America, and when and how? Jeffreys has suggested expeditions (return journeys) across the Atlantic by Arab-Africans to account for the pre-Columbian presence of American maize in the Old World.

A thesis published in Algiers in 1930 by a French commandant, Jules Cauvet, lends further support to this suggestion. While involved in another study, Cauvet noted that "the ethnic names of certain Berber groups were the same as those of certain American Indian tribes."[58] The Berbers are a mixed race of Arabs who live in North Africa. They originally came from Northern Asia, India and the Caucasus, and have also mingled with Negroid tribes in the Saharan deserts. They lived in the medieval period at the northern boundary of the Mali empire and paid allegiance to the black emperors of Mali. Because of their original "Asian" background before their intermingling with other Caucasoid and Negroid elements, Cauvet found it necessary to cross-check Asian ethnic names to see whether these similar names among the Berbers and the Americans arose as a consequence of "a simultaneous arrival of groups from Asia."[59] This check could not ex-

plain these astonishing parallels. Few could be accounted for by
virtue of the early Asiatic element in the Berber background.

"Certain American ethnic names," Cauvet said, "are only duplicated among the Berbers and are not found anywhere else in the
world; certain other [American] names have undergone Berber
transformations; the origin of a number of names is attested by
the grouping of names of collectivities in the vicinity of their
point of origin."[60]

Cauvet examined the origins of 77 such similar names of tribes
on both sides of the Atlantic. Among the 77 he was able to distinguish five categories.

Of the 77, he found as many as 46 names of American tribes
that seemed to come directly from Africa. He cites the following
examples in this category: the Azlantecas of America (the Atlantes
mentioned in Herodotus); the Baquetias (the ancient Bacouates);
the Barcas (the Barcadjenna mentioned by Arab writers); the Bu-
coyas (the Bokkoya of the Rif in North Africa); the Guisnais (the
Gueznaïa of the Rif); the Gualis (the Guellaïa of the Rif); the
Chorti (the Chorta mentioned by Arab writers); the Guamares
(the Ghomara of the Rif and the island Gomera); the Guanchas
(the Guanches of the Canary Islands); the Huares (the Hoouara
of Morocco) etc.[61]

Cauvet explains how some of these names found among Ameri-
cans belong to "inland" as well as "coastal" Atlantic Berbers:
Berber tribes moved around; "inland" tribes took part in expedi-
tions organized by coastal tribes; Arab-African expeditions to
America drew upon people from all over the Berber complex in
Africa.[62]

In the other four categories of names, he places those which
"certainly come from the East but might have got to America
from Europe as well as from the Berbers" (examples are the Antis,
Atures, Dorins, Gabilanes, Ges, Jibaros, Lipis, Parisis, Saracas,
Samagotos, Tames, Zamoras),[63] those that are "also Berber but
seem certainly to have come to the Americas from Europe" (Cam-
pas and Utes), those that "might equally have come from Asia
as from Africa" (Coras, Chalcas, Kutchines, Katamas)[64] and those
whose origins remain unsure but are found nonetheless duplicated

in America and North Africa (Amalecitas, Cesares, Faraones, Gergecensenos, Matemates and Outtaouts).[65]

Cauvet's study is massive. It runs to half a thousand pages. These in brief, however, are his main discoveries. Some of the ethnic names he has turned up could have traveled to America during the medieval contact period between Africans and Americans. One is the Galibis, for a small tribe in Brazil (in a province once known as Portuguese Guyana) from the Galibis in the Mali university town of Timbuktu. Another is the Marabitine tribe of the Sudan, which he compares with the Marabitinas and Maravittinas, also of former Portuguese Guiana (in Brazil), Marabi-os (Nicaragua) and Maravigene (Venezuela).[66]

There are many more, but these should suffice. Anthropologists have often found ethnic names important in following the migrations of peoples. Like the names of individuals, they are the last linguistic elements to go, even after the foreign tongue has been abandoned, forgotten or absorbed. Linguistic studies among the Gullah blacks in the Sea Islands, for example, although related only to post-Columbian migrations, show how thousands of West African names have been retained as "secret names" among them.[67] People drop a great deal when they settle in an alien environment and intermarry with the women or the culture of native populations. The last thing they drop, however, is names. Names can therefore often be used to track down their identity, as detectives track down the identity of suspects from fingerprints.

But these many identities in names are not simply the result of one migration of Arabs or Africans to America, nor in fact to a one-way traffic of people and culture to the American continent. Cauvet does not rule out American contact with Africa and mentions "four documented instances of Americans shipwrecked on the shores of the Old World."[68] These were rather rare events, much rarer than African accidental shipwrecks, because the pattern of winds and currents favors the possibility of the one over the other. Nevertheless, they sometimes happened.

The Gulf Stream departing from Florida provides a return route back to North Africa and parts of Europe. At Spain the Gulf

Stream divides in two directions, one continuing around the British isles on to Germany and Denmark, and the other bending south to Africa. This would explain American aborigines' being found in Berber territory in North Africa.

Two anthropologists have demonstrated that certain people living in the Sahara possess American Indian traits. "Not only do they have similar names and naming methods but tribal groups are also designated by the same titles, differing only in the aspects of an occasional prefix or suffix. Furthermore, the womenfolk of the same region in all appearance could easily be mistaken for American Indians . . . these nomads reside in tents rather than mud-brick houses as do most of their neighbors."[69]

Among the documented instances of Americans landing in the Old World is an incident in the life of Quintus Metellus Celer, governor of Cisalpine Gaul in 62 B.C. and governor designate of Transalpine Gaul prior to his death in 59 B.C.

A chief from somewhere just outside of the Roman world made him a present of some shipwrecked sailors, who created a sensation. After some communication could be established with them they were questioned closely, and on the strength of this, Metellus concluded that they had been blown by a storm from "Indian waters" and eventually cast up on a shore in Germany [this would agree with the drift of the Gulf Stream current from America, a branch of which proceeds to Germany]. These so-called "Indians" were brought across the Alps *from the Atlantic side* by the Suevians, a tribe which lived in northeast and southwest Germany. The Americans were shipwrecked near the mouth of the Rhine and were taken up that river and across the Alps. Celer related the incident to a friend, Cornelius Nepos. Nepos included it in a geographical work which, though lost, was cited by subsequent historians, Pomponius Mela and Pliny. Records of the incident were therefore preserved, and these writers used the information as proof that the ocean extended continuously around the north of Europe to India. "One thing is certain," comments Professor J. V. Luce, who has investigated the matter, "no one from India could have taken this route at this date."[70]

Where, then, did these shipwrecks come from? An examination

of all the facts (drift of ocean currents, point of entry into Europe, physical appearance, etc.) establish them as Occidental Indians (that is, Americans) as against Oriental Indians (Asians from India).

These Americans came too early to have been the carriers of the maize grain to the Old World, but they might have brought in the pineapple. Their visit occurred in 62 B.C. About a hundred years later (79 A.D.) a catastrophe struck the Roman city of Pompeii. Excavating under the volcanic dust archaeologists turned up a mural which depicted this plant, completely unknown in the Old World. It has been confidently identified as the American pineapple by Casella, an authority on Pompeii, and has been accepted as such by plant taxonomist E. D. Merrill[71] (who had argued in the past against pre-Columbian contact between the Old and New Worlds).

It would be an irony, indeed, to find that Americans "discovered" Europe many centuries before Europeans "discovered" America. But the whole notion of any race (European, African or American) discovering a full-blown civilization is absurd. Such notions should now be abandoned once and for all. They presume some innate superiority in the "discoverer" and something inferior and barbaric in the people "discovered." These notions run through the works even of pioneers like Wiener, Cauvet and Jeffreys. What I have sought to prove is not that Africans "discovered" America, but that they made contact on at least half a dozen occasions, two of which were culturally significant for Americans.

The African presence in America before Columbus is of importance not only to African and American history but to the history of world civilizations. It provides further evidence that all great civilizations and races are heavily indebted to each other and that no race has a monopoly of enterprise and inventive genius. The African presence is proven by stone heads, terra cottas, skeletons, artifacts, techniques and inscriptions, by oral traditions and documented history, by botanical, linguistic and cultural data. When the feasibility of African crossings of the Atlantic was not proven and the archaeological evidence undated and unknown, we could in all innocence ignore the most startling of coincidences.

This is no longer possible. The case for African contacts with pre-Columbian America, in spite of a number of understandable gaps and a few minor elements of contestable data, is no longer based on the fanciful conjecture and speculation of romantics. It is grounded now upon an overwhelming and growing body of reliable witnesses. Using Dr. Rhine's dictum for phenomena that were once questionable but are now being empirically confirmed, truly it may be said: the overwhelming incidence of coincidence argues overwhelmingly against a mere coincidence.

NOTES AND REFERENCES

1 M. D. W. Jeffreys, "Pre-Columbian Arabs in the Caribbean," *The Muslim Digest*, 5 (I), August, 1954, p. 26.
2 G. F. Hourani, *Arab Seafaring in the Indian Ocean in Ancient and Early Medieval Times*, Princeton University Press, 1951. See Appendix.
3 Ibid., p. 107.
4 Ibid., pp. 56–59.
5 Ibid., p. 109.
6 Hui-Lin-Li, "Mu-lan-p'i: A Case for Pre-Columbian Transatlantic Travel by Arab Ships," *Harvard Journal of Asiatic Studies*, 23, 1961, pp. 114–126.
7 Ibid., p. 125.
8 Ibid., p. 126. Hui-Lin-Li bases this statement on Edrisi's account, which is translated by R. Dozy and M. J. Goeje, *Description de l'Afrique et de l'Espagne par Edrisi*, Leyden, 1866.
9 Jeffreys, op. cit., pp. 25, 26.
10 Cyrus Gordon, *Before Columbus*, New York, Crown Publishers, 1971, pp. 71, 72, 73. (Gordon provides illustrative reproductions of the Piri Reis map, showing the correct longitudinal relationship between the Atlantic coast of South America and the Old World.)
11 Arthur James Weise, *Discoveries of America to 1525*, New York, G. P. Putnam's Sons, 1884, pp. 66–68.
12 Gordon, op. cit.
13 Cartographers projected the Piri Reis map onto a grid. It

then appeared virtually identical with a United States Air Force map of the world on an equidistant projection based on Cairo. See Comparative Maps in Erich von Däniken's *Chariots of the Gods?* (the Bantam Books paperback edition, 1974, translated by Michael Heron). His explanation of this phenomenon, however, on pp. 14–15, involves extraterrestial visitors and takes no cognizance of the sophisticated level of Arab cartography and geographical knowledge in pre-Columbian times.

14 See Weise (note 11 above), but see also H. F. Tozer, Biblot Tannen, 1964, pp. 167, 172, 343.

15 Gordon, op. cit., p. 68.

16 Gaston Edouard Jules Cauvet, *Les Berbères en Amérique*, Alger, J. Bringan, 1930. See Avant Propos.

17 Hui-Lin-Li, op. cit.

18 Hourani, op. cit., pp. 63, 66.

19 Alain Bombard took 65 days in 1952, sailing from Casablanca in North Africa on a raft to Barbados. Amerigo Vespucci took 64 days, even though he started out from a more advantageous position off the African continent. In a letter to Lorenzo di Pier Francesco de Medici in 1502 he writes: "We departed from the Cape Verde very easily . . . we sailed on the wind within half a point of southwest, so that in sixty-four days [delayed by the doldrums] we arrived at a new land which, for many reasons . . . we observed to be a continent." For the latter, see Frederick Pohl, *Amerigo Vespucci, Pilot Major*, New York, Columbia University Press, 1944, p. 130. Hannes Lindemann made the journey in 1955 in an African dugout in 52 days.

20 For reference to Buzurg (ibn-Shahriyar of Ramhurmuz) see Hourani, op. cit., p. 98. Also see Varthema in Hakluyt Society, 1st Series, Vol. XXXII, p. 161 (ship holding 400 men).

21 Li, op. cit., p. 125.

22 Friedrich Hirth and W. W. Rockhill (eds. and trans.) *Chao Ju-kua: His work on the Chinese and Arab trade in the twelfth and thirteenth centuries, entitled Chu-fan-chi*, St. Petersburg, 1911, pp. 33–34.

23 Li, op. cit., p. 122.

24 Li, op. cit., pp. 122, 123. See also L. W. Bailey, "The Domesticated Cucurbitas—I," *Gentes Herbarum* 2, 1929, pp. 63–115.
25 Li, op. cit., p. 123.
26 Li, op. cit., p. 124.
27 Ibid.
28 M. D. W. Jeffreys, "How Ancient is West African Maize,"
   Africa, January, 1963, p. 116.
29 Ibid., p. 120.
30 F. Willett, "The Introduction of Maize into West Africa: An
   Assessment of Recent Evidence," *Africa*, 32, No. 1, January,
   1962.
31 Ibid.
32 C. Bertagnolli, "Delle vicende dell' agricoltura in Italia" in
   L'Agricoltura Italiana nell' età Moderna, Firenze, 1881. Jeffreys, *How Ancient is West African Maize*, p. 126.
33 Jeffreys, op. cit., p. 121.
34 Idem.
35 Jeffreys, op. cit., p. 127.
36 H. Lains e Silva, "Nomes vulgares de algumas plantas de São
   Tomé e Principe," *Garcia de Orta*, Lisboa, 1959. Jeffreys, op.
   cit., p. 121.
37 J. W. Blake, *European Beginnings in West Africa 1458–1578*,
   London, 1937. Jeffreys, op. cit., p. 121.
38 O. Ribiero, "Cultura do milho economica agraria e povo-
   mento," *Biblos*, Vol. 17, No. 2, Lisboa, 1941, pp. 657–663. Jeffreys, op. cit., p. 124.
39 Jeffreys, op. cit., p. 123.
40 Leo Weiner, *Africa and the Discovery of America*, Philadelphia, Vol. 1, Innes & Sons, 1920, p. 118.
41 A. J. H. Goodwin, *South African Archaeological Bulletin*, Vol.
   8, No. 29, 1953. Jeffreys, "Pre-Columbian Maize in Africa," pp.
   965–966.
42 R. F. Burton, *Abeokuta and the Cameroon Mountain*, London,
   1863. Jeffreys, op. cit., pp. 965–966.
43 S. O. Biobaku, in his Lugard lectures published in Lagos,
   1955, suggested that the founders of Yoruba civilization in
   Southern Nigeria reached their country between A.D. 700 and

A.D. 900, coming originally from the Middle Nile. The emphasis on eastern origin is clear and insistent with the Yoruba. (This point is made by Basil Davidson, *The Lost Cities of Africa*, Boston, Little Brown, 1959, p. 60.)

44 A. Babalola, *West African Review*, Vol. 23, No. 292, 1952, and Jeffreys, "Pre-Columbian Maize in Africa," *Nature*, 172, 1953, p. 965.

45 P. A. Talbot, *Southern Nigeria*, Oxford, 1926, and Jeffreys, op. cit., p. 965.

46 Jeffreys, op. cit., p. 965.

47 Ibid.

48 E. Axelson, *South-East Africa, 1488–1530*, London, 1940, p. 132, and Jeffreys, "Who Introduced Maize into Southern Africa?" *South African Journal of Sciences*, 63, January, 1967, p. 30.

49 J. L. L. Duyvendak, *China's Discovery of Africa*, London, 1949, p. 30, and Jeffreys, op. cit., p. 28.

50 Jeffreys, op. cit., p. 30.

51 R. Summers, *Inyanga*, Cambridge, 1958, p. 241. H. Wild, *Botanical Notes Relating to the Van Niekirk Ruins in Inyanga*, Cambridge, 1958, p. 176. See Jeffreys, op. cit., p. 37.

52 M. D. W. Jeffreys, "Pre-Columbian Maize in Southern Africa," *Nature*, 215, August, 1969, pp. 695–697.

53 H. J. Kidd and H. C. Reynolds (trans.), N. N. Kuleshov, "Some Peculiarities of Maize in Asia," *Annual of the Missouri Botanical Garden*, 41, No. 3. See Jeffreys, "Pre-Columbian Maize in Asia," in Riley et al. (eds.) *Man Across the Sea*, Austin, University of Texas Press, 1972, p. 380.

54 Jeffreys, op. cit., p. 382.

55 Jeffreys, "Pre-Columbian Maize in Asia," in Riley et al. (eds.) *Man Across the Sea*, Austin, University of Texas Press, 1972, p 399.

56 Idem.

57 Idem.

58 Cauvet, op. cit., p. 9.

59 Idem.

60 Ibid., p. 432.

61 Ibid., p. 446.

62 Ibid., p. 447.

63 Ibid., p. 448.

64 Ibid., p. 449.

65 Idem.

66 Ibid., pp. 101–102.

67 Lorenzo Dow Turner, *Africanisms in the Gullah Dialet*, Chicago, University of Chicago Press, 1939. Reprinted by Arno Press, New York, 1969.

68 Cauvet, op. cit., p. 9.

69 Harold Lawrence, "African Explorers in the New World," *Crisis*, June–July, 1962, Heritage Program Reprint, p. 10.

70 J. V. Luce in Geoffrey Ashe (ed.) *The Quest for America*, New York, Praeger Publishers, 1971, pp. 90, 91

71 For reference to Casella and E. D. Merill, see Stephen Jett in Riley et al. (eds.) *Man Across the Sea*, Austin, University of Texas, Press, 1972, p. 26.

POSTSCRIPT
ON OTHER FINDS

The negro started his career in America not as a slave but as master.
—R. A. JAIRAZBHOY, *Ancient Egyptians and Chinese in America*

The startling fact is that in all parts of Mexico, from Campeche in the east to the south coast of Guerrero, and from Chiapas, next to the Guatemalan border, to the Panuco River in the Huasteca region (north of Veracruz), archaeological pieces representing Negro or Negroid people have been found, especially in Archaic or pre-Classic sites. This also holds true for large sections of Mesoamerica and far into South America—Panama, Colombia, Ecuador, and Peru . . .

—ALEXANDER VON WUTHENAU, *Unexpected Faces in Ancient America*

I let the grains filter slowly through my fingers like sand falling in a measured drip through the neck of an ancient hourglass. Some of the grains at the bottom of the grave reminded me of that sunless, ashen powder one finds on the floor of abandoned ant heaps. They were mixed now with a darker, heavier, more brittle soil, but when the grave had first been opened, the layer in which I now buried my hands had been dated circa 1250 A.D. Within that layer had been found the bones of two Negroid skeletons.

I looked up from the pit, strewn with the irreverent debris of beer and soda cans, at the pure unlittered pool of the Caribbean sky. My guide called down to me from the edge of the pit. Her voice was clear above the muffled hammer of the sea in the bay outside, and the closeness and immediacy of this vital cry against the whisper of the unseen ocean in Hull Bay flooded me with a sensation of the overlapping of the visible and the invisible, of modern substance and ancient shadow, of the far and the familiar centuries. I felt as though the hands through which I now sifted this thirteenth-century dust were branches drawing sap from the grafted tree of my Carib and African ancestors.

I had come to the Virgin Islands a year after the Smithsonian had reported the Hull Bay find.* According to the Associated Press report on the discovery, the skeletons of two Negroid males in their late thirties had been found buried in soil layers dated 1250 A.D. Clamped around the wrist of one of the skeletons was a ceramic vessel of pre-Columbian Indian design. Examination of the teeth of the skeletons indicated "dental mutilation characteristic of early African cultures."[1] The find must have generated considerable excitement at first, since the area adjoining the grave had been acquired at the cost of hundreds of thousands of dollars. By March, 1976, however, when I visited the site, a blanket of secrecy had descended. The grave had degenerated into a garbage dump. I learned from information filtering out of the Smithsonian that interest had evaporated because the skeletons found in the grave could not be properly dated. Salt water had seeped into the bones, disturbing the carbon content, leading to wildly fluctuating readings of skeletal age. Also, and this is most revealing, a nail had been found near one of the skeletons,

---

* My visit to the Virgin Islands was sponsored jointly by the Environmental Studies Program on St. John and the College of the Virgin Islands on St. Thomas. Mrs. Doris Jadan, President of E.S.P., had invited me to study the petroglyphs carved at the bottom of an ancient freshwater pool in the Reef Bay Valley. Some of these I identified as African. The central plaque was distinguished from the others by the Gye Nyame sign (of Ashanti origin), a sign of power overturned and reasserted, as well as by a medieval West African dating code of solar dots and lunar curves inscribed along the waterline.

indicating (said the informant) that the find was most certainly post-Columbian.

In matters of this nature it is wise for the Smithsonian to tread with great caution. The disturbance of the bones by seawater makes one aspect of the evidence inconclusive, but the other features—the pre-Columbian ceramic vessel, the age of the soil layers, the evidence of an unusual dental ritual not associated with Africans of slavery times—strongly suggest a pre-Columbian context. In other words, *nothing* in the evidence associated with the skeletons suggests a post-Columbian dating. The find at Hull Bay remains, therefore, an open question. Further diggings in that area may establish the pre-Columbian presence of Africans in the Virgin Islands, after all. But the matter is being prematurely closed by a conspiracy of silence, a spate of insidious rumors, and by apparent ignorance of African metallurgical history. For to assume that a nail found beside an African skeleton is proof of a post-Columbian dating is absurd. Apart from the possibility of accidental intrusion from a higher stratum (such a tiny object can easily slip through a crack in the earth), the even more real possibility that pre-Columbian Africans were acquainted with iron nails has not been considered. Why should a nail pose insuperable problems to Africans whose smelting of iron dates back to 650 B.C. at Meroe in Nubia* and to 200 B.C. at Nok in Nigeria? Are we to believe that the medieval West African who could devise metal implements refined enough to perform eye-cataract surgery in the thirteenth century was incapable of making a nail?

The find at Hull Bay, however, is only the most recent in a series of discoveries of Negroid skeletal remains in pre-Columbian strata in the New World. I have already noted some of these

* In fact an isolated iron spearhead was found in Nubia by the Randall Mac Iver and C. L. Wooley archaeological team in a stratum dating back to the Twelfth Dynasty. This is four hundred years before tiny iron implements for use in ritual ceremonies appear in Egypt in the tomb of Tutankhamen (late Eighteenth Dynasty) and more than a thousand years before iron began to become common in the Egyptian world, which was in the Twenty-Fifth Dynasty under the blacks. See A. Lucas, *Ancient Egyptian Materials and Industries*, London, Edward Arnold, 1926, pp. 196, 197.

among the Olmecs (as cited by Andrzej Wiercinski and Frederick Peterson) and the Pecos River valley skulls of a later period (as cited by Earnest Hooton). Some theorists (H.S. Gladwin in *Men Out of Asia* and his latter-day disciple, Legrand Clegg II, in his article "Who Were the First Americans?")[2] point to "proto-Negroid" or "proto-Australoid" finds among some of the Pacific migrants to America twenty thousand years ago. These finds are almost exclusively of an Australoid pygmy type and are mostly confined to the Pacific coast. They cannot account for the presence, influence and distinctive racial-cultural characteristics of Negro-African types found much later in either the Olmec or medieval Mexican cultures. They are therefore peripheral, if not irrelevant, to our study.

In the first place, they are different in stature and cephalic shape from the Olmec Negroid types reported by Wiercinski at Tlatilco, Cerro de las Mesas and Monte Albán; second, they belong to a period in world history when the so-called "Africoid" or "proto-Australoid" base (to use terms coined by these theorists) could equally be traced even to some tribes in the Baltic region and northwestern Russia;[3] third, they had mixed and melted into the billion-bodied Mongoloid gene pool for at least 20,000 years (to judge from the datings given to these very early remains of the glacial epoch)—far too long to emerge suddenly as clearly defined, highly distinctive Negro-African faces such as we find in the colossal black dynasts of the Olmec civilization; fourth, the Negro-African portraitures in stone, clay, copper, gold and copal found in pre-Columbian America are distinguishable as Nubian-Egyptian and West African types not simply and solely on the ground of their Negroid physiognomy but because of identifiable cultural items—helmets, coiffures, headkerchiefs, caps, compound earrings, tattoos and scarification—associated with particular historical periods and particular peoples. Also, they are found mainly along the Atlantic seaboard at the terminal points of winds and currents which bear from Africa all that remains flying and afloat, not only gourds and men and ships but even "the seasonal dust-cloud, drifting out of the great ocean of Sahara—the harmattan."[4]

The pre-Columbian blacks reported by Mongoloid Americans and enshrined in their oral traditions are clearly not the primitive "proto-Australoids" of the Ice Age. No oral traditions in the world go back that far. If they did, we would expect the Mongoloid Americans to preserve legends also of their primordial Pacific homelands before the crossing of the Bering Straits. A look at their oral traditions makes it very clear that the black figure to which they refer was an unusual outsider, in most cases an object of mystery and reverence, and, moreover, a figure who began to feature prominently in their world in *historic* times (that is, from the Olmec civilization onward). Unlike the short-statured Pacific Australoid negrito, he was taller than the average Amerindian, although the historian Carlos C. Marquez does make mention of a few "small black men" seen in Darien (now Panama) by the American tribes who first settled there.[5]

Nicholas Leon, an eminent Mexican authority, reports on the oral traditions of the native Americans, according to some of whom "the oldest inhabitants of Mexico were Negroes." "The existence of Negroes and giants," he continues, "is commonly believed by nearly all the races of our soil and in their various languages they had words to designate them. Several archaeological objects found in various localities demonstrate their existence, the most notable of which is the colossal granite head of Hueyapan, Vera Cruz, and an axe of the same located near the city. In Teotihuacan abound little heads of the Ethiopian type and paintings of Negroes. In Michoacan and Oxaca the same have also been found . . ."[6]

The reference to giants is interesting, since many continental Africans are much taller than the native Americans. Vespucci mentions a strange race of tall men sighted on a Caribbean island (now known as Curaçao), and his distinguished biographer, Frederick Pohl, believes that these men were blacks. In a letter to me Pohl wrote: "Vespucci is accredited first explorer to reach Curaçao ('Island of Giants') and did so in 1500. His 'Letter from Seville' describes the giants (even the women) as a head and a half (or foot and a half?) taller than any of the Spaniards with him. Spaniards in his day in Spain saw many Moors, and Indians were of a different color also, and so negro giants were described only by height, not by color . . . Amerigo does give the color of the Indians of Trinidad in the same letter. His letter, written 5 or 6 months after his landing on Curaçao, was to his patron in Florence, and he could easily have failed to put in details we wish he had given."[7]

After completing the present work, I fell upon an extraordinary little volume, which is really a chapter in a larger work, *Old World Origins of American Civilization* by R. A. Jairazbhoy.[8] Jairazbhoy claims that the Olmecs burst in on the Mexican Gulf Coast circa 1200 B.C., and that it is just after their appearance that "all kinds of civilised activity appears including massive organisation of labour, a trade network, ceremonial centres with pyramids, colossal sculpture, relief carving, wall painting, orientation of structures, gods and religious symbolism, an obsession with the Underworld, representation of foreign racial types, hieroglyphic writing and scribes, seals and rings, use of iron, and so on." He attributes *all* these to Old World migrants who came to America in that period (circa 1200 B.C.), but admits "few artifacts so far found go back to the first generation migrants."[8] In fact, *none* indicating an Old World influence do go back to 1200 B.C. Hard carbon datings of artifacts associated with outside influences begin in the 800–700 B.C. period, though the cultural complex known as Olmec has its beginnings in an earlier stratum (1200–1100 B.C.).

Because of Jairazbhoy's hypothesis—that the journey from Egypt to the Gulf of Mexico had to be made circa 1200 B.C. to coincide with the first Olmec settlements—he is led into strange speculations about the role and fate of the black figure in the reign of Ramses III, the Egyptian Pharaoh of the 1200 B.C. period. Since the Negroid figure, according to him, was a slave and mercenary in that period, but appears as a figure of great authority and power among the Olmecs, he speculates that they came to America under the supervision of Northern Egyptian overlords, and were either made military governors of the Olmec by these overlords (of whom he admits there are no sculptural traces)[9] or that the blacks mutinied and killed their overlords.[10] The latter suggestion is even more problematic, since it would mean that all the complex Egyptian elements he mentions were transplanted here by soldiers. The so-called overlords, which would include the high priests, would in all likelihood have perished in the mutiny or been relegated to a role of little or no influence.

These matters can be explained far more simply and without recourse to such speculations. First of all, the native Americans were not savages when the Nubian-Egyptian party arrived, and while one may speak of profound outside influences upon the Olmecs, one should make allowance for the existence of a native civilization (however less advanced) in the Gulf Coast area before the coming of the outsiders. To date the coming of the outsiders, therefore, in the reign of Ramses III because it coincides with the very beginnings of Olmec civilization is quite unnecessary, apart from the fact that the hard carbon datings of the Negroid figures in the Olmec heartland—La Venta—are 800–700 B.C. Second, the prior existence of a civilization among the Olmecs explains why there is an incorporation of Egyptian elements with native modifications rather than a wholesale replica of Egyptian civilization, although there are a number of identical traits shared by both cultures, reinforcing the evidence of an intimate and prolonged contact. Third, it is dangerous to take so literally, as Jairazbhoy does, the legend of a Ramses III expedition to "the inverted waters" or the "Mountain to the Far West of the World" believed to be the entrance to the Underworld. Couched in this vague mythological language, legends of this nature abound among the sunworshipers of Egypt. Fourth, all the main Ramessid traits traceable to Olmec culture were equally in vogue in the Twenty-Fifth Dynasty of the blacks, and some that had lapsed in the Ramses period were revived by the Nubians. Finally, the blacks emerge in America as "tough warrior dynasts" (to use Michael Coe's phrase) because that is precisely what they were in the Mediterranean of the same period (800–700 B.C.).

Bearing in mind these reservations, one may still point to a great deal of valuable evidence Jairazbhoy presents for an Egyptian contact and influence upon the Olmecs.

He notes that Tanis was the place from which Egyptian ships

went out on distant expeditions. Taniś is also the place where
he cites colossal sculptured heads in stone, some representing
Negro-Nubians, similar in style and size to the ones found in the
Olmec world. This is particularly interesting in view of the fact
that the black kings made Tanis their capital, and Taharka not
only concentrated his military and administrative elite in that
Delta city, but built a new pharaonic palace and gardens there.
Jairazbhoy also highlights an oral tradition among the American
Indians that may indicate the place where the migrant party
from Egypt may eventually have landed, and the number and
type of ships in which they may have traveled. It appears from
this oral tradition (if it relates to the Egyptian flotilla lost off
North Africa) that they were blown off-course into the North
Atlantic current and made their landfall at a place called Panuco
(north of Veracruz) in seven wooden ships or galleys.[11]

This oral tradition recorded in the *Popul Vuh*, the bible of the
Quiche Maya, also mentions "black people, paleskinned people"[12]
as among the people who came to this land from the sunrise.
This would fit in with a Nubian-Phoenician crew. While oral
traditions are sometimes difficult to date, and most literal events
in the *Popul Vuh* only go back thirteen generations to about the
first decade of the fourteenth century, some of its recorded traditions do go back to the earliest American civilization, and Jairazbhoy points to a number of datable clues.[13] He demonstrates
remarkable similarities between several deities in the Egyptian
Underworld and those in Olmec Mexico. At least half a dozen
of these gods present in comparative analysis such a startling
identity of arbitrary elements in unique combinations that it is
difficult to see how independent cultures having no contact or
other means of diffusion could duplicate them. These clusters of
identical traits go beyond the universal generalities and symbols
common to the world's religions. (See examples in Plates 35 and
36 of this volume.)

He also draws attention to almost identical ritual practices and
funerary customs shared by both cultures, as well as similar names
for religious objects and concepts. One or two examples of these
rituals may be seen in the phallic cult (Plate 33) and the Opening

of the Mouth Ceremony (Plate 37). The most striking linguistic identities lie in the names (allowing for slight phonetic and morphemic transformations) for sun (Mexican and Peruvian *Ra* from Egyptian *Re* or *Ra*); for sacred incense (Mexican *copal* from Egyptian *kuphi*)*; for paradise (Peruvian *yaru* from Egyptian *iaro* or *yaro*); for the sacred crocodile barque (Mexican *cipak* or *cipactli* from the Egyptian *sibak*).[14] The Mexicans and Egyptians also share the same hieroglyph for sun, and the origin of heart-plucking in Mexico can be traced back to the heart-plucking of enemies of the sun-god in the Egyptian underworld.[15]

I have already noted the similarity between the royal litters and parasols in the two cultures. Jairazbhoy also mentions the double-crown of Egypt, which appears on an Olmec dignitary who is proferring an object to a seated Negroid figure.[16] Von Wuthenau has also noted the pharaonic cap itself on a Nubian figure in Mexico.[17] The Nubian sistrum, a musical instrument, is noted as being in use among the American Indians of Yaqui territory, with a similar religious function.[18]

The new light Jairazbhoy sheds on the skeletal evidence of the Polish craniologist Weircinski is of great importance in clearing up confusions over the Atlantic origin of the Negroid population among the Olmecs. He highlights the fact that 13.5 percent of the skeletons examined in the pre-Classic Olmec cemetery of Tlatilco were Negroid, yet later at Cerro de las Mesas in the Classic period, only 4.5 percent.[19] This indicates that the Negroid element intermarried until it almost fused with the native population. The female found in the graves in the pre-Classic period next to the Negroid male is very distinct from the male (native female, foreign male) but becomes similar to the male in the later Classic site, indicating progressive intermixture and the growing absorption of the foreign Negroid element into the largely Mongoloid American population. This evidence makes it very clear that the Olmec Negroid element was a distinctive outside element that came, conquered and crossbreeded in the

---

* Also the ritual incense spoons are of the same form, and incense in both places is used in the form of balls.

Olmec time period, rather than proto-Australoid or proto-Negroid aborigines who may have trickled into America from the Pacific in the very ancient glacial epoch. According to these skeletal statistics, the latter would have disappeared 'millenia ago into the American gene pool; therefore it can only be concluded that Atlantic migrations from the African continent are responsible for the black pre-Columbian presence in America from the Olmecs onward.

Notes

1 The Associated Press report first appeared in The Washington *Post*, February 29, 1975, p. A17.

2 Harold S. Gladwin, *Men out of Asia*, New York, McGraw Hill, 1947, and Legrand Clegg II, "Who Were the First Americans?" in *The Black Scholar*, September, 1975.

3 Roland B. Dixon, *The Racial History of Man*, New York, Scribner's, 1923, pp. 409–410.

4 Edward Braithwaite, *Rights of Passage*, Argo DA 101 (1968), sleevenote.

5 Carlos C. Marquez, *Estudies arqueologicas y etnograficos*, Mexico: Bogota, D. E. Editorial Kelly, 1956, pp. 179–180.

6 Quoted in J. A. Rogers, *Sex and Race*, New York: published by the author, 1942, Vol. 1, p. 270.

7 Frederick Pohl, personal communication dated February 17, 1976.

8 Chapter 3 of *Old World Origins of American Civilization*, Vol. I, published separately under the title *Ancient Egyptians and Chinese in America*, Totowa, New Jersey, Rowman and Littlefield, 1974, p. 7.

9 Ibid., p. 20.

10 R. A. Jairazbhoy in *The New Diffusionist* (April, 1972) as quoted by Alexander von Wuthenau, *Unexpected Faces in Ancient America*, New York, Crown Publishers, 1975, p. 125.

11 Jairazbhoy, *Ancient Egyptians and Chinese in America*, p. 8.

12 Ibid., p. 17, and *The Popul Vuh* (5128 f). "White" for color of skin is an anachronistic translation.

13 Jairazbhoy, op. cit., pp. 10–11.

14 Cyrus Gordon, *Before Columbus*, New York, Crown Publishers, 1971, p. 135.

15 Jairazbhoy, op. cit., p. 69 (Fig. 68).

16 Ibid., p. 29 (Fig. 15).

17 Alexander von Wuthenau, *Unexpected Faces in Ancient America*, New York, Crown Publishers, 1975, p. 229.

18 Jairazbhoy, op. cit., p. 37. Also see K. G. Izikowitz, *Musical and Other Sound Instruments of the South American Indians*, Wakefield, Yorkshire, 1970, p. 151.

19 Jairazbhoy, op. cit., p. 20. R. A. Jairazbhoy has given notice in a private communication (June 5) that he will present further evidence on behalf of the Egyptian and Nubian presence and influence in Mexico circa 1200 B.C. to the 42nd Congress of Americanists in Paris in September, 1976, in a talk entitled "Ramses III in person in Mexico." Professor Van Sertima will also present a body of new evidence in support of the case for that presence and influence circa 800–700 B.C. to the 19th Annual Meeting of the African Studies Association in Boston, November, 1976, in a talk entitled "The African Presence in Ancient America."

INDEX

ABOUT THE AUTHOR

IVAN VAN SERTIMA's pioneering work in linguistics and anthropology has appeared in numerous anthologies and journals. He is a regular contributor to the *Inter-American Review*, has published a collection of poems, critical essays and a *Swahili Dictionary of Legal Terms*, and has written on the subject of the African presence in Pre-Columbian America for *The New York Times*. Professor Van Sertima teaches at Rutgers University.